THE NEXT CHAPTER

WRITING IN RETIREMENT

Julie A. Gorges

Julie A. Gorges
Visit my website at https://juliegorges.com/

Printed in the United States of America

First Printing: October 2024
I-Form Ink Publishing

ISBN 978-0-9763274-9-3
Library of Congress Control Number: 2024906425

Dedicated to my grandchildren, Eden, Rowan, River, and Paige, who have brought me much joy in my golden "retirement" years.

* * *

Dedicated to my sons, Jonathan and Christopher, who helped me with technical issues publishing this book, and my daughter-in-law, Johnni, who has been a wonderful addition to our family.

* * *

Dedicated to my compassionate husband for all his love and support throughout my writing career and in all things.

* * *

And, finally, this book is dedicated to those of you living the second half of your life to the fullest. May you continue to courageously chase all your dreams!

ABOUT THE AUTHOR

Julie A. Gorges is an international award-winning author and a member of the Authors Guild. Hundreds of her articles and short stories have been published in national and regional magazines including *Woman's World, True Romance*, and *Cricket*. She received three journalism awards from the Washington Newspaper Publishers Association and her blog, *Baby Boomer Bliss*, was recognized as one of the top 50 baby boomer blogs on the web.

OTHER BOOKS BY JULIE A. GORGES

FICTION

Just Call Me Goody-Two-Shoes

Time to Cast Away

NON-FICTION

I'm Your Daughter, Julie: Caring for a Parent with Dementia

Ten Secrets to Losing Weight After 50

Residential Steel Design and Construction

"Start writing, no matter what. The water does not flow until the faucet is turned on."

— LOUIS L'AMOUR

CONTENTS

INTRODUCTION:

PURSUE YOUR PASSION

While many retirees are focused on saving enough money for their golden years, it's also important to plan what you'll do with all that extra free time. At first, you may be happy going to the movies, reading novels, gardening, and hanging out in a hammock. However, now that people live longer, these pursuits won't likely keep you entertained for the next 20 to 30 years.

After a while, you may want something more exciting and fulfilling to keep you busy. Of course, spending more time with family, traveling, and volunteering are all worthwhile goals. In addition to these activities, however, some retirees aspire to become writers in retirement.

Does that describe you?

WERE YOU MEANT TO BE A WRITER?

Have you always fantasized about becoming a writer? Are you distracted with thoughts about story plots, characters, poems, writing your life story, or ideas for a blog?

Are you captivated by the power of words and drawn irresistibly to bookstores and libraries? Do you have a notebook filled with scribblings or lose track of time when writing in a journal? Did you love to write as a child and long to revisit that creative and enchanted place?

You are probably a natural-born writer if you answered yes to any of those questions. If that's the case, writing is a calling that pulls at your soul.

If you feel this way, believe me, I understand. As a writer, I'm addicted to words.

And no wonder.

Words evoke imaginations and create wondrous worlds to explore. Words can be powerful, exciting, healing, motivating, hopeful, and inspirational. And sometimes words can even be magical.

I started down the path of becoming a professional writer more than 30 years ago and still love the endless possibilities this art form offers.

OVERCOMING OBSTACLES

If you dream of writing a book, you're certainly not alone. Author Joseph Epstein wrote in a *New York Times* article, "Eighty-one percent of Americans feel they have a book in them – and that they should write it." Others dream of starting a blog, becoming a travel writer, or seeing their byline on a magazine article.

Unfortunately, most people don't attempt to live out their cherished dreams. Why not?

Many people don't know where to start. Others allow self-doubt and a fear of failure to stop them from moving forward.

Is that you? If so, that's where I come in. As an author, blogger, and freelance writer, I want to help all of you harboring a burning desire to write and turn your dreams into a reality. In this book, I'll provide the inspiration and motivation you need while sharing my knowledge and experience to help you begin your writing journey.

This book contains a wealth of information to help any aspiring writer. But, if you're retired or looking for an encore career, this is written specifically with you in mind. You finally have the time and freedom to pursue your passion. After years of keeping your nose to the grindstone to make a living, haven't you earned that luxury?

Even if you're not retired yet, you can begin learning about writing and publishing. Or move forward and start your writing career right now as time permits. No time like the present!

WHAT ARE YOUR GOALS?

This book will help you explore all your options and then guide you through steps to accomplish your goals.

Is it your dream to write the great American novel? Begin an encore career as a freelance writer? Share your knowledge and experience with a self-help book and teach online classes? Write travel articles in exchange for meals and lodging? Become a playwright or publish a memoir?

I'm here to help.

Or perhaps you don't want to commit to the discipline of writing a book or the deadlines of being a freelance writer. Your goal is not to earn money, but to find a pleasurable and fulfilling way to spend your leisure time. Maybe you're interested in writing poems, penning an autobiography or family history for future generations, journaling, or blogging to inspire others. You want the freedom to write whenever the muse hits - and when you're not busy with your family and friends, volunteering, playing with your grandchildren, or traveling around the world.

I'm here to help you too.

Whatever your dreams, this book is for you.

NO EXCUSES!

You may have a million reasons for procrastinating. Sure, we're all busy, but dig deeper and you may discover that you're using appointments, errands, or chores as an excuse to postpone chasing your dream.

Is it possible that you're afraid of failing?

Maybe you don't have a college education or don't think your writing skills are good enough. Without connections in the publishing world, getting published seems impossible. You envision a massive pile of rejection letters if you pursue your dream of becoming a traditionally published author. You're afraid friends and family will snicker if you admit you want to become a writer.

If that's the case, I can certainly relate.

When I started writing in the early 1980s, I didn't have a college degree or any connections in the publishing business whatsoever.

Keep in mind that options existing today weren't available back then. Self-publishing was expensive, and blogging wasn't even invented yet. Writers were pretty much at the mercy of book publishers and magazine editors.

I was definitely afraid of failing. Wasn't it better to continue dreaming and keep my aspirations private? If I dared to write that book dancing around in my head and submitted it to agents and publishers, I just knew it would sit in a huge slush pile. Getting a short story or article published in a magazine seemed like an impossible dream.

My excuses continued. If countless rejections came my way, I'd probably be so discouraged I'd give up and watch my precious dreams fade away. If I expressed my dreams of becoming a professional writer out loud, I was sure that friends and family would roll their eyeballs.

Let's face it. Even though I've always loved writing and dreamed about turning my passion into a career, I put a lot of self-imposed barriers on myself.

Oh, I dabbled a bit in my 20s. I took a few writing classes at the local college, wrote a short story, jotted down some ideas for a novel, and penned some poetry. I attended a writer's conference and listened with envy as authors explained their secrets to success.

But to move beyond that was scary.

I was perfectly comfortable just dreaming about becoming an author one day. It was fun envisioning my novel on the shelves of Barnes and Noble and my first book signing.

Content with fantasizing, I put my ideas for a novel aside and didn't submit any of my work for publication. I'd get distracted by life, which was easy with a job and two kids in tow. Sometimes, months would go by before I'd write something. After all, writing was just a silly hobby.

Then I attended a writer's seminar – just for fun, of course, I told myself – and told a woman about my idea for a novel during lunch break. She asked me a simple but profound question. "What are you waiting for?"

Oh, I had a million excuses for not pursuing my passion. But the woman forced me to ask myself some important questions.

Did I want to go to my grave with regrets that I never followed my dreams? Sorry that I never even tried? Would I wonder what I could have accomplished if only I had mustered up enough courage and perseverance to break through my self-imposed barriers?

With those questions bouncing around in my head, I bravely moved forward.

I took another writing class at my local college, checked out every writing book at the library, and finished two correspondence courses. I wrote regularly and started submitting my work.

Admittedly, some of my fears did come true during those early years. Turns out chasing your dreams isn't easy. I gathered enough rejection letters to wallpaper a room. Many people gave me cynical looks when I dared to share my dreams of becoming a published writer. Many, many times, I became discouraged and swore off writing.

But in the end, I tenaciously pressed forward. Am I happy I persevered and faced down all those nagging self-doubts and fears?

You bet!

Eventually, I sold one of my short stories to a literary magazine for a whopping $22 and couldn't have been more thrilled! That began my exciting career in writing. Ultimately, I lived out the dream of seeing my books on Barnes and Noble's shelves along with book signings at their stores.

During the past three decades, I co-authored a book published by a New York publishing house, landed a well-known literary agent, published two young adult novels and three nonfiction books, won three journalism awards while working as a reporter, and had thousands of articles published in magazines, newspapers, as well as online magazines and websites. One of my books, *I'm Your Daughter, Julie*, even won a grand prize in an international writing competition.

My point is not to brag but to prove that anything is possible if you take that first step.

So, I'll ask you the same question: What are you waiting for? When I started writing, I was working a secular job and raising two young sons. If you're retired, you'll be ahead of the game with more freedom and time.

Of course, I can't promise that you'll achieve fame and fortune, but aren't you curious about what could happen if you just take that first step? Maybe you're thinking, "I don't have any grand goals. I just want to write." That's fine too. Just get started.

Because this is the point. You don't need to have an English degree or natural talent coming out your ears. And you don't need a prestigious career to enjoy the process and joy of writing. If you want to be a writer, you only need to write.

YOU'RE NEVER TOO OLD!

Think it's too late to get started? Perish the thought.

The good news is that writing has no barriers. Race, sex, background – and age – are not important. Anyone can write.

Becoming a writer requires the same process, whether you're 20 or 80 years old. In fact, with all the life experience, knowledge, wisdom, patience, and perseverance you've attained over the years, you'll have a distinct advantage over younger writers.

Need some reassurance? There are plenty of famous writers who found success later in life. Here are just a few examples:

- Frank McCourt launched his literary career at age 66 by writing the Pulitzer Prize-winning memoir *Angela's Ashes*. "I'm a late bloomer," he told the *New York Times* in an interview.
- Mary Wesley, author of *The Camomile Lawn*, which later became an Emmy-nominated TV mini-series, wrote her first novel at age 70. She went on to sell three million copies of her books, including 10 bestsellers.
- Laura Ingalls Wilder, the author of the *Little House on the Prairie* series started writing books at age 63.
- Sue Monk Kidd's first novel, *The Secret Life of Bees*, was published when she was 53. The book spent over one hundred weeks on the *New York Times* bestseller list, sold more than four million copies, and was made into a movie.
- Helen Hoover Santmyer's novel, *And Ladies of the Club*, became a bestseller when she was 88.
- Anna Sewell, the English novelist, wrote *Black Beauty* in her 50s.

Consider Linda Lombri and Virginia Cornue who took up writing in their post-retirement lives as mystery writers. Both fans of the Nancy Drew series when they were young, reimagined her into a trio of female baby boomer characters. "Not only are we reinventing ourselves, we have our characters reinventing themselves as well," says Cornue in an interview for *USA Today*.

On a personal note, my father, John Hacker, took up writing later in life. At the age of 65, he co-wrote a book with me that McGraw Hill published. Afterward, we started our own publishing company, and he published two more books. He conducted several seminars, and we did a few book signings together. And, believe me, he had an absolute blast doing it!

Of course, not all older writers are authors. Take a quick look around the Internet, and you'll find plenty of older writers happily typing away on their keyboards, sharing their lives and wisdom on blogs.

David and Carol Porter were in their 50s when they sold their mortgage business, downsized to a smaller home, and retired early to see the world. They had barely started checking countries off their bucket list when the stock market crashed destroying nearly half their life savings.

Instead of wallowing, the couple started a successful blog, *The Roaming Boomers,* and began operating a travel agency from their home. And they started traveling again. They didn't allow their age or bumps in the road to keep them from living their dreams.

BENEFITS OF WRITING IN RETIREMENT

Need more inspiration? Writing just happens to offer a slew of benefits for retirees, some of which you may not have considered:

- Mental Stimulation

  One study published in *Neurology* reported that those who read and wrote later in life could slow their memory decline by 32 percent compared to people with average mental activity. Curiosity and creativity have been proven to improve cognitive function. You can have fun writing and improve your mental capabilities while you're at it!

- Supplements Your Income

  Maybe you didn't save enough for retirement. Or you would like to earn some extra money to travel or spoil your grandchildren. Writing offers opportunities to do so with a flexible schedule.

- Social Opportunities

  People often think of writing as an isolating activity with countless hours spent alone sitting at a computer. But it doesn't have to be that way. If you take classes, join a local writing group, attend a writer's conference, or man a booth at a book fair, you'll have opportunities to meet people with similar interests. Researching books or articles often includes interviewing fascinating people. Blogging is an interactive experience that puts you in touch with your readers and other bloggers. If you start an author's Facebook page, you'll be in touch with even more people.

- Therapy

Writing has been linked to well-being, improved mood, and stress reduction. Trust me, writing is a therapeutic way to express and release negative emotions, heal from grief, and relive joyful moments. While reading provides a welcome respite from my troubles, writing is my real escape. I become so focused on the creative process that my problems fade away for a while, giving me a much-needed and welcome break.

- Preserves Memories

Writing a memoir or autobiography, or keeping a journal, will help you remember important events and feelings that may otherwise fade or disappear. As an added benefit, future generations can read about important family events, learn about your life, and benefit from your valuable wisdom and experience. If you've done something unusual, led an inspirational life, or can write about life's events in a humorous or quirky way, you may even be able to sell a memoir.

- Inspires Others

How-to or inspirational books, articles, and blogs have the power to educate, motivate, solve problems, and even change lives. Writing is a great way to share the wisdom you've gained over the years to help others. Some of my readers have left comments on my blog, *Baby Boomer Bliss*, letting me know that I have, in some small way, inspired them, provided useful information, or made them laugh. That always lifts my spirits and brings me joy.

- Clarifies Life

Writing puts life's events into perspective and can inspire you to move forward to achieve your dreams. Since you can't write about every event, idea, thought, and feeling that pops into your head, writing a memoir, journaling, or blogging provides a filter for determining what is most meaningful to you. Writing about your life can help you decide whether you're headed in the right direction.

- Fun Perks

Sometimes, unexpected freebies come your way. For example, I was asked to write a book review for the late 1960s teen idol Bobby Rydell's new autobiography. I received a free autographed book, and he agreed to do an interview for my blog. When I offered to write a review for one of his concerts near my home, I received two free front-row tickets valued at $160 to see Rydell perform with Frankie Avalon and Fabian. I was even given a backstage pass to meet Rydell in person. So much fun and a once-in-a-lifetime opportunity since he recently passed away.

WILL AI MAKE WRITERS UNNECESSARY?

Artificial intelligence (AI) has been all over the news lately, so I wanted to briefly comment on how it impacts the future of writers.

Recently, a group of famous fiction writers joined the Authors Guild in suing OpenAI, alleging the company's technology illegally uses their copyrighted work.

Hollywood screenwriters succeeded in securing significant guardrails against the use of AI after a 148-day strike.

No doubt, as AI technology evolves, this issue will come up again in the future.

So, will AI make writers defunct? In my opinion, no.

AI tools can help writers in many ways, such as bringing ideas to fruition, checking spelling and grammar, and suggesting book titles.

"My belief is that just as spelling and grammar checking software lifted some of the load off our [authors] shoulders, software can do the same when we're stuck in a scene, struggling to describe an object or a setting, or just not sure how to inject something fresh into a tired plot line," says Amit Gupta, creator of Sudowrite.com in an Alliance for Independent Authors article, "AI for Authors: Practical and Ethical Guidelines."

Although AI can write entire articles, blogs, and even books, there are things that AI cannot achieve. AI cannot replace a human touch or an emotional connection with readers. A cookie-cutter, machine-generated work doesn't have a unique and identifiable voice. That's why I'm not worried.

Chapter 3 discusses the pros and cons of using this technology, along with some tools you may want to try.

For now, keep in mind that there's a big difference between "AI generated" (artificial intelligence created the text) and "AI-assisted" (a human created the text, and artificial intelligence helped improve the writing).

HOW TO USE THIS BOOK

You may have noticed from the Table of Contents that this is a comprehensive book. Don't be overwhelmed.

Of course, it's your choice, but I wouldn't try reading the entire book at once. Instead, start with the first section, which provides general information all writers can benefit from – no matter what genre you choose. You'll find inspiration for ideas, tips for creating the perfect writing workspace, the right technology to help you write, ways to learn more about the craft of writing, and ideas for developing a consistent writing routine.

Then, you can start exploring your options. Skim the Table of Contents and focus on one or two areas you'd like to examine first. Perhaps you want to write poetry but have no interest in freelance writing. By all means, skip that section. You'll find each section can stand alone.

Not sure which avenue to pursue as a writer? There's no rush. Experiment to find the right path for you. See where your natural talent lies and what type of writing you enjoy the most.

Ask yourself a few questions to help you choose what to explore first:

- What have you always dreamed of writing?
- What appeals to you about each possibility?
- Do you want to write for your own pleasure or reach a broad audience?
- Do you need extra income to supplement your social security checks, or are you simply looking for a creative way to spend your spare time in retirement?

Take it from me, if you keep your mind open, you may be surprised where your writing journey takes you. In my 20s, I wrote short stories and novels for young adults. I never considered writing anything else. Then, an article I wrote for a magazine article writing class was published in a regional parenting magazine. That opened my eyes to other possibilities and changed the direction of my career. And you know what? I discovered that I enjoyed writing nonfiction just as much as fiction.

Nonfiction can educate, motivate, heal, and even change lives. Human-interest articles I later wrote as a newspaper reporter and as a contributing writer for a print magazine were fascinating and inspiring. Not to mention, nonfiction is a lot easier to sell than fiction.

Ultimately, I've written everything from a technical book to romantic short stories to humorous articles about menopause. My point? Don't limit yourself to one kind of writing. Have fun experimenting. Enjoy the journey. Whatever you decide, this book can open doors, empowering you to reach your goals with step-by-step guidance.

Lucky you, today, many new and exciting opportunities are available. For example, self-publishing has never been easier. Options discussed in this book include Kindle Direct Publishing (KDP), which enables authors to publish and sell digital, paperback, and hardcover versions of their books on Amazon at no cost whatsoever. Easy-to-use tools are available for beginners.

Below are some avenues of writing you may want to consider:

- Write a Novel

  Maybe you've been carrying around an idea for the next great American novel for years. Are you a great storyteller with a vivid imagination? Do your grandchildren prefer stories you create instead of stories from books? Is an idea for a story stuck in your head and you can't get it out? Whether you try to find a traditional publisher or self-publish a book yourself, now is the time to live out your dreams. Learn how to write a novel in Chapter 6 of this book.

- Create a How-To Book

  With four or five decades of experience, no doubt, there's something you do better than most people. Why not share that valuable knowledge and expertise to improve other people's lives? Are you an expert on a specific subject? Is there a perplexing question you know how to answer? Do you have an idea that will benefit your readers in a profound way? Then you have a purpose and writing a nonfiction book can fulfill it. See Chapter 7 for more details.

- Start a Blog

  Blogging can be a great place to voice your unique ideas, thoughts, and feelings. Do you want to inspire and touch the lives of others in a positive way? Are you looking for a great interactive experience that may also bring in a little money over time? Do you want to document your life in an empowering way while improving your writing skills? Is it your goal to explore career and business opportunities, promote a book, or start an online course? Blogging doesn't have to cost anything and can help you do all these things. Read all about it in Section V.

- Become a Freelance Writer

  Maybe you're considering an encore career or supplementing your social security checks. Writing jobs are needed for a wide variety of subjects, interests, and hobbies. Websites connect writers with clients, making freelancing easier than in the past. Do you want to experience the thrill of seeing your byline for the first time? Are you looking for a flexible schedule? Do you want to get paid for what you love to do? With the right strategies, you can start building your writing career. Section IV will get you started.

- Write a Family History, Memoir, or Autobiography

  Do you want to preserve your family legacy for future generations? Learn about your ancestors? Gain a clearer vision of your personal identity and insight into your past? Do you feel a burning desire to tell your personal story? Do you want to heal from a traumatic experience and want to help others do so as well? Writing your life story can achieve all these things and more. Chapter 8 is for you.

- Draft a Play

  Are scripts dancing around in your head? Maybe you're fascinated with learning the skill of transforming stories for the stage or screen. Become a playwright. Even if your traditional play doesn't end up on Broadway, there are other opportunities to experience the thrill of seeing your work produced on stage in community theaters, schools, or other amateur productions. Or simply write a play for your grandchildren to perform. They'll love it! Or maybe you picture your story on the big screen or on TV. Do you fantasize about making it in Hollywood or having your work turned into the next great indie project? Check out Section IX.

- Pen Some Poetry

  Do you have a love affair with the beauty of words? Do you want to explore your feelings and ideas with style and rhythm, inspiring others? Do you want to have a deeper understanding of language and become a better writer? Poetry is your ticket. If you'd like to share your poems, many literary magazines and online publications accept poetry. Or perhaps you'll want to self-publish a book of poems. You could even share your art by crafting your own greeting cards. Section VII provides more details.

- Start a Journal

Keeping a journal is a personal journey and a window into your soul. A journal can help you learn about yourself, express your feelings, reduce stress, help solve problems, remember important events in your life, and outline goals. Do you want a place where you can be yourself without fear of judgment and experience your deepest thoughts and feelings? Is it your goal to get into the habit of writing on a regular basis? Perhaps a standard diary doesn't interest you. Keep in mind gratitude journals, travel journals, idea journals, child or grandchild journals, and inspirational journals are also available. Read Section VIII and start journaling now.

- Publish an eBook

Do you find writing a full-length book overwhelming? eBooks can be 50 pages or less and take much less time and effort to write. Do you want to write an eBook to help boost another business venture? Or to gain valuable experience launching, marketing, and selling a book? Creating an eBook is a cheap and fast way to get published and accomplish these goals. With Kindles, iPads, and Nooks, digital books are becoming more popular all the time. Even if a print book is still your dream, an eBook can help you see if there is interest in your subject, build an audience, and move you closer to your publishing goals. If you have a blog, offering a free eBook to subscribers is a great way to develop an email list that can help you sell future books. Chapter 11 describes how to achieve this goal.

- Write Travel Books or Articles

Do you dream about wandering the world and sending back tantalizing tales about your adventures? Is it your desire to inspire others to explore, experience new things, and appreciate different cultures? Do you want to combine your love of writing and traveling? If you can establish yourself as an expert, in time you may earn money writing for travel magazines, local newspapers, online publications, and other media outlets. If you gain a following on a travel blog, you may become eligible for complimentary meals and lodging. Section VI was written just for you.

Contemplate your choices. Experiment with one of the above or a combination of two or three. Eventually, you may want to give them all a try. Why not?

After reading about your chosen avenue(s) of writing, be sure and come away with an action plan for achieving one goal. What is one thing you can do in the next 30 days to move towards your dream of becoming a writer in retirement?

As a side note, you'll discover that different parts of this book can help you achieve the same goal. What do I mean?

Maybe you want to write a novel. But before approaching traditional publishers you want to journal to get into the habit of writing regularly, do some freelance writing to build a portfolio, and start an author's website with a blog to look professional. You have everything you need to get started in this book.

In that sense, this book is a one-stop shop!

To give you another example, let's say you want to become a travel writer. You take the following steps:

- You start with Section VI to learn more about this genre.
- Excited and ready to begin writing, you decide to create a travel blog to showcase your work. Section V gives you the information you need to get started.
- Later, you feel more confident about trying to sell your articles to print or online travel magazines and read Section IV on becoming a freelance writer.
- After gaining some experience, the idea of writing a travel memoir sounds appealing, so you study how to write a memoir in Chapter 8.
- Once you've finished writing your book, you can't decide whether to approach agents and traditional publishers with your manuscript or self-publish. Chapter 9 helps you decide which route to take followed by chapters explaining how to do both.
- Once your book is published, you read Chapter 12 on how to market and promote your travel memoir.

So, are you motivated and ready to begin your fulfilling journey of becoming a writer?

As Mark Twain said: "The secret of getting ahead is getting started. The secret of getting started is breaking your complex overwhelming tasks into small manageable tasks and starting on the first one."

If you want to fast-track down the exciting path of becoming a writer, this is the book for you. Let's start one step at a time.

WHAT WRITERS IN RETIREMENT HAVE TO SAY...

SANDRA BENNETT, AWARD-WINNING CHILDREN'S AUTHOR

I have always wanted to write for children, ever since my teacher college days. Once I retired from teaching, it was time to stop dreaming and talking about it and do it.

Working from home or wherever I am when traveling is a great benefit. Your time is your own, so you can write at any time of the day that suits you.

Once you leave the workforce, you lose contact with most colleagues. Writing has meant making new friends and connections with like-minded people. I have developed amazing new friendships that I value and appreciate. It's wonderful to have friends who can help and support each other as we all understand the need to write.

Writing for kids means I get to do author visits at schools, so even though I am no longer teaching, I am still able to connect with kids.

My advice: Stop daydreaming and just do it. Join writing groups online to encourage and support you. Research, learn, do a writing course or two, and read. Read in the genre you want to write in and study what works. Learn what you do and don't like and then go for it.

Read and write as often as you can, even if no one else ever sees your writing. Most of all have fun and enjoy the process and journey whether the end goal is publication or not.

* * *

CAT MICHAELS, AWARD-WINNING INDIE AUTHOR

My passion for storytelling began in childhood, as I filled notebooks with tales of wagon train adventures in the Old West. As an angsty teenager, my journals became my confidantes, capturing the turmoil and uncertainty of adolescence. As an adult, I started in education and took a turn into the corporate world, where I honed my writing skills crafting press releases, staff newsletters, and trade magazine articles.

However, I wanted a deeper connection with the written word, one beyond the boundaries of corporate communication and learning guides.

The digital revolution ignited my entrepreneurial spirit, coinciding with the rise of self-publishing platforms that democratized storytelling. I delved into family lore, crafting engaging chapter books in the award-winning "Sweet T Tale" series for young readers, writing under the name Cat Michaels. When the pandemic hit, I explored a new challenge, and I embraced contemporary fiction. My small-town, beachy romances are brimming with swoon-worthy moments, feel-good vibes, and happily-ever-afters.

Being an Indie author is an exhilarating journey that allows me to harness my creativity to connect with readers on a deep level, sharing stories that resonate, inspire, and bring joy. It's a privilege to impact lives through the power of storytelling.

* * *

ROSIE RUSSELL, AUTHOR AND ILLUSTRATOR OF CHILDREN'S BOOKS

At the end of working in our school district for 15 years, I became a grandmother and watched our grandson weekly.

I knew one of my favorite things to do when visiting classrooms was reading and investigating parts of authors' stories. As I read to our grandson every day, the thought occurred to me how much I enjoyed sharing stories with him and so many others throughout my life. That's how I began looking into writing, illustrating, and publishing my own stories for young children.

I have more time and much more patience to learn new things. When raising our sons and attending school and sports functions, the time for other things was just not there. Once things slowed down, I had more time to think and found ways to make it happen. I'm busier than ever now, but it's a different kind of busy.

Writing is a wonderful means of expression. It has made me a better observer and a more critical thinker. I was fortunate that I have always loved to write, so doing so as an aging boomer comes easily to me.

That isn't always the case. If you're new to writing, read a lot, learn all you can, and then start writing. To be the best at it, keep writing every day!

* * *

BARRY SILVERSTEIN, AUTHOR, BLOGGER, AND FREELANCE WRITER

Writing had always been part of my career as a direct marketing and advertising professional. In fact, I wrote my first book about business-to-business direct marketing during that time.

I decided to retire early, in my late 50s. Since I loved to write, it seemed like a natural progression to become a freelance writer of blogs, articles, book reviews, and books.

As a freelancer, I am my own boss and write on my own schedule, writing from anywhere. Since I write part-time, it's an ideal lifestyle for maximum flexibility, allowing for volunteering and travel.

I find that writing as you get older has great intellectual benefits. Writing blogs demands that you keep current. Writing book reviews means you must read and digest lots of information. Writing books involves research and organizational skills. All these things keep an aging mind active and sharp.

PART I: GETTING STARTED

CHAPTER 1:

INSPIRATION FOR IDEAS

Have you heard this quote by Jack London? "You can't wait for inspiration. You have to go after it with a club." I don't believe in paralyzing writer's block, and it sounds like Jack London didn't either.

Maybe you already have tons of ideas bouncing around in your head. If that's the case, you're ahead of the game.

However, some beginning writers aren't sure how to start. Where can you find ideas for writing projects? The answer is anywhere and everywhere.

The following is a list of places where you can start looking.

EXPLORE YOUR MEMORIES

If you're older, you have the benefit of a lifetime of meaningful experiences and emotions to draw upon for inspiration. Start by making some lists:

- Search and make note of those enlightening moments, traumatic events, and significant turning points in your life that changed you forever. Include the painful, humiliating, frustrating, fearful, and confusing moments as well as the thrilling, joyful, exhilarating, and inspiring times.
- Jot down life lessons, adventures, secrets, and childhood memories.

- Make note of what made you laugh the loudest and memories that reduce you to a bucket of tears.
- List people who have had the most impact and influence on your life – good and bad. Your first love, a friend, a stranger that helped you, or even an enemy that provided compelling life lessons. Maybe someone you never met affected your life in a meaningful way. Jot down fascinating personality traits and interesting quirks of people you know.

All these recollections can be used in a novel, memoir, children's book, magazine article, blog, or poem.

Do you need help jogging your memories?

- Listen to music from a bygone era.
- Look at photos.
- Dig up old love letters and correspondence from friends and family.
- Talk to friends and family who share your memories.
- If you kept a journal, lucky you! You have an instant channel to take you back in time. I used portions of my teen diaries to write my first young adult novel, *Just Call Me Goody-Two-Shoes.* I landed a literary agent who praised me for using an authentic voice that my journals inspired me to create.

Remember, if you have a traumatic story, other people can benefit from learning how you overcame challenges and failures to move forward and live a fulfilling life. Maybe you lost a parent in death while still young, went through a harrowing divorce, or were diagnosed with a chronic disease with no hope of a cure.

Dig beneath the surface. Tap into the raw emotions you felt. You may have the outline of a compelling memoir, the basis for a protagonist's problem in a novel, or an intriguing topic for a nonfiction book, article, or blog.

For example, caring for my mother, who had Lewy Body dementia (a cruel combination of Alzheimer's and Parkinson's), and her eventual death was one of the lowest periods in my life. Yet, I chose to share my experiences and life lessons in my book, "*I'm Your Daughter, Julie: Caring for a Parent with Dementia*," to help other caregivers. The process helped me heal and the book won a literary grand prize award. Most importantly, I had the deep satisfaction of hearing from caregivers describing how my book helped them. Knowing that putting my painful experience into words made a difference during a difficult time in their lives made it all worthwhile.

You may feel more comfortable using your traumatic story in a novel. If so, you don't need to describe the exact event. Use your experience as a starting point. As

Nancy Ellen Dodd writes in *The Writer's Compass*, "It doesn't have to be factual, in fact, it will probably be much stronger if it is metaphorical because you can then write about it more objectively, and you can get to the deepest, most painful, most vulnerable part of the truth. It's not as much about what you've experienced as it is the depth of that experience and the truths it reveals to you."

You can even use the same memories more than once in different ways. For example, let's say you had a heartbreaking relationship that ultimately failed. Consider how you might use this memory:

- Write a novel about two people who love each other deeply but, for whatever reasons, break up and move on with their lives.
- Change the ending and write a romance novel about how they overcame all the obstacles and lived happily ever after.
- You may have learned an important life lesson from that relationship. Turn the experience into an article or blog, describing what you learned and revealing how it can benefit others.
- This experience can be the basis of a memoir if the life lesson was repeated often during your lifetime.
- Pen a heartfelt poem about the struggles of loving the wrong person.

USE YOUR BACKGROUND

List all your jobs, skills, interests, travels, and adventures.

Are you an expert on a specific subject? Do you have practical and cost-effective solutions to problems that businesses in your industry commonly face? Your knowledge and experience could give you an advantage when submitting articles or book proposals as a beginning writer.

If you're obsessive and knowledgeable about a subject – whether it's traveling, sailing, quilting, extreme sports, or photography – your enthusiasm can help you write with passion and conviction. You might choose to write a book, start a blog, freelance for a print or online magazine, or perhaps a character in a novel will share your fascination.

Tip: If you plan to submit a nonfiction book to publishing houses, try to find a unique angle on a subject to help you stand out from the crowd. For example, my father is a civil engineer who designed a building system for energy-efficient steel-framed homes. I was able to sell several articles to building magazines on this subject. Although there were several books on building steel-framed homes, none tackled the subject of how to make steel, which conducts heat, more energy-efficient. I wrote up a book proposal for a nonfiction book which McGraw Hill accepted. My father and I co-wrote the book and were well compensated. As a bonus, we had a great writing credit to add to our resumes.

PROWL THE INTERNET

This one is a no-brainer. The Internet provides a treasure trove of ideas with endless variations on any subject. Story possibilities are waiting to be discovered right at your fingertips. Where should you start looking?

- News stories on the Internet can inspire ideas for novels. Keep an eye out for absurd or bizarre news items and poignant human-interest stories. Everything from a double homicide to a neighborhood do-gooder to a corporate conspiracy may spark your creativity.
- Maybe you're researching a subject on the Internet and discover a related fact and think, "Now, there's a great story idea." Go with it! Take note of any surprising or interesting fact, event, or anecdote that arbitrarily pops up.
- Blogs and forums are available on every subject under the sun and may give you an idea for a nonfiction book or article.
- Learn from publishers who know how to find interesting story ideas to attract readers. Write down magazine, newspaper, and blog headlines along with book titles on subjects that interest you. Change one word for a different spin on a current topic.
- Use Google Alerts. Choose a subject that interests you, type in a keyword, and you'll get emails when articles on your subject appear on Google. If you have a blog, you'll never run out of ideas.
- Search the web for creative writing prompts that many sites offer for free. These prompts can help you explore ideas you may not consider on your own. A couple of sites include https://www.writersdigest.com/prompts and https://blog.reedsy.com/creative-writing-prompts/.
- Inspiration is not only found in the written word. If you're stuck, you may get an idea from a photograph, map, or an old legend you see online.

READ, READ, READ!

As Stephen King advised: "Can I be blunt on this subject? If you don't have time to read, you don't have the time – or the tools – to write. Simple as that."

If you're a writer at heart, you probably already love reading. I certainly do! Use that passion to your advantage:

- A topic or phrase you find in a book may inspire your own story.
- Study the author's plot and think of a different twist. For example, the book *Wicked* is based on characters created by L. Frank Baum in *The Wizard of Oz.* (Just keep in mind, if you decide to use material directly from the source, be sure the work is in the public domain.)
- Analyze your favorite novels and make a note of the reasons why you love them so much. Scrutinize characters and see what brings them to life. You may even combine character traits from different books when creating a protagonist.

Don't limit yourself to just novels. Non-fiction can provide inspiration as well.

- Reading about a historical event may motivate you to create a fictional story using the first-person viewpoint. Or maybe you'll write a novel describing how life would be different if the incident never happened.
- As mentioned in the last section, read newspaper and magazine articles about crimes of passion, human-interest stories, and current topics for inspiration. Use your imagination and embellish away!
- Even a fable, poem, proverb, or quote may get your creative juices flowing.

Ray Bradbury once advised a group of inspiring writers at a writer's conference I attended over 20 years ago: "Read one short story, one essay, and one classic poem every night for a thousand nights." In other words, be inspired by great writing. Note how the author uses voice, rhythm, and writing style to engage readers and pay attention to sentence structure and word choice. Apply these techniques in your work.

DO SOMETHING EXCITING AND WRITE ABOUT IT

As Benjamin Franklin once famously said, "Either write something worth reading or do something worth writing."

In other words, if you want to make your writing more interesting then make your life more interesting.

Writing is a great excuse to do all those fun things you want to experience in retirement. Be like Ernest Hemingway who spent as much time living an exciting life filled with adventures as he spent penning novels.

Make a bucket list and do those things you've dreamed about for years. Push your limits and get out of your comfort zone. Then write about your adventures in a nonfiction book, memoir, blog, or magazine article. Or use the experiences to help define a character in a novel.

Be creative and think outside the box. Need some ideas? Here are some to consider:

- Move to or visit a foreign country. Write about your experience in a travel blog or memoir. Or use your intimate knowledge of the country for a setting in a novel.
- Become a missionary or volunteer for disaster relief and share life lessons in a non-fiction book or memoir. If you're writing a novel, use the experience to help create a character.
- Conquer your fears. Afraid of heights? Go tree camping, attempt zip-lining, or ride in a hot-air balloon. Afraid of making a public spectacle of yourself? Act in a play, give a speech, or sing Karaoke. Immediately afterward, jot down how you were able to face your fears and how you felt afterward. Write about your experiences in a blog or use those feelings in a novel or poem.
- Perform one act of kindness each day for a year. Describe how it changed their lives – and yours. The experience could be the basis of an inspirational story.
- Work 10 bizarre jobs like a professional mourner, line-stander, street performer, or dog surfing instructor (and earn some cash while you're at it). Use one of the jobs in a novel, or write a nonfiction book or an article about your experiences.

Living life to the fullest will not only provide you with a constant barrage of things to write about. It will also give you a life worth remembering.

BE A LITTLE NOSY

There's nothing more inspiring than humans themselves. If you look carefully, you'll find plenty of dramatic material all around you:

- Maybe one of your friends, neighbors, or family members has an interesting, tragic, or inspiring story. Use it as an anecdote in a nonfiction book, article, or blog with their permission. Or use your imagination. Change the characters and location, twist the truth, and dramatize events until they are no longer recognizable. Then, use the fictionalized story in a novel.
- Read your local newspaper. If you live in a small, rural community, all the better! You may know the personalities of the people involved, what caused an event, and the devastating consequences. Ask, what would have happened if the people or sequence of events happened differently and take the story in an entirely new direction. You may have the beginnings of a novel that is more riveting than real life.
- I'm not advocating eavesdropping, but sometimes you can't help overhearing conversations. Especially these days when people talk freely, loudly, and publicly on their cell phones. Hey, if you happen to hear an interesting story or a bit of riveting dialogue, discreetly jot it down for inspiration later.
- Be observant. Go to a public place with lots of people. Imagine what their lives are like and create backstories. People-watching can also be helpful when describing a character's looks, gestures, dress, or grooming. Write down descriptions of quirks, mannerisms, strange clothes, and any unusual ways of eating, walking, or talking that you can use later.

ASK QUESTIONS

"The most important of the questions is just 'what if,'" prolific writer Norman Gaiman writes on his website. "What if you woke up with wings? What if your sister turned into a mouse? What if you all found out that your teacher was planning to eat one of you at the end of term - but you didn't know who?"

The list of "what if" questions is endless. What if a conspiracy theory were true? What if birds started screaming instead of singing? What if there were really monsters living underneath beds? What if you could write a letter to your past self? What if a historical event had never happened?

To show you how well this works, think of famous movies that asked the question "What if?" *Jurassic Park* asked: What if dinosaurs still roamed the earth? *The Matrix* asked: What if our world is actually a computer stimulation? *The Sixth Sense* asked: What if a little boy could see dead people but no one else could?

Or ask why. Children often do this. Have the same kind of curiosity and see where it leads you. If you read a disturbing news story, ask yourself why and how it happened. What were the possible motivations for the crime? Why did the victim react in a specific way? What other possible outcomes could have resulted if the victim had acted differently?

Explore all the possibilities and you may have a story idea.

WATCH MOVIES OR TV

Writers can be a bit snobby about reading good literature, but quality movies and TV shows can provide ideas as well.

Take a different spin or combine plots from movies or shows for a novel. Or use a personality trait for one of your characters.

Even a TV show or news program may inspire you. Bestselling author of *The Hunger Games*, Suzanne Collins, found the idea for her book series from channel surfing. "I was flipping through the channels one night between reality television programs and actual footage of the Iraq War when the idea [for *Hunger Games*] came to me," she says in an interview for *The New York Times*.

No plans to write a novel? You could use an interesting quote from a character in a movie to launch a blog post or inspire a journal entry.

JOIN A WRITING GROUP

A writing group allows you to brainstorm with other writers. Some groups provide writing prompts, props, or writing assignments to trigger ideas.

Try to find a group that not only talks about writing but puts pen to paper while sitting together. That way you go home with a page or two of scribbled notes to get you started.

Other writers may help you discover a new path, take a different direction in your story, or try different types of writing.

How can you find a writing group in your area?

- Google your city and "writing groups" to help you find a local group.
- Contact your local library or bookstore since many host groups.
- Your local college or university may have writing groups or programs open to the public.
- Explore retirement communities that have a focus on fostering creativity. These communities sometimes organize writing workshops and events.
- Check your local newspaper for announcements about meetings.
- Online writing groups are also available. Look for groups on social media sites. I'm part of a Facebook writing group that has been inspirational and provided lots of support.

BRAINSTORM

Try writing whatever pops into your head with reckless abandon. Tap into the subconscious. Don't think, pause, self-edit, or judge your ideas. Just let random thoughts flow from your mind onto paper. Quantity is more important than quality at this point.

Here are a few ideas to get you started:

- Write down a theme for a novel, plot ideas, snippets of conversation, character descriptions, and scenes the minute they pop into your head.
- Scribble notes about topics for nonfiction books, blogs, or articles that you would like to explore in the future. Jot down already-known facts, parts of an outline, people you may want to interview, and possible questions to be researched.
- Use a mind map drawn in a tree-shaped format. Write down your subject at the center, add branches and subbranches, and fill with ideas and sub-topics associated with your topic.
- "Word storm" by taking a one-word topic and adding a word or phrase. Say you want to write about hiking. You might come up with phrases like

benefits of hiking, best hiking trails for beginners, hiking equipment, or hiking for those aged 50-plus.

- Play a game of free association. Open a dictionary, pick a word, and write down all your thoughts and associations that come to mind. Your notes may be funny, shocking, sobering, or hysterical. Most of it might not be helpful, but you never know. You may find an idea or insight you can develop into a writing project if you're lucky.

ATTEND A WRITER'S CONFERENCE

Not only will topics of discussion at a writer's conference provide ideas, but other attendees can provide inspiration as well.

Romance suspense *USA Today* bestselling author, Charlotte Byrd, who has sold more than 2 million books, discovered her phenomenally successful path after talking to another author at a conference.

"I've written a lot of other types of projects, including short stories, literary fiction, and my PhD thesis," she explains. "When I attended a writer's conference, I met a romance author who told me about how successful she has been writing and publishing romance books and I decided to try my hand at that. I love thrillers with a good love story so that's how I found my niche as a romantic suspense author."

CHANGE THE SCENERY

If you're stuck and can't settle on one idea, try stepping away from your computer:

- Get up, take a walk, and enjoy nature. When you're not trying to force ideas, some wandering can stir up random thoughts that come unexpectedly.
- Travel somewhere – whether that means visiting a different country and culture, hiking a new trail, or visiting a nearby town you've never seen before. Let your mind meander, be curious, and see what new ideas pop into your mind.
- Express yourself creatively in different ways. Play the piano, arrange flowers, or create pottery. Look at beautiful artwork or play classical music

that stirs your soul. You might be surprised at what arbitrary thoughts pop up when you relax and get your creative juices going.

Even if you're not successful, at least you've taken a much-needed break and your mind may be more cooperative when you sit down at the keyboard again.

Finally, don't forget why you chose to write in the first place. Don't put too much pressure on yourself. Simply enjoy the process. Writing should be a time of joy, exploration, excitement, passion, and discovery. Don't lose sight of this fact, and inspiration often comes on its own.

KEEP A WRITING JOURNAL

So, maybe you've used some of these suggestions and developed some great ideas. Don't let those inspirational flashes escape. Write them down!

Keep all your ideas in one place. When your muse dries up, you can return to your journal full of ideas and inspiration.

Any plain notebook or even your cell phone will do, although a beautiful leather journal may be more motivating. Always keep your journal with you and by your bedside at night.

WHAT WRITERS IN RETIREMENT HAVE TO SAY...

ROSIE RUSSELL

I find the biggest thrill when I'm inspired by a pleasant memory from childhood or writing about special people and pets in my life.

There are literally stories everywhere you look. The ones that keep nagging at my heart are the ones I know I must find a way to write.

* * *

CAT MICHAELS

Tap into your own experiences and passions to create stories that resonate with your readers. Discover the sweet spot where your interests align with their desires–what do they want to learn about, and be entertained by?

My upbringing along the Atlantic instilled a deep love for the coast. I spent summers as a kid exploring the beaches, just a 15-minute drive from home. This connection to the sea is reflected in my children's tales and sweet contemporary romance novels, both set in charming coastal communities near my North Carolina home.

Plus, both genres share a common thread of hope and happy endings, reflecting my belief in a brighter future.

* * *

SANDRA BENNETT

Inspiration comes from everywhere.

My grandkids, nature, the environment, holiday destinations, conversations, and interacting with children in general.

* * *

BARRY SILVERSTEIN

The world around me is my greatest inspiration. I try to keep up with current events, changing technology, and culture. Especially information that relates to boomers, since I blog and write books primarily for that audience.

A lot of my blogging comes from my own personal experience.

The subject matter for my books is typically related to small business and brand marketing, topics I am very familiar with.

CHAPTER 2:

CREATE A WRITING WORKSPACE

Mark Twain wrote to William Dean Howells and described where he wrote most of his famous novels:

"It is the loveliest study you ever saw...octagonal with a peaked roof, each face filled with a spacious window...perched in complete isolation on the top of an elevation that commands leagues of valley and city and retreating ranges of distant blue hills. It is a cozy nest and just room in it for a sofa, table, and three or four chairs, and when the storms sweep down the remote valley and the lightning flashes behind the hills beyond and the rain beats upon the roof over my head—imagine the luxury of it."

Oh, I love the romantic vision of that little writer's retreat, don't you?

Most of us don't have the luxury of a writing studio with a majestic view like Mark Twain. But that doesn't mean we can't create a tranquil, comfortable place to pen our own masterpieces.

As a writer, I want my office to not only be functional, but inspirational too. A place that invites me to come in and enjoy the simple satisfaction and joy of writing. I couldn't be happier with my writing space now in the corner of our sunroom. I have plenty of light, an inspiring and relaxing view out the window, and my beloved collection of books nearby.

BENEFITS OF A WORKING SPACE

You probably want a dedicated writing space, even if it's simply a small desk in the corner of a room.

Why?

- An area free from noise and distractions with easily accessible tools will make you more productive.
- You'll be inspired by the beautiful surroundings you create.
- Sitting down in a peaceful writing environment will put you into the right mindset, helping you move from a hectic everyday life to a creative zone.
- Finally, a workspace helps you and others take your writing seriously. You can let people know when you're in your writing space and encourage them to leave you alone with your muse.

With these advantages in mind, let's discuss ways you can create the perfect space - whether it's the luxury of your own office or a writing nook in the corner of a room.

GO FOR COMFORT

As you age, it's more important than ever to opt for an office chair that supports your back and encourages good posture. A chic upholstered dining room chair may look fantastic but will kill your back.

Your desk and keyboard should be at a comfortable height to reduce muscle stress and strain. You may even opt for a standing/sitting desk if you plan to write for long periods of time to prevent getting stiff from sitting too long.

If you have the luxury of a dedicated room for your office, consider adding a pretty, nice comfy chair or small sofa with an ottoman. A place where you can curl up with a laptop, jot down ideas on a tablet, or proofread.

If you want to go all out, add a small coffee or end table to hold snacks and drinks, a fashionable lamp for extra lighting, a cheerful rug, and a throw to keep you warm.

You'll never want to leave!

LET THERE BE LIGHT

Proper lighting to reduce eyestrain is also essential as you get older. If possible, put your workspace near a window or French door for some natural light. Place your desk so that the window is in front of your desk or to the side to avoid glare on your computer screen – and so you can enjoy the view outside.

If you must depend on artificial light, be aware that existing overhead or recessed lights usually won't do the trick. An adjustable desk lamp can put light exactly where you need it. Avoid putting a light source behind you, creating an annoying glare on your computer monitor.

GET ORGANIZED WITH STORAGE

Good organization can help you focus and increase efficiency.

You don't need expensive storage products to accomplish this feat. If you're on a budget, get creative.

"Build" your desk with file cabinets for storage as a base underneath and a decorative wood door, a piece of granite, or a laminate countertop for the desktop.

If you're using the guest bedroom for an office, consider installing a shelving system in the closet for storing office supplies that are out of sight when not in use. If that's not an option, an old antique dresser can be a charming place to store writing materials.

You'll want the items you use daily to be handy. Vertical file folders can hold important papers within arm's reach, and a pretty basket can keep your mail and notes under control.

Keep your space simple and uncluttered. Basic tools like pens, paper, folders, and a few reference or how-to books on writing will do the trick. Remember that all the latest technology and shiny gadgets won't make you a better writer.

BE A BOOK WORM

This is optional, but books bring an inspirational quality to a room. If you visited my home, you would quickly see that I'm an enthusiastic collector of old books.

I feel like Lew Wallace, the author of *Ben-Hur*, who wrote to Susan Wallace, from Constantinople in 1885, "I know what I should love to do - to build a study; to write, and to think of nothing else. I want to bury myself in a den of books. I want to saturate myself with the elements of which they are made and breathe their atmosphere until I am of it. Not a bookworm, being which is to give off no utterances; but a man in the world of writing - one with a pen that shall stop men to listen to it, whether they wish to or not."

Books are not only beautiful to look at but can also be useful. Of course, reference books are essential. But you might also pick up a bestselling novel to see how your favorite author resolved a tricky plot line. The first edition of an old classic book may inspire you with its lyrical language. When you feel discouraged, just glancing at a novel on a shelf can provide reassurance that your name will be on the cover of a book one day.

If you're limited in space, a floating shelf above your desk can display your favorite books to motivate you.

CHOOSE PRETTY ACCESSORIES

Make the space your own so you'll enjoy time spent writing there. Choose furniture and accessories that reveal your style and personality.

Think about colors, textures, and items that inspire you and provide a sense of well-being. Since nature can help you feel calm and centered, consider adding plants or fresh flowers. Or decorate with natural materials like sisal or wood. Browse Pinterest for inspiration. Fun accessories might include:

- a fashionable lamp
- a decorative waste basket
- trendy notepads
- a colorful pencil holder
- a cherished family knick-knack.

Of course, be careful not to clutter your working area with too many decorative items which can become messy and distracting.

SURROUND YOURSELF WITH INSPIRATION

Post inspirational sayings, photos, or a favorite piece of art above your desk for extra motivation.

When I started writing, I had a board above my desk with clippings, acceptance letters, and even encouraging rejection letters to help me remember successful moments. You know what? It helped.

On the practical side, some writers hang whiteboards above their desks that they update regularly. Visibly seeing plot ideas, deadlines, or your progress can also inspire you.

WHAT IF YOU DON'T HAVE ANY SPACE?

If you have an extra room to create a charming retreat – wonderful. But you don't need much space to set up a writing area. I've seen photos of charming offices created inside of walk-in closets or writing nooks in quiet attics. If you have an unused alcove or corner available in a favorite room, why not set up your desk there?

If you don't have any room whatsoever for a designated writing space, don't despair. Perhaps you live in a multi-generational home with grandchildren running around. A quiet area is simply not available.

Don't give up on your dreams. Remember, writing can be done on a dining room table amidst chaos if necessary. I did just that when I started writing and my children were young.

Fortunately, a laptop can go anywhere. Maybe you'll start writing in bed, then move to a couch or desk when people aren't home. Feel a need to get out of a noisy house? You can always write at your local Starbucks. Prepare a tote with pens, paper, and your laptop ready to go when the muse hits.

Author Nancy Ellen Dodd writes in her book *The Writer's Compass* that she knew someone who "threw a giant bean bag into a corner with a CD player at arm's reach for music and that became her writing space."

Hey, whatever works.

CHAPTER 3:

EMBRACE TECHNOLOGY

If you're serious about writing, try to get comfortable with technology. You may envision click-clacking away at an old manual vintage typewriter like Jessica Fletcher in *Murder She Wrote*. Or romantically penning a novel in a leather-bound journal sitting under your favorite tree. While these nostalgic visions may be appealing, let's get practical.

As you age, your hands tend to cramp up when handwriting for long periods of time. And do you really want to go back to the days of a manual typewriter with whiteout to correct errors?

A computer allows you to easily correct mistakes, rearrange paragraphs or chapters, spell check, and research the Internet – to name just a few advantages. On top of that, handwritten or typed manuscripts sent to an agent or traditional publisher from a first-time author will likely end up in a trashcan without so much as a glance. Even if you plan to self-publish, manuscripts need to be uploaded to a computer for easy transfer. Believe me, I'm technically challenged, but I realize that computers and software programs are invaluable to me as a writer.

Hopefully, you already have a computer in your home you can use for writing. If you have a reliable computer that meets your needs, stick with it. There's no need to buy a new one simply for writing. Although several years old, I still use a custom-built desktop PC that my brother helped build.

If you don't have access to a computer and want to purchase one, choices abound. Should you buy a desktop computer, laptop, or Chromebook? That depends on your needs, preferences, and budget constraints. You'll want to choose carefully. Having the right computer can make a difference in how efficiently you work and make your writing journey more productive and enjoyable.

Let's discuss some of your choices.

DESKTOP COMPUTERS

Desktop computers typically have more spacious keyboards and larger monitors than laptops, which can be gentler on your body and eyes, especially if you plan to write for long periods of time.

As *Consumer Reports* points out on their website: "Compared with a similarly priced laptop, a desktop PC typically delivers more power, more storage, and more ease when it comes to upgrading components."

If you don't have space for a full-size tower, compact desktops require less room. Keep in mind, however, that these computers offer less flexibility. For example, although the small Apple Mac Mini performs very well, according to *Consumer Reports*, you won't be able to upgrade the memory or storage.

In general, writers require a system that offers a comfortable and ergonomic writing environment, reliability, and sufficient performance for word processing and other potential tasks such as research. A moderately-priced computer from a reputable manufacturer is likely to meet these requirements adequately.

If you plan to transcribe spoken words into written text through voice dictation, many computers are equipped with built-in speech recognition features. Additional specialized software, such as Dragon NaturallySpeaking, Otter.ai, and Google Docs Voice Typing, can be installed to provide extended functionality. When selecting a computer for voice-to-text software, ensure that it meets the software's technical requirements.

Of course, the number of options available can make decisions hard. Before purchasing a computer, do your research. Read reviews and consider warranty and support options before making a purchase.

LAPTOPS AND CHROMEBOOKS

A laptop may be a good choice if you travel a lot, prefer to move from room to room when writing, or portability is important. Personally, I use a Dell Inspiron 16-plus for these types of situations.

Chromebooks may be tempting if you're on a tight budget since they are often half the price of a Windows laptop. In addition, Chromebooks are smaller and lighter than laptops, which makes them more portable.

However, at the time of this writing, Chromebooks have limitations, including the following:

- If you're accustomed to Windows or MacOS, which allows users to install a wide range of applications, including traditional desktop software, Chromebook's minimalist operating system may not have all the functionality you need.
- Chromebooks use cloud-based apps. As a result, they are almost unusable without the Internet and have limited support for USB peripherals.
- Chromebooks typically have limited internal storage. Users are encouraged to store their files on Google Drive or other cloud services.
- You can't print directly to any printer on your network. The printer needs to be supported by the Google Cloud Print service.

In conclusion, if you require a wide variety of applications and offline functionality, a traditional laptop might be a better fit. However, if your tasks are primarily web-based and you prioritize affordability and simplicity, a Chromebook could be a suitable option.

Consider the following features when choosing a portable computer for writing:

- Keyboard: A comfortable and responsive keyboard is crucial for long writing sessions. If possible, try typing on the keyboard before making a purchase.
- Portability: If you plan to carry your laptop a lot, a lightweight and compact design may suit you better.
- Battery Life: A long battery life is beneficial for writers who work on the go or in places where power outlets may not be readily available.
- Display: Look for a comfortable laptop with a larger screen suitable for long writing sessions to minimize the strain on your eyes. A high-resolution display can make writing more enjoyable.
- Performance: For writing tasks, a mid-range processor is usually sufficient. More powerful configurations may be necessary if you plan to use demanding applications.
- Storage: Consider the storage capacity based on your needs. Keep in mind that USB hard drives are accessible for computers and cloud solutions like Dropbox, Google Drive, OneDrive, and similar options are available for expanded storage capabilities.

SOFTWARE PROGRAMS

Once again, the "best" choice of software depends on your specific needs and preferences. Try different options to see what works best for your writing style.

Here are some of your choices:

- Microsoft (MS) Word: MS Word is still the word processor used by most writers today. Widely compatible, the interface is easy to use and familiar to most users. What you see on the screen is what your book will look like when you print it out. However, MS Word isn't really designed to handle large projects like books. For example, it takes time to scroll through hundreds of pages or rearrange chapters. Requires a subscription.

- Scrivener: Designed for writers, this software organizes complex projects, such as novels, nonfiction books, and screenplays. It's available for both Windows and macOS. Scenes or chapters can easily be rearranged by dragging and dropping them. Other features include setting targets and deadlines and a bird's eye view of your entire project available in corkboard mode. On the downside, there is a steep learning curve for new users. Requires a one-time payment of $49 at the time of this writing.

- Google Docs: The best free writing software for collaboration. A great choice if you are co-writing a book, viewing suggestions from editors, or gathering feedback from beta readers. Google Docs also has a built-in voice typing feature. Requires Internet access for full functionality. Does not require a subscription.

- Atticus: A book formatting tool that helps you export your book into beautiful formats for both print and eBooks. Atticus also functions as a word processor, allowing you to directly write your book using the software if preferred. Works for every platform (Mac, Windows, Linux, Chrome). Requires a one-time payment of $147 at the time of this writing.

- Vellum: Another book formatting tool well-known for producing gorgeous books with beautiful aesthetics. If self-publishing, this is software worth considering. A one-time cost of $199 for eBook generation and $249 for paperback formatting is required at the time of this writing.

AI TOOLS

Should you use artificial intelligence (AI) writing tools? That depends. Just so you know, if you use spell-check, you're already using AI. However, as I pointed out earlier, there is a huge difference between "AI generated" (AI wrote the entire book) and "AI-assisted"(you wrote the book but used tools to improve it).

When I started writing this book, I hadn't tried AI-generated tools yet. There was something about using AI that made me feel like it was cheating and not producing truly unique work.

However, many experts disagree and believe that writers' access to these powerful tools can make work more productive, effective, and even creative. After doing some research and talking to other writers, I've been experimenting with some AI tools that can help:

- brainstorm ideas
- develop new storylines
- rewrite phrases using an active voice
- check grammar
- help with sensory details
- suggest book titles
- error-check
- rewrite awkward passages
- improve blurbs
- provide useful feedback
- generate questions for beta readers

An advantage of using AI-generated ideas is that you save time and energy that usually would be spent brainstorming. Theoretically, this could give you more time to focus on creating original content.

As a bonus, AI can come up with story directions you may not have considered. Even if the ideas for a plot or characterization aren't viable, the suggestions may stimulate your creativity to help you come up with a different spin that works. This helps immensely if you have a bad case of writer's block.

Nonetheless, this is a slippery slope. Using generated text to write entire articles, blogs, or books and passing it off as your own writing is unethical in my opinion. Call me old-fashioned, but I became a writer because I actually enjoy the process of writing.

As you can imagine, using these tools has turned into a controversial and sometimes contentious issue. Recently, several authors sued OpenAI for "systematic theft on a mass scale," the latest in a wave of legal action by writers concerned that AI programs are using their copyrighted works without permission. As the lawsuit proves, when using these writing tools, you must ensure that you have not unwittingly infringed upon someone else's copyright.

Other disadvantages of using AI-generated text include:

- Although AI-generated content is no doubt efficient and fast, on the downside, it can be plagued by errors, inaccuracies, inconsistencies, and outdated material.
- Relying on AI may make your writing appear stilted, artificial, robotic, or repetitive. Remember, AI recycles phrases and descriptions based on what it's "learned" from data which can keep things stale.
- AI-generated stories lack a human touch that resonates with readers and a unique voice that only you can provide.

Be aware that the publishing world has taken notice and is responding to the wave of new books written using generative AI tools. For example:

- Amazon added a new artificial intelligence policy for authors using its Kindle Direct Publishing (KDP) platform. The policy requires authors to inform them when AI-generated content is used, defined as follows: "If you used an AI-based tool to create the actual content (whether text, images, or translations), it is considered 'AI-generated,' even if you applied substantial edits afterward." However, you are not required to disclose AI-assisted content, which Amazon distinguishes as follows: "If you created the content yourself, and used AI-based tools to edit, refine, error-check, or otherwise improve that content (whether text or images), then it is considered 'AI-assisted' and not 'AI-generated.' Similarly, if you used an AI-based tool to brainstorm and generate ideas, but ultimately created the text or images yourself, this is also considered 'AI-assisted' and not 'AI-generated.'" Before publishing, you will be asked: "Did you use AI tools in creating texts, images, and/or translations in your book?"

- If you plan to submit your book to agents and publishers, there's a good chance you'll be questioned whether you used AI in your story and to what extent. You'll probably find that – while disapproving AI-generated books – most do not object to authors using AI tools to enhance creativity and improve the quality of writing.

- Interestingly, Upwork, a freelance writing site, acknowledges on their web page that AI writing tools "help writers and bloggers do their job better—not replace human intelligence or the creative work that writers do so well." My latest client on Upwork asked that I not submit anything AI-generated. However, he didn't object "if I chose to leverage AI tools in my creative process if the result was 'uniquely me.'"

Keep in mind that AI detector tools can help uncover the probability of AI-generated content. At the time of this writing, these tools do so by analyzing specific patterns, attributes, structure, syntax, and stylistic elements indicative of AI authorship. However, as AI technology continues to grow, AI detector software will likely become even more sophisticated and accurate.

Ultimately, whether you choose to use AI is up to you, your agent or publisher, and your freelance clients. By using AI as a tool to enhance your writing and not as a crutch to do the work for you, AI can potentially enrich your writing to better your craft. Weigh the pros and cons, and be careful how you use this technology.

Most programs have free trials if you want to check out these tools for yourself. Here are some you may want to try:

- ChaptGPT: An AI chatbot that can assist with generating and organizing ideas, researching, creating characters, developing outlines, enhancing settings, suggesting titles, and, yes, even creating drafts of content. Be careful since using this tool can easily skirt plagiarizing if misused. Free with premium features available for $20 a month.

- Grammarly: Offers grammar and spell-checking tools and enhances writing style by offering suggestions related to repetitive words, incorrect punctuation, or consistency. Best of all, it's free, although premium features require a subscription of $30 per month. I used Grammarly to help edit this book as an experiment and was pleased with the results.

- Jasper: One of the biggest names in AI text generation, this tool has countless features to help you with every aspect of your writing, from brainstorming ideas to editing your final draft. Since Jaspar can generate content of any length, use it with caution to maintain originality and quality. A downside is that Jasper is one of the priciest AI tools on this list at $39 to $59 per month, depending on which plan you choose.

- ProWritingAid: Like Grammarly, ProWritingAid is a comprehensive writing tool that helps improve grammar, style, and readability. It includes checks for grammar, style, overused words, and more. It also provides in-depth reports on your writing. Subscriptions range from $10 to $12 a month.

- Sudowrite: This software can be helpful for fiction writers. It helps with outlines, plot points, character arcs, themes, pacing, revisions, and more. Again, use wisely since Sudowrite will write entire passages for you. They claim on their website that if you "start with your own work" then "you'll only get completely original suggestions." Subscriptions range from $10 to $44 a month.

Before we leave the subject of AI, many authors are excited about using AI art to create cover art and illustrations for their books. There are dozens of AI art tools out there. Here are some you may want to check out:

- Dall-E 2
- Fotor AI image generator
- Adobe Firefly
- Midjourney
- Canva
- Stable Diffusion

What about copyright laws regarding AI art? In a Kindleprenuer article, "AI Art for Authors: Which Program to Use, Copyright and Use Cases" writer Jason Hamilton states: "In most countries, there are no rights granted to AI-generated art, so all images are essentially in the public domain." Nonetheless, he warns: "There is a limit to this. For example, if you generate a recognizable image of Batman, you could not commercially use that art, because you obviously aren't the rights holder for Batman." It's dangerous to use the likenesses of public figures in your AI art as well, he adds.

At present, there is limited legislation addressing this issue. We'll likely see the development of more laws if legal action is initiated against those involved in the creation of AI art.

Given the evolving nature of AI and the legal landscape surrounding it, try to stay informed of new developments.

CHAPTER 4:

LEARN ABOUT THE CRAFT OF WRITING

You may want to write purely for your own pleasure. Perhaps you plan to start journaling, pen a short story, or write poetry for your eyes only. Learning about writing techniques and the publishing world gives you a headache just thinking about it.

If that's the case, feel free to skip this chapter. Simply enjoy the creative process and wonder of writing. You may enjoy reading a how-to writing book like this one or join a writing group for fun. Nothing wrong with that.

On the other hand, if you plan to submit manuscripts to agents or traditional publishers, write for a print or online publication, or self-publish a successful book, consider continuing to educate yourself after finishing this book. You may need to brush up on your spelling and grammar skills, learn to write more clearly and precisely, and edit your work to meet professional standards. If so, retirement is the perfect time to learn and acquire new skills. Before you balk at this idea, remember that learning can be enjoyable and good for your brain, especially as you age.

What are some of your options to hone your craft?

SIGN UP FOR COLLEGE CLASSES

Often, retirees can take college-level classes at deeply discounted affordable prices and sometimes even for free. Some colleges offer senior citizen tuition waivers to retirees past a specific age and who meet other requirements.

The American Association of Community Colleges introduced the Plus 50 Initiative in 2008 to help colleges learn how to provide what older students want. As a result, those over 50 usually find flexibility in terms of degree programs, online and weekend courses, and accelerated classes.

Most schools provide low-cost, non-credit adult continuing-education courses without tests or grades. My first writing class was of this variety and gave me a great start on my journey.

If you live close to a college, schools sometimes host authors and invite residents to take part. Some colleges allow retirees to use the libraries and other campus perks.

TAKE AN ONLINE COURSE

Not everyone can go back to school; maybe you don't want to. If you prefer, you can take online courses on your computer without ever having to leave the comfort of your home.

Whether you're interested in writing a novel, freelancing, blogging, or reviewing forgotten grammar rules, options abound. Countless online courses are offered on the Internet by knowledgeable instructors and professional writers.

Back in the day, before these options were available, I took two correspondence courses from Writer's Digest School – one on writing fiction and one on writing nonfiction. These valuable courses helped me get started on my career path.

You're fortunate that technology has improved teaching methods and made learning much easier.

EDUCATE YOURSELF

Maybe you don't want to commit to something so formal. What are some different ways to educate yourself on the craft of writing?

- Visit your local library or bookstore and read books about writing. When I started, I enthusiastically checked out every book my library had on the subject. If you can afford it, books can also be purchased. Used books are available on Amazon for a reasonable price.
- Expand your mind with websites dedicated to the art of writing, audiobooks, podcasts, blogs, and TED talks.
- Study *The Elements of Style* by Strunk and White, which every writer should have on their bookshelf.
- Subscribe to a magazine like *Writer's Digest*, *Poets & Writers,* or *The Writer* to stay up-to-date.
- Learn from other writers. Read and analyze both good and bad writing. Note what works – and what doesn't.

Be like Louis L'Amour, one of America's most prolific and beloved authors who educated himself. In his memoir, *The Education of a Wandering Man*, L'Amour describes how he learned to write from reading and experience. "I have never had to strive to graduate, never to earn a degree," he wrote. "The only degrees I have are honorary, and I am proud to have them. I studied purely for the love of learning, wanting to know and understand. For a writer, of course, everything is grist for the mill, and a writer cannot know too much. Sooner or later everything he does know will find its uses."

ATTEND A WRITERS CONFERENCE

Writers conferences provide valuable ideas, training, and insights about writing and are an excellent way to continue your education and improve your craft. Some conferences feature different categories and levels of writers, while others focus on a genre, such as romance novels or children's books.

These events usually offer lectures, panels, workshops, and advice from best-selling authors, literary agents, and editors. Many speakers will answer questions you have about writing and publishing.

Some conferences offer appointments to meet editors or agents who will look at your work for an extra fee. This can be a good option instead of mailing a manuscript that may land at the bottom of a slush pile.

As a bonus, you can enjoy the luxury of immersing yourself solely in your writing for a few days. You'll also have opportunities to meet other writers at various stages of their careers who are often happy to share tips.

These conferences cost money, of course. If you're on a budget, search for local conferences to avoid travel costs. You might also consider attending only part of a writer's conference if that's an option. Remember that dinners, special sessions, or meetings with editors and agents usually cost extra.

Online writers conferences are also available if preferred.

SIGN UP FOR A WRITING WORKSHOP

Writing workshops provide an opportunity to receive specific feedback from other writers and an instructor.

Unlike a writing course or conference with lectures, these workshops focus solely on your work in progress. Often, writers develop their craft together in the spirit of discovery and solidarity.

Some well-known workshops operate annually for an intense week or two, while local writer's groups usually host more affordable one- or two-day workshops. Assignments and critiques may be included. Online workshops are also available.

JOIN PROFESSIONAL ORGANIZATIONS

Joining professional writing societies can be valuable for writers looking to connect with peers, access resources, and stay informed about industry trends.

Here are some well-known writing organizations you might consider joining:

- Historical Novel Society (HNS)
- Horror Writers Association (HWA)
- International Thriller Writers (ITW)
- Mystery Writers of America (MWA)
- National Association of Memoir Writers (NAMW)
- Poetry Society of America (PSA)
- Romance Writers of America (RWA)
- Science Fiction and Fantasy Writers of America (SFWA)
- Sisters in Crime
- Society of Children's Book Writers and Illustrators (SCBWI)
- Western Writers of America (WWA)

These organizations often offer benefits such as networking opportunities, conferences, writing resources, and access to a community of professionals in the field. Before joining, consider your writing goals and choose an organization that matches your genre or area of interest.

BECOME A MEMBER OF A WRITING GROUP

Writing groups tend to be more casual and intimate. Typically, a small group of writers meet regularly in someone's living room or café to discuss issues relating to writing and publishing.

Members encourage each other, share contacts and ideas, and read and critique each other's work. Writing can be lonely at times, and these groups can provide much-needed support. A simple Internet search can help you find local groups.

These days, Facebook groups often serve as online writing groups. I'm part of one of these groups, and it's been invaluable.

PRACTICE, PRACTICE, PRACTICE

No one improves at a sport, skill, or craft without practicing. Writing is no exception. The best way to learn the craft of writing is by practicing the art - no fairy dust involved.

Try to write something every day – whether it's a chapter of your novel, a blog, an entry in your journal, or a poem.

Develop your own style. Don't worry if you hate your first attempts. You'll make mistakes and learn from them. Have fun and enjoy the process.

CHAPTER 5:

DEVELOP A WRITING ROUTINE

Whether you plan to write that novel you've been dreaming about for years or create a book of poems from a pile of index cards in your nightstand drawer, think about making a commitment. Developing a regular schedule can help you accomplish your goals.

Don't be frightened by this idea. I know, if you're retired, you've probably had enough of appointments and calendars during your career. I'm not talking about buckling down at a computer for hours and hours. You can work out a system that fits your retirement lifestyle. Just try and be consistent.

Here are a few tips to help you achieve your dreams.

DEDICATE TIME TO YOUR CRAFT

Even if it's only 15 minutes a day, commit to a specific amount of time and then stick to it. Make it a goal to be productive during that time. Let your family and friends know so they'll respect your valuable time dancing with your muse. You'll be surprised how fast the words add up – even if it is a short amount of time. Chip away at your dream bit by bit.

Of course, you might feel more ambitious. Perhaps you want to spend a few hours – or more – a day to knock out that novel. If that's the case, try writing in half-hour intervals so you don't burn out. Set a timer, and when your time is up, take a 10 or 15-minute break. This is a healthy thing to do as we age anyway. Stretch, sit in the sun, take a quick walk, or make a cup of tea. When your break time is over, start again. Complete as many half-hour sessions as you desire.

Choose a time to write that best works for your unique body rhythms. Does your brain work best early in the morning when you're feeling more energetic? Or are you more inspired to write when you have activities to reflect on at the end of the day? Everyone is different. Experiment to see what time of day works best for you.

CREATE A WRITING RITUAL

This is optional but can be fun. I'm talking about a simple writing routine that signifies the beginning of a writing session and entices your muse to kick into gear.

Your writing ritual can be any action or habit that separates you from everyday life as you begin writing. Perhaps it's something simple like clearing your desk, making coffee, listening to music, or sharpening your pencil. Anything that triggers a signal to your brain that it's time to get creative.

Of course, you're welcome to try a more elaborate writing routine if desired.

The writing habits of some famous writers were downright quirky. Victor Hugo, the author of *Les Misérables* and *The Hunchback of Notre-Dame*, famously had his servant take all his clothes away for the day and leave him naked with only pen and paper. That way, he was forced to sit down and write. I'm not that dedicated and will never write in the buff but to each his own.

Author and poet Maya Angelou rented a small, simple room with just a bed and bathroom in a hotel for a few months at a time. Dedicated and serious about her craft, she arose at dawn to write at least five hours daily. Angelou always kept a bottle of sherry, a Bible, a deck of cards, and a dictionary with her. Interesting combination, right?

I've heard of writers who drink a different flavor of tea each morning, write in a new place each day on "inspirational field trips," or light a scented candle to enjoy aroma therapy while getting into the groove.

You get the idea. In other words, experiment, have some fun, and see what summons your muse.

GIVE YOURSELF DEADLINES

I know you're retired, and the word "deadline" seems like a nasty word. But try to look at deadlines differently. Not to be dreaded but embraced to achieve your goals.

As the article, "Why a Writer Without a Deadline is Looking for Trouble" by Austin Vosler on *Writer's Digest's* website points out: "Too many writers say they are going to write a book and, after starting strong, find excuses as to why they stopped (or are on a super-long pause from writing books). There are legitimate reasons that could prevent you from book writing—help needed in the family, a health issue, etc. But if you're serious about writing a book, you must make time for it. Deadlines will push you to do just that."

Consider some positive aspects of setting deadlines:

- Setting a timeframe can help you finish your writing project in a reasonable time. As a professional writer for more than 30 years, I know for a fact that deadlines work.
- Writing under a deadline may force creative ideas to come to the surface. Remember when you had a college essay due the following day? Sometimes, writing under pressure brings out the best in you.
- Successfully meeting a deadline gives you a feeling of satisfaction and accomplishment, like checking items off a bucket list. And wait until you see the result of a finished writing project!

When setting deadlines, here are a few tips to keep in mind:

- Be realistic. How much time can you credibly devote to writing in a day? How many days a week do you want to write so it won't interfere with retirement activities like spending time with your family and traveling?
- Break down deadlines into smaller, doable goals. Setting a goal to write an entire book in one month will probably not work. You're likely to get discouraged and give up your project altogether. Instead, make it a goal to write one chapter a week or one page a day. You can also use word counts as deadlines. For example, "I will write 500 words a day" to measure your progress.
- Write down your deadlines in a calendar. Consider letting friends and family know about your goals so they can hold you accountable.

- When you meet deadlines, celebrate your progress. Take time to give yourself a pat on the back or a small treat for finishing a chapter or another accomplishment. Then, move to the next leg of your writing journey.

If you're feeling ambitious and need a kick in the pants, some writers enjoy participating in National Novel Writing Month. Commonly known by the acronym NaNoWriMo, this event occurs annually every November.

The goal is to write 50,000 words by writing every day for a month—about 1,700 words a day. Writers type their work directly into the NaNoWriMo website, and if they reach 50,000 words at the end of the month, they are considered winners. This program keeps you accountable and connects you to other writers.

PART II: WRITE A BOOK

CHAPTER 6:

WRITE A NOVEL

If you're retired, your life has undoubtedly been full of commitments and obligations. This is the perfect time to write that novel you've dreamed about for decades. You deserve to do something that brings you joy and makes you feel alive at this stage of life.

Just be sure to write a novel for the right reasons. Don't write a book because you think becoming an author will make you rich or famous. If that's your goal, you're likely to be disappointed. And don't write a book to impress your kids, grandkids, or friends.

Write for you. Pen that novel because you:

- love to write
- want a creative outlet
- feel a need to share your thoughts and feelings
- want to feel fulfilled when readers are moved to tears or laughter by your story
- hope to motivate people to rethink their lives and see the world from a different perspective
- look forward to the thrill of becoming an author and seeing your name on the cover of a book
- want to look back at your life with a sense of accomplishment and a smile on your face, knowing you had the guts, dedication, and perseverance to realize your goal

Ready to get started? Let's make that cherished dream come true for you one step at a time.

CHOOSE A GENRE

The term "genre" is another word for category and simply refers to the type of story you'll be writing.

Some classifications include adventure, romance, mystery, fantasy, thriller, suspense, historical, horror, science fiction, chick lit, juvenile, and young adult.

Maybe you don't want your book to be put in a box or limited by the confines of a specific genre. If you're going to write as an artist for your own pleasure, you don't need to worry about choosing a particular genre. There's certainly nothing wrong with that, especially during your retirement years when you're supposed to be having fun.

On the other hand, if you want to submit a mainstream novel to agents and publishers, you should rethink your strategy. Professionals typically specialize in a few specific genres. A manuscript must fit the type of book they represent or it will probably land in the trash.

Perhaps you plan to self-publish your book. Even so, if you plan to approach bookstores and sell your novel on online platforms like Amazon, your manuscript should fit into a specific category.

Need some help choosing a genre? Here are some tips:

- Learn about each genre before deciding. Read a few bestsellers in different categories.
- Understand your preferences before putting pen to paper. For instance, do you find romance novels moving, or do you think they're silly? Do thrillers keep you turning the pages well into the night, or do you hate to be scared? When people ask about your favorite books and authors, do you think of children's books or young adult novels? Likewise, what kind of movies and TV shows do you watch? If you lean toward mysteries, thrillers, or science fiction, that's probably where your passions and interests lie. Remember, you'll spend a lot of time and work – as well as your heart and soul – into a book. If you absolutely loathe reading a particular type of book, how will you write a quality novel in that category? You'll hate every minute. So, pick a genre that you feel passionate about and will enjoy creating.
- Think about what piques your curiosity. You may want to try a historical novel if you love reading biographies and visiting historical sites or

museums. A character-driven thriller might be your calling if you're fascinated by what motivates people.

- The genre you choose should come most naturally to you. Don't try to copy a bestseller you think will earn millions. That rarely works anyway.
- Stay flexible. The importance of experimentation shouldn't be overlooked. Write a few chapters or short stories in different genres and see what most appeals to you and where your talent lies. Finding out what you're good at writing can take some time. But through trial and error, you'll eventually find your niche. Be patient and enjoy the process.

Once you've chosen a genre, study books in your category. Learn about basic writing techniques and necessary elements. Consider your target audience – your readers' age, gender, background, and interests. Ask yourself what readers want and expect from your selected genre.

For example, a person reading a romance novel will expect a hero and a heroine who fall madly in love but face a problem or situation that causes conflict, tension, struggles, or dangers that keep them apart. On the other hand, a person reading a thriller will want plenty of suspense, intensity, a sense of looming danger, unpredictable passages, increasing tension, and an evil adversary.

Don't worry, you can still write in your unique voice in an exciting way without straying too far from basic formulas.

Can you combine elements from different genres? Sure. Many authors do so successfully. For example, popular romance subgenres include historical, suspense, fantasy, contemporary, science fiction, young adult, and paranormal. If you choose this route, make sure one genre dominates and the two categories blend seamlessly.

CONSIDER A THEME

Put simply, a theme is what you want to say in your book. What is your novel about – I mean, *really* about? Your theme should be the pulse of your story, giving your novel substance and deeper emotional impact. It can help your story become more cohesive, engaging, and meaningful.

Don't be scared off by the idea of coming up with a literary theme. It doesn't have to be complicated.

Think about Nicholas Sparks' successful novels that simply center on love and loss. Many popular themes can be explained in just a few words or less – good versus evil, survival, betrayal, the loss of innocence, vengeance, forbidden love, deception, triumph in the face of adversity, or redemption.

Themes are often based on life lessons. Therefore, you may be drawn to a theme influenced by your experiences, beliefs, or ideals. Or maybe you'll explore a universal theme such as why a good person does bad things, the dangers of ignorance, or the illusion of power.

Remember, your theme shouldn't be preachy with a simplistic black-and-white answer. As a famous movie director, Sam Goldwyn, once said, "If I wanted to send a message, I use Western Union." Step out of your comfort zone. Raise fascinating questions and explore all the sides and aspects of your theme.

While a theme is not absolutely necessary, it can make the difference between pure fluff and an engaging book your readers will think and talk about long after reading. As a bonus, a theme can also be used as a foundation to pitch your book to agents, publishers, and readers.

What if you can't come up with a theme?

Don't stress. A theme may evolve subconsciously as your novel progresses. Some books have multiple themes. Start writing and see what happens.

PLOT YOUR STORY

Basically, a plot is a series of events - or scenes - that focuses on a character's efforts to solve a problem or achieve a goal.

Many people are overwhelmed when thinking about plotting a novel. If that's how you feel, consider using a simple "three-act structure" that divides the story into three parts.

Keep in mind that this isn't your only option. Many contemporary novelists have successfully broken away from this basic structure and used unorthodox ways to organize their books.

But to give you the basics, the classic three parts of a novel include:

THE BEGINNING

The beginning of your novel should accomplish some specific goals. For example, you should:

- acquaint readers with the main character
- set the tone for your story
- introduce important secondary characters
- reveal the setting and time period of your novel

But that's not all.

More importantly, you must share what the character cares about or fears the most. What are your character's deepest longings? How is your character dissatisfied with life? What does your character value the most? What does your character think is the worst thing that could happen?

You must also grab the reader's attention. Include an exciting incident that propels your character's journey or adventure at the beginning of your book. This event should reveal your main character's goal and hint at the predicaments or challenges ahead.

THE MIDDLE

This part will be the longest section of your book. Conflicts, obstacles, and challenges come into play. Your goal is to make it as difficult as possible for your main character to solve a problem or achieve a goal.

Depending on the type of novel you're writing, you might use a vicious villain, an overwhelming obsession, a powerful organization, an inanimate force, or even a terrifying alien to block your character's path and cause lots of trouble.

Perhaps you've personally faced struggles, setbacks, and complications that could be used. If so, this can add a realistic touch to your character's plights.

Whatever you do, don't be easy on your character. As the author, it's your job to create a series of events and people that change your character forever.

How can you make your character's life miserable? Here are some ways:

- create a potent antagonist with a strong motivation to oppose your character
- make the conflict personal
- give your character personality flaws that make the journey more difficult
- present a moral dilemma with intolerable choices
- raise the stakes by making your character's desire an obsession
- let psychological, ethical, or cultural issues cause confusion and self-doubt
- keep your character off-balance with shocking events
- allow your character to question long-held beliefs

Remember, good stories involve a logical, cohesive series of events. Keep it real. Make sure each scene has a purpose and keeps the story moving. One scene should trigger the next and be propelled by a character's motivation.

Of course, stories have lows, highs, ebbs, and wanes. But overall, the action, energy, and urgency should increase in the middle of your story.

Build suspense and excitement by creating challenges that seem impossible to overcome. Give your character temporary victories and then snatch the triumphs away. Create even worse complications. Use surprises, twists, and turns to keep your story from becoming too predictable. Make it seem impossible for your character to succeed and your readers won't be able to put your book down.

Consider including subplots in the middle section. These secondary storylines can give different insights into your theme, main character, and events in the story. Subplots are often character-specific, so think about how each character's backstory might come into play. Subplots should be weaved in seamlessly and help advance your story instead of distracting from it.

THE END

The pressure has been building and now it's time for an explosion during a crisis point. Reaping all the consequences, your character must find the courage to achieve the desired goal. Perhaps an action must be taken or a life-changing decision must be made.

Once the pivotal moment has occurred, the tension falls dramatically. Your character must have a revelation, epiphany, or transformation and understand the truth of your chosen theme.

The conclusion of your story should also wrap up any loose ends, provide necessary resolution, and clarify the motivation for your character's actions and behaviors.

Be sure to reach a conclusion compatible with your theme and plot that will satisfy readers.

Following this structure will give you a basic outline for your book. Should you take it a step further? Do you need to develop an elaborate outline explaining each scene and all the details in your plot?

Authors' opinions differ widely on this subject. Here are your choices:

- In-depth plotting: If you have organizational skills, you may enjoy detailing the sequence of events in exact order. Some authors use a computer for this purpose, utilizing software programs or templates. Others prefer the old-fashioned method, using index cards, a notebook, or files to accomplish this feat.
- Planning: You can take the middle ground. With a general idea of how you want the story to progress, scribble some general notes and allow the plot to develop as you write. This is my preferred method.

- Pansting: This basically means writing by the seat of your pants. You have an idea but sidestep the logical part of your brain and use intuition and creativity to wrench the story from your subconscious. In other words, you wing it and just start writing. Surprisingly, prolific author Stephen King, rarely plots out his stories from start to finish before writing them. He wrote in his book, *On Writing*: "I distrust plot for two reasons: first, because our lives are largely plotless, even when you add in all of our reasonable precautions and careful planning; and second because I believe plotting and the spontaneity of real creation aren't compatible." Not surprisingly, King is also a big fan of the element of surprise. His philosophy: "If you as the writer can't guess what will happen next, then the reader sure won't."

The technique you choose depends on the type of novel you're writing and your personal preference. As you write, you'll find what works best for you.

CREATE COMPELLING CHARACTERS

Fictional characters are your story's lifeblood. Even with a fantastic plot, readers won't keep turning pages unless they care what happens to your characters. Think about your favorite books. Undoubtedly, the characters leaped from the page, intriguing, vibrant, and relatable.

If you're fortunate, characters will spring to life by themselves, reveal interesting traits, and speak and act of their own accord. But don't count on it. I love this idealistic and romantic idea, but unfortunately, this doesn't happen often – at least not to me.

More likely, you'll take a basic idea for a character and use techniques to bring that fictional person to life. Where can you find those first seeds of inspiration?

- Your plot line will probably require specific personality traits and that's an excellent place to start.
- Many beginning writers use facets of their personality. This is almost inevitable. Creating characters from your own imagination means a bit of you will likely sneak in. If you choose this route, only take the most intriguing and unique parts of you. And don't put too much of yourself into a character. If you become too attached, you may not allow bad things to happen including struggles, failures, or heartbreaks, which is necessary for a good story.

- Be a careful observer of human behavior and recreate interesting people in your life. This can include people you love as well as loathe. Use their strongest and most interesting traits and qualities. Just be sure to add plenty of embellishment so your character becomes unrecognizable.
- A character may be inspired by someone you read about in a newspaper, magazine, or on the Internet. Or even a historical person.
- Although you don't want to copy characters from other novels or movies, there's nothing wrong with using one or two of their personality traits as a springboard for your own characters.

Once you have a general idea of what your characters are like, you'll need to flesh them out. Consider creating a chart for each character to accomplish this task. This tool can also help you keep track of all the details associated with each character ensuring consistency.

Of course, you'll include basic information such as the protagonist's name, age, height, weight, ethnicity, general physical appearance, marital status, children, pets, education, background, work history, religion, social status, physical condition, place of residence, style of clothes, and income level.

Then, you'll need to dig deeper. How?

- Determine the character's motivations, goals, ambitions, deepest fears, regrets, strengths, weaknesses, beliefs, values, struggles, and innermost longings.
- Think about your character's specific personality traits, attitudes, and opinions. What makes your protagonist angry, happy, or scared? Cry or laugh? How does your character react to change? What's your character's best trait? Worst? What personality trait would your character most like to change? Is the character an optimist or a pessimist? Demanding or empathetic? Sensitive or thick-skinned? Cautious or adventurous? A realist or a dreamer? An outgoing extrovert or a shy introvert?
- Make note of your character's inner circle including close family members, dearest friends, and worst enemies. Examine what these relationships reveal. For example, has a childhood trauma or dysfunctional family affected your character's outlook on life?
- Add a few distinguishing details – or tags – to set your characters apart. These can include unusual physical traits, clothing, hairstyles, facial expressions, gestures, scent, quirks, voice, mental state, posture, and mannerisms.
- Know your protagonist's back story including events that happened before your story begins. Don't include every single detail of your character's past

in your book, of course, but let the events shape your character. How have your character's background and past experiences influenced desires, fears, motivations, and the type of person your protagonist eventually became? What life lessons did your character learn in the past that determine current decisions? What shameful secret is the character fervently hiding from the past?

- While main characters may be strong and even heroic, be sure to give them flaws and shortcomings. Is your character vulnerable, impulsive, self-destructive, stubborn, inconsiderate, arrogant, opinionated, aloof, or careless? Let your character make mistakes or fail miserably because of these weaknesses and suffer the consequences. Your characters' defects will make them relatable and become part of what your readers love about them.
- Give your character internal conflicts based on their background. What traits make your character stop and reassess relationships, examine issues from different angles, battle doubts and fears, waver between choices, or question what seems to be true?
- Each character should have a unique voice. A character's manner of speech can reveal background, education, and personality. For example, does a character stutter while looking down, dominate the conversation while constantly interrupting people, make outrageous or prejudiced statements, or use fancy words to impress people?
- Describe personal habits. Details count. What are your character's talents, hobbies, vices, likes, and dislikes? How does your character spend free time? What kind of food and music does your character prefer? What does your character spend money on? What does your character find frustrating? What's your character's favorite book or movie? What is your character's morning routine?
- Be sure and create three-dimensional characters with depth. Stay away from stereotypes. Make the nerdy college professor in a shabby suit dance on tables. Create a ruthless CEO who secretly has a soft spot for kittens. Combine traits in unexpected ways to make characters more realistic and memorable.

Fill out as much of this character chart as you feel is required. Obviously, minor characters need less fleshing out.

These charts don't have to be boring. Feel free to get creative. If you're a visual person, draw pictures of your character. Include facial expressions and body language that reveal their personality. Create a Pinterest vision board and pin images of people that match how you envision your characters. You could include clothes they'd wear, cities and houses where they'd live, bars or coffee shops they'd frequent, or images that capture their status in life.

Keep a character chart flexible. Perhaps you'll discover different traits suit your story better. Go ahead and make the changes. In fact, as your novel progresses, let your character evolve and adapt as necessary. Remember, real people never stop changing, and neither should your characters.

ESTABLISH A VIEWPOINT

Viewpoint (sometimes called point of view or POV) refers to the mind of the character(s) through which the story is told.

This can seem complicated sometimes, so I'll try and keep explanations as simple as possible.

One tip before we get started: Once you choose a point of view, stick with it for the entire novel. This is important. Be consistent. You should establish which point of view will be used in the first few paragraphs.

The three most common viewpoints are as follows:

- First Person

  In this case, the central character tells the story, using the pronoun "I." Everything a reader sees, hears, and experiences in the story comes through the main character. The advantage of using the first-person viewpoint is the intimacy and emotional impact it creates. You give the reader a detailed look into the heart and mind of your character. For beginning writers, using the first-person viewpoint keeps things simple since the story is told from just one person's perspective. On the downside, this point of view can be limiting. As a writer, you can't reveal the thoughts and feelings of other characters, although you can share how your main character understands and interprets them.

- Third Person

  This is the most common type of viewpoint used in novels. The author narrates the story using third-person pronouns like "he," "she," and "they" or refers to characters by name. The focus is mostly on the main character's thoughts, emotions, and actions. This enables a reader to closely identify with the protagonist. But, if necessary, you have the option of using another character's point of view. For example, in a thriller you may want your reader to know that the main character is in danger but, to add suspense, you don't want your protagonist to be aware of it. Or maybe you need to show your reader something that happens when your main character isn't present or share two different perspectives of the same story. If you choose this route, be careful not to jump from one character's head to another too often or in the same scene which will confuse readers.

- Multiple Viewpoints

  This viewpoint is used to tell a story from the perspective of several characters but stays with one character for a considerable length of time – usually for an entire chapter. Be sure and clarify which viewpoint character you're using within the first few sentences. Keep the number of viewpoint characters to a minimum. The more viewpoint characters you use, the less time the reader can get to know – and care about – each one.

If you're unsure which viewpoint to use, choose what comes naturally to you. If you're still confused, write a scene from different viewpoints. Read the scenes out loud and see which one works best for your story.

WRITE COMPELLING DIALOGUE

Well-written dialogue can advance your story and give insight into your characters. However, writing realistic and captivating dialogue isn't always easy.

Here are some tips to keep in mind:

- Dialogue must have a purpose. Conversations should provide essential information, add suspense, or give depth to characters. Avoid filler words, meaningless discussions with little or no point, or small talk – like you may hear while eavesdropping. You can do better than that.
- Keep dialogue brief and concise. Characters shouldn't give long, stiff speeches. Never use ten words when five words will do. If you can do the job with a simple gesture like a shrug, even better.
- Avoid boring conversations at all costs. Remember when you were first attracted to someone and you tried to make the conversation interesting, fresh, or funny? Do the same thing in your novel.

- Keep conversations natural. That means avoiding dialogue with complete, formal grammatical sentences. Very few people talk that way in real life. "Do you want to go to the park?" sounds stiff. "Want to go to the park?" is better.
- Break up blocks of dialogue. Use physical details, descriptions, and the character's thoughts to interrupt long discussions. Vary the length of sentences.
- Give your characters a unique voice when talking. For instance, perhaps your character has favorite words or phrases used frequently. A regional accent can make a voice distinctive, but only if you know the accent and slang well. Use sparingly since this kind of dialogue can quickly become annoying.
- Include any unusual mannerisms or facial expressions your character exhibits while talking.
- Remember, even silence can speak volumes. Not responding to someone's remark may imply anger, disapproval, condescension, frustration, or contempt.
- Don't overdo dialogue tags – variations on "he said" and "she said." You want your readers to pay attention to what the character is saying, not focus on colorful but strange dialogue tags. When I started writing, I found a list of 99 ways to say, "he said." As a result, my characters bellowed, babbled, beamed, bawled, and blurted. I was proud of myself until an editor told me to knock it off. You can throw in an occasional "whispered" or "yelled" but keep it simple and stick to basic tags for the most part.
- Avoid words that end with "-ly," reiterating the obvious with adverbs. "I got the job!" she said happily. "I can't believe you cheated on me," he said angrily. "My mother died," she said sadly. Good dialogue should let readers know how the character feels without you telling them.
- Don't allow dialogue to give away too much information at once, making readers feel like they're being fed important facts. Let the story unfold naturally.
- Beginning writers sometimes fail to punctuate dialogue correctly. Remember, quotation marks surround the dialogue as well as the comma or period at the end. "I don't believe you," she said. If you're not using a dialogue tag: "I don't believe you."

In the editing process, read your dialogue aloud to identify problem areas such as pacing, punctuation, and flow. Eliminate any repeated words or accidental rhymes.

PROVIDE RIVETING DESCRIPTIONS

A picture is worth a thousand words, which might make you think that writing can't compare with visuals in a movie. Yet, writers have one advantage over cinematography. You can create vivid mental images in the minds of your readers with the power of imagination.

How?

- Make sure you give your readers a sense of place at the beginning of your book. Choose a country, state, region, and town. Does the story occur in a hectic city, a quiet rural area, near the serene ocean, or in the pristine mountains? Which place serves the story best? When does the story happen? One hundred years ago, presently, or in the future?
- Use all your senses. What are some of the sounds your character would hear in an eerie town? How does the frigid lake water make the character feel? What does the dense, mossy forest smell like?
- Set a mood. Does your character find the setting relaxing or does it feel dangerous? Is your character chilling at a tranquil beach, listening to crashing waves with a cool breeze, and snuggling in the arms of a loved one? Or is your character's heart beating fast, stuck inside a closet that smells like dead rats, listening to heavy footsteps approaching?
- When appropriate, describe trees, flora, climate, bodies of water, or nearby mountains. Research will be needed so your descriptions are accurate and give your story credibility. If you have traveled or lived in the place you are describing, all the better. If not, the Internet is a great place to start your research. Or visit a library and enjoy the ambiance while you browse through books about your selected location.
- Whenever you start a new scene, let readers briefly know where the characters are and then sprinkle more details throughout. For example, if your characters are at a lively diner, briefly describe the loud, cheerful place as they enter. Later, mention a sassy waitress who interrupts an intense conversation. When they leave, indicate that one of the characters is too cheap to leave a decent tip.
- Paint a dynamic picture with strong, active words to heighten tension and pique curiosity. An excellent example of this is the scene in Margaret Atwood's *The Handmaid's Tale*, when Offred describes her room: "Above, on the white ceiling, a relief ornament in the shape of a wreath and in the center of it a blank space, plastered over, like the place in a face where the

eye has been taken out. There must have been a chandelier once. They've removed anything you could tie a rope to."

One warning: People today don't want endless, meticulous descriptions of settings that bring the story to an abrupt halt. Less is more. Don't get carried away. Ensure the descriptions enhance and support your story and are important to its theme.

CHOOSE AN INTRIGUING TITLE

You want a captivating and distinctive title that provokes interest and curiosity. Something that will entice people to click the "buy" button to read your book.

How do you find the right title? Start by brainstorming potential ideas and writing them all down. If you need some inspiration, one logical place to start searching is inside the pages of your book.

For example:

- What is your book about? Think *The Hunger Games* by Suzanne Collins, *Murder on the Orient Express* by Agatha Christie, or *The War of the Worlds* by H.G. Wells.
- A character's name can work, especially if he or she has a quirky name like *Forrest Gump* by Winston Groom or *A Man Called Ove* by Fredrik Backman.
- Is there a line of dialogue or a sentence that is thought-provoking, powerful, or poignant? The title *Silence of the Lambs* by Thomas Harris is derived from dialogue when the main character describes how she was traumatized by screaming lambs about to be slaughtered.
- A phrase or metaphor that sums up the idea or theme of your novel can be provocative. *The Thorn Birds* by Colleen McCullough is an example. Harper Lee's *To Kill A Mockingbird* represents a central theme and a meaningful piece of dialogue.
- Perhaps a character trait can be turned into a title, like my young adult book, *Just Call Me Goody-Two-Shoes*, which describes the protagonist.
- Consider a descriptive sentence or word that creates a particular emotion or mood based on your novel like Stephen King's book, *Misery*. Or Mary Higgins Clark's *Pretend You Don't See Her*, which immediately sets a mysterious tone.

- A catchy phrase with some alliteration can stick in readers' minds. For example, *Run Rabbit Run* by John Updike, *Pride and Prejudice* by Jane Austin, and *B is for Burglar* by Sue Grafton.
- Sometimes famous books use a time period like George Orwell's *1984* or even a time of day like *Twilight* by Stephanie Meyer.
- Be evocative to hook readers with a title like *The Particular Sadness of Lemon Cake* by Aimee Bender. The title is both allegorical and literal. Or *John Dies at the End* by David Wong which makes readers immediately wonder: Does John really die at the end? If so, how?
- Use a setting with some embellishments like *Cold Mountain* by Charles Frazier, *Picnic at Hanging Rock* by Joan Lindsay, or *Peyton Place* by Grace Metalious.
- Character motivation or a revelation can inspire a title like *Atonement* by Ian McEwan.
- Some titles are based on a main character's occupation. For example, Margaret Atwood's *The Handmaid's Tale* or Arthur Golden's *Memoirs of a Geisha.*

A title may also be inspired by a phrase in a book, song, or poem. *Fault in Our Stars* by John Green was inspired by Shakespeare's *Julius Caesar.* John Steinbeck's book title *Of Mice and Men* is based on a Robert Burns poem. *Love the One You're With* by Emily Giffin was inspired by a song written by Stephen Stills. The title of my second young adult novel, *Time to Cast Away*, was taken from a Bible verse.

If you still need help, study the names of popular books similar to your novel. What are common words and phrases they use? Of course, you never want to choose the same title as a well-known book, but this may give you some ideas for your own original and unique title.

AI tools and book title generators found on the Internet can also help.

Whatever you choose, make sure your title is a sensible length, clear, and concise. Avoid titles that are too broad or don't accurately represent your novel. A bit of mystery isn't bad, but your title should match the genre and tone of your book.

Once you've narrowed down your choices, search Amazon and Google to see if the title has been used before. Although titles cannot be copyrighted, your title should be distinctive to eliminate confusion.

If your book is traditionally published, consider the title you choose a "working title." The publisher may change the title for better marketability.

ESTIMATE WORD COUNTS

Many new writers are puzzled when it comes to the length of a book. How long should a novel be?

If you're writing for your own pleasure, the answer is however long you like. On the other hand, if you want to submit your novel to agents and traditional publishers or sell a self-published novel to online retailers, you'll want to aim for the norm.

To keep it simple, an adult novel is typically 70,000 to 90,000 words. That's around 300 pages of double-spaced type.

That being said, the length of a novel can vary depending on the genre. A romance reader may be happy with 50,000 words. On the other hand, an epic fantasy novel may have as many as 120,000 words due to complex storylines and the number of characters involved.

For children's books, keep the following word counts in mind:

- Picture Books: 300–800 words
- Early Readers: 200–3500 words
- Chapter Books: 4000–10,000 words
- Middle Grade: 25,000–40,000 words
- Young Adult: 50,000–80,000 words

Microsoft Word and Google Docs have word count options to help you keep track of your word count.

To figure out how many pages these word counts represent, keep in mind the average single-spaced document typed in a standard 12-point font contains about 500 words per page. The average double-spaced document has about 250 words per page.

EDIT YOUR NOVEL

You'll want to edit your manuscript before you self-publish your book or start submitting it to agents and publishers. You've probably made some changes as you wrote the story, but now it's time to fine-tune your book.

Many people look at the editing process as a chore. Personally, I enjoy polishing my words until they shine. With the right attitude, you can learn to enjoy this necessary part of writing.

The best way to find mistakes and needed changes is to look at your story with fresh eyes. That means putting your manuscript in a drawer for at least a few days, preferably longer. In *On Writing*, Stephen King says he puts finished drafts in a drawer for at least six weeks before looking at them again. I do the same.

When it's time to start editing, begin with major corrections. Search for confusing storylines or holes in your story, pacing problems, a weak opening or ending, a lack of character development or motivation, or any inconsistencies.

Eliminate unnecessary scenes or characters. Don't make the mistake of falling in love with your words. Be brutal. If a scene, paragraph, or sentence doesn't progress the story, take it out.

Finally, look for spelling, grammar, and punctuation errors, inconsistencies in tense, awkward sentences, repetitive words, and overused words and phrases. Using AI tools such as Grammarly can be helpful at this point.

The final step to editing is having others read and critique your work, sometimes referred to as "beta readers." Friends and family can help, but only if they can be honest without hurting your feelings. Writing groups often provide critiques to members. If you have other writer friends, perhaps you can trade critiques. I belong to a Facebook writing group and we often volunteer to be beta readers for each other.

If you plan to self-publish or submit your novel to agents and/or traditional publishers, you may want to hire a professional book editor. You can find an abundance of choices on the Internet. When I wrote my first novel, I used Writer's Digest's critique services and was pleased with the results.

CHAPTER 7:

WRITE A NONFICTION BOOK

Why write a nonfiction book?

Here are a few reasons:

- to share your life experience or valuable knowledge you've gained during a lifelong career to transform the lives of others
- to earn some extra income
- to attract people to an existing business
- to establish yourself as an authority and open doors to possible paid speaking engagements or to teach online classes
- to aim for literary acclaim while extensively exploring and researching a subject that fascinates you

Whatever your motives, I'm here to help you accomplish your goals. Let's get started!

SELECT A TOPIC

If you want to write a book for your own satisfaction and are not overly concerned with how it sells, pick any subject that tickles your fancy.

However, if your goal is to make money and write a successful nonfiction book, you must carefully select a topic. It helps to remember why people buy nonfiction books in the first place.

Readers want to:

- find solutions to problems
- discover valuable life lessons and improve their lives
- learn new skills
- gain insight into a subject they're passionate about
- be entertained
- learn from history for a better understanding of the world
- experience personal growth
- expand their horizons

You may already know the subject of your book. But what if you're not sure? Here are a few ideas to help you choose a topic:

- Look into your background. Do you have special knowledge that will be useful to others? Have you won any honors or received special recognition that would make you an expert on a subject? Do you know how to do something in an unknown, unique, and effective way?
- What life experiences do you have that could benefit others or broaden their understanding of the world? Remember, even your failures can provide inspiration for a book if you can help others avoid the same mistakes and share insightful life lessons. If you're funny and can write about your life experiences in a fun, quirky, and entertaining way, humor is always in demand.
- What if you think nothing in your background is interesting enough to write a whole book about? You can write about a topic you know little about but feel excited enough to research extensively. What fascinates you? For example, you may want to write a book about a historical event and are willing to devote time to locating people, finding unique interpretations of history, as well as researching letters, diaries, newspapers, and other documents. Go for it! You aren't necessarily limited to what you already know.

- Research a current topic. What concerns people the most right now? Which subject will be the most valuable to them? Think back to this past month. What did you hear or read about that piqued your curiosity and made you want to know more? Would other people be interested to learn about the subject as well?

If you choose a popular subject like weight loss, finances, or self-improvement, check out what books are already available. Then, search for a fresh angle that will make your book unique. For example, although there are several books about steel-frame construction, I discovered that none addressed energy-efficiency issues. Finding a different angle helped me get a contract with one of the major publishing houses.

When you're just starting, a niche publication with a regional slant may do well for kids, seniors, singles, etc. Submit to smaller publishers within your chosen area. *The Complete Guide to Self-Publishing* by Marilyn Ross and Sue Collier suggests combining a regional topic with new trends, adding that "there is a keen interest in regional cookbooks, restaurant guides, and history books about specific areas."

CREATE AN OUTLINE

Once you choose a specific topic, brainstorm what areas you'll explore in detail. Write down everything that pops into your head. Perhaps some of your unused ideas will end up in a different book.

Next, create order out of chaos. Edit your list and create an outline or table of contents. Include all the major topics you plan to cover and sub-categories that help explain or clarify your subject. Be sure to cover your subject thoroughly so readers will be satisfied.

Include:

- answers to common questions and concerns
- necessary actions or changes your readers need to make
- common misconceptions and myths
- mistakes, challenges, or obstacles your readers may encounter
- any unique advice, process, or methodology that can help readers
- valuable tools and resources.

If you're having trouble outlining your book, AI tools can help. Also, there's nothing wrong with visiting Amazon and searching for similar books. Browse through their table of contents (use the "Look Inside" feature that allows you to preview pages) to inspire your own ideas.

Visit popular chat rooms, discussion groups, or forums relating to the topic you want to write about and take note of what questions people are asking. What are their concerns, interests, and perplexing problems?

Creating an outline may feel a bit cumbersome, but a few hours of outlining your book saves you countless hours later when it's time to write it. Instead of wasting time staring at your monitor with a crippling case of writer's block, you'll know what to write each day following the blueprint you created.

START YOUR RESEARCH

Perhaps you've already done some research for the book. If you're a public speaker, you probably have material from a PowerPoint presentation or handouts. If you've started a blog, perhaps you've written articles on your subject. Or you may have information from personal experience that needs to be written down. If so, that's a great place to start.

After you utilize what you already have or know, research can begin.

Of course, the Internet is an unlimited free source of material. Learn to use search engines effectively and you'll have instant access to data, statistics, anecdotes, expert opinions, contact information for potential people to interview, and much more.

Government agencies, both in print form and online, have a wealth of free information available through various departments, agencies, committees, boards, and services.

Don't forget your local library. When I started writing 30 years ago – before online research was readily accessible – the research librarian at my local library was my best friend. These librarians are still a valuable resource as walking databases. Use them!

Periodical magazine and newspaper indexes and online databases can help you find articles on your subject. Use the *Subject Guide to Books in Print* to see what books have been written on your topic. The *Encyclopedia of Associations* is helpful to find associations or groups dedicated to your subject. Not only will they have information on their websites or printed material, but they may be able to help you find experts to interview later. In the future, you may want to rent members' mailing lists to assist with marketing efforts.

You can also visit local bookstores or online book retailers to purchase relevant books or magazines if you have money to spare.

FIND EXPERTS TO INTERVIEW

Sure, you can simply provide your own advice and use quotes from other sources like books, magazines, and websites, by giving proper credit (more on that later).

But if you want to be traditionally published, consider interviewing experts on your subject. In other words, talk to real people. Interviews can help sell a book as well as verify and validate information. Even if you are self-publishing, remember that direct quotes from experts will earn your book more respect.

How can you find experts? These days you have plenty of options.

- If you're writing a book related to your career, you probably know people willing to be interviewed.
- If not, free online services like Profnet and HARO help connect writers with expert sources. The advantage of these sites is experts respond to your requests. That means they're interested in talking to you. As a result, you're not wasting time trying to contact people who don't wish to be interviewed.
- With just a bit of research, experts can be found everywhere – universities, associations, professional organizations, and consulting firms. Many databases list experts along with professional qualifications and contact information. Popular ones include https://www.experts.com/ and https://www.expertclick.com/.
- Google your topic. For example, searching "diet experts" or "astronomy experts" will bring up several links and some may include contact information. Many professionals are happy to help for visibility and exposure.
- Reach out via Facebook, Twitter, Instagram, LinkedIn, or other social media to connect with potential sources.

When approaching an expert, be upfront. Immediately state your name, the topic of your book, and the deadline (if you have one). Be willing to accommodate a person's preferences and conduct the interview by email, phone, Zoom, Skype, or in person.

If an expert agrees to be interviewed at a specific time, be punctual. You may be nervous, but remember, most people are eager to talk. Your ability to interview will evolve and improve over time.

Here are some tips to keep in mind:

- Prepare for the interview beforehand. Get the basics including the correct spelling of a person's name, job title, education and work background, location, and if applicable to your book, family status or hobbies. The Internet has made doing a bit of digging simple with social media sites including LinkedIn.
- Be sure and prepare a list of questions. Listen to answers carefully with interest. You'll get a better interview if you're not thinking about what you'll say next. Ask for clarification on information you've gathered or quotations. This will show that you've spent some time doing your homework which facilitates trust and shows that you're prepared and professional. If you don't understand something, ask for more explanation. Don't be afraid to ask different questions or use follow-up questions.
- Look for and note subtle details during in-person interviews to help readers visualize the story being told.
- Be careful. Never change the meaning or essence of what the expert said.

This is a personal choice, but I like to tape my interviews. Be sure and ask for permission before beginning the interview, however. Many states require that you notify people when using recording devices or taping a phone conversation. Informing participants that the conversation will be recorded not only helps you comply with legal requirements but also fosters transparency and ethical communication.

As a courtesy, always send your sources a thank-you note and a copy of your finished book.

USE ANECDOTES

The definition of an anecdote is "a short amusing or interesting story about a real incident or person."

Don't you love to hear stories about people who've been in your shoes, had the same problems or issues, and overcame them successfully? Anecdotes provide:

- hope that you can put the information to use in your own life and experience similar results

- personal stories that prove strategies and tips in your book work in the real world
- added interest and sometimes humor

Where can you find anecdotes?

- Narratives can be based on your own experiences and observations.
- You can use anecdotes from books, magazines, or websites if you give proper attribution (see the next section on how to do so).
- Social media and online forums on your subject can be helpful. Once again, give the person proper attribution – but only after getting permission.
- If you're writing a historical book, documents such as diaries, family histories, and letters, can be used as sources for anecdotes.

An anecdote attained from an interview or from someone you know will add a personal touch. Here are some ideas for sources:

- If you know someone personally who had an experience related to the subject of your book, ask if they'd be willing to share their story. If you're writing about a sensitive or personal topic, offer to use a pseudonym or omit their profession or location if desired.
- Perhaps family and friends know someone in their everyday life who could contribute a relatable story.
- Ask people you know if they'd be willing to try your strategies and share their honest opinions and results.

When adding anecdotes, weave in literary devices that add interest such as dialogue, characterization, description, and personality insights.

Don't sweat it if you can't come up with anecdotes right away. You may choose to get your facts down first and then go back and see where it would make the most sense to add supporting examples.

GATHER QUOTES FROM OTHER SOURCES

Relevant quotes from reliable sources such as books, magazines, and websites can give your book authenticity and credibility. Be sure to fact-check your sources to ensure quotes are accurate.

Be aware, there are some rules regarding giving attribution:

- If quoting from a book, include the author's name and book title.
- When quoting from an article, include the author's name and title, the article title, and the name of the publication or web page.
- Most style manuals recommend italicizing the titles of books and other complete works like newspapers and magazines and putting the titles of articles in quotation marks.

To give you an example of how to weave these attributions into your manuscript, let's suppose you want to quote from this book. You might write: In her book *The Next Chapter: Writing in Retirement,* Julie A. Gorges points out (or explains, suggests, states, believes, etc.) that "relevant quotes from reliable sources such as books, magazines, and websites can give your book authenticity and credibility." Or you could include the quote first: "Relevant quotes from reliable sources such as books, magazines, and websites can give your book authenticity and credibility," states Julie A. Gorges in her book *The Next Chapter: Writing in Retirement.*

Keep track of your sources. When using online sources, it helps to cut and paste URLs in your manuscript with the information below to properly give attribution. Or you can paste the URLs separately in a Word document or Scrivener's – whatever works best for you. If you're using a lot of quotes from various sources, you may want to include a bibliography or list the sources in footnotes or endnotes.

One important caveat before you start using quotes in your book: Please be aware that within copyright law, the use of quotes is an extremely gray area.

Under the "fair use" defense, you may make limited use of an original author's work, such as quoting from a book, magazine, or website without asking permission. That is if you follow a few vague rules. Is it your aim to make a profit from the quote? Will your book stop people from buying a book you're quoting from because you've made it unnecessary? If that's the case, "the fair use" rule may not hold up in court.

And what exactly does "limited use" mean? How much can you quote from a publication without getting in trouble? That's a tricky question. Unfortunately, no legal rules provide an exact number of words you can use in a quote. Some experts estimate you can use up to 300 words from a book or 50 words from an article in a quote if you give credit and attribution to the source. However, that figure is certainly not set in stone and doesn't guarantee fair use.

Paraphrasing an idea – significantly – can help you avoid copyright problems but must be used with caution.

If you want to use more than the recommended amount of material, you can formally request permission to quote from the publisher. Be aware, that this may take months and often a fee will be involved.

Since I'm not qualified to give legal advice, it's best to consult a lawyer with experience in publishing if you have any concerns. Since that's expensive if you're unsure of what you can use legally, utilize the rule: "If in doubt, leave it out." Determine if you really need to use a specific quote and if it's worth the risk.

CHOOSE A BOOK TITLE

Do not underestimate the power of a title. A title can make or break a book. Keep these tips in mind:

- Be specific. Your title should promise to improve readers' lives in some way. People will want to know: What's in it for me? If your book title doesn't immediately answer that question, you've probably lost them. Hopefully, you had a hook in mind when you wrote your book. Consider using part of it in your title. Your goal is for a customer browsing Amazon to see your title and think: "I need that!"
- Steer away from titles with long, fancy words that no one understands or titles that don't accurately represent your book. Use simple words and clear language so readers understand what your book is about and how it benefits them.
- That being said, you can use catchy, clever, or humorous words that make your title memorable and create curiosity. Just be sure to pair it with a descriptive subtitle that explains what your book is about and how it solves a problem. For example, my book *I'm Your Daughter, Julie*, has the subtitle: *Caring for a Parent with Dementia*.
- Include relevant keywords – a word or phrase associated with your book that people will use when searching online or on Amazon. If you need some ideas, look at Amazon's top-selling books on your topic and see what words and phrases appear frequently in the titles, subtitles, book descriptions, and book reviews.
- Stay away from weak words. Instead, use words with an emotional trigger and a sense of urgency. For example, which intrigues you more? Something that is "good" or something that is "amazing?" Persuasive words like transform, conquer, discover, essential, improve, crucial, proven, secret,

ultimate, fun, increase, valuable, incredible, effortless, and risk-free can be effective.

Interestingly, a Lulu study found that the title's length does not affect a book's likelihood of becoming a best-seller. What makes the difference is whether the title catches readers' interest, addresses a need, and motivates readers to buy the book to satisfy their curiosity.

SET AN APPROXIMATE WORD COUNT

Have a general idea of the total word count for your book when you get started. This will help you meet the expectations of agents, publishers, bookstores, online retailers, and readers. As a side benefit, having an approximate word count makes it easier to set daily or weekly goals.

So, how long should your book be? Remember that a printed book should be at least 100 pages long if you want the title to fit easily on the spine of the book.

Although there are no hard and fast rules regarding the specific word length, the following are some general guidelines for different types of nonfiction books:

- The average how-to/self-help/motivational book is between 30,000 and 70,000 words. Keep in mind that readers don't want to go through an overwhelmingly lengthy book to find out what they want to know. So, don't make it too long.
- A standard business, educational, political, psychology, or history nonfiction book can be a bit longer, between 70,000 and 80,000 words.
- eBooks can be as short as 3,000 words or the same length as a full-length printed nonfiction book. In general, I'd aim for at least 10,000 words. But if you can do your subject justice with a shorter eBook, then it's better not to ramble on aimlessly just to achieve a specific word count.

As I pointed out in the last chapter, Microsoft Word and Google Docs have word count options. To figure out how many pages these word counts represent, remember that the average single-spaced document typed in a standard 12-point font contains about 500 words per page. The average double-spaced document has about 250 words per page.

By the way, don't be overwhelmed by these word counts. If you wrote 193 words five days a week for one year, you'll achieve 50,000 words. Or if you're ambitious, write 1,667 words per day and you'll have a rough draft in a month. Not so bad.

START WRITING

When writing your rough draft, don't stop to fix typos, and grammatical errors, or fact-check. You'll have plenty of time to revise and edit later.

Pretend you're having a conversation with a friend who is looking for advice and you're simply sharing your insights and suggestions.

Many people who want to write a book start but never finish. This is where they usually get stuck. Just keep writing. Follow your outline and add appropriate research, details, quotes, and anecdotes as you go along.

EDIT YOUR BOOK

Woo-hoo! You finished your first draft. Take a break and celebrate before starting the editing process. That way, you can look at your work with fresh eyes.

When you're ready, take a broad view of your book. Will your book meet a reader's needs, wants, and expectations? Did you include the necessary information to answer questions that may arise? Are there areas that need more details, research, or anecdotes? Is the language appropriate for your audience and does it convey the right feeling? Is any part of your book confusing?

Now is the time to be ruthless and courageously look objectively at your writing. For the best results, you must become your own harshest critic. Don't fall in love with your own words. Did you include unnecessary or distracting material that doesn't support your subject? Do parts of your book drag as you drone on and on needlessly? Is any part of your book redundant? Look for ways to shorten paragraphs, sentences, and even words.

Read your manuscript aloud and note any sections of your book that seem too long, too short, or in the wrong place.

Be sure to fact-check carefully. Use multiple sources and make sure they are credible.

Next, it's time to start proofreading. You can start by using the grammar and spell check tools on your word processing program and AI tools. However, this probably won't catch all the errors and typos. Try printing your manuscript and editing it on paper with a pen. This will help you catch mistakes you may have missed on the computer.

If your eyes are starting to cross, take a break. Come back in a few days or even a few weeks so you can look at the material objectively and with a new perspective. Try editing your book in a different location. Move to the couch or take your manuscript to a coffee shop.

Self-editing is a hard skill to learn, but well worth the effort. You want to send your best draft to beta readers. Or if you send your book to a professional editor, you can save money and time.

FIND BETA READERS

Just as with fiction writing, once you've self-edited your book to tighten it up and fix any glaring errors, it's time to have other people look at it. Getting feedback is an important part of the writing process. You need to know what's working and what isn't, what's appealing to people, and what's boring them or turning them off.

As mentioned in the previous chapter, friends and family can help if they can be truthful and objective. If you are part of a writer's group, members may offer to critique your book. If you have a Facebook author's page, your fans and audience may volunteer to help you.

Ask your beta readers to read your book thoroughly and to spend some time thinking about it. It might help to give your beta readers a list of questions to answer such as:

- Does the book need more details?
- Does it contain unnecessary information?
- What doesn't make sense or is confusing?
- What was their favorite and least favorite part of the book and why?
- Did they have any questions that didn't get answered?
- What did they want to know more about? What parts of the book bored them?
- Do they have any suggestions on how to improve your book?

In addition, ask them to point out any typos, errors, or other glaring issues they may notice.

If you're serious about the publishing business, consider hiring a professional editor and a cover designer for your book.

CHAPTER 8:

WRITE YOUR LIFE STORY

Writing down your legacy can be a satisfying and rewarding experience in many ways. As Anais Nin said: "We write to taste life twice, in the moment and in retrospect." Whether you want to write a family history, an autobiography, or a memoir, here are some benefits:

- Revisiting precious memories can bring joy.
- Writing down painful experiences can be a therapeutic way to heal and lead to understanding, self-acceptance, and peace of mind.
- Documenting life lessons and how you overcame mistakes and hardships can give you the confidence to face future challenges.
- Sharing your life stories can benefit others as they learn from your experiences.
- Loved ones will likely cherish having a family history available and learning more about your unique story.

Those who have succeeded at writing their life story can attest to these benefits. Jeannette Walls, author of the wildly successful memoir *Glass Castles*, says in an interview for *Reader's Digest*: "I'm constantly urging people, especially older folks, to write about their lives. It gives you new perspective. It was hugely eye-opening for me and very cathartic. Even if the book hadn't sold a single copy, it would still have been worth it."

Don't be overwhelmed by the thought of writing about your entire life. You don't need to put down everything you've ever experienced. In fact, an assortment of well-chosen vignettes will be more interesting to readers than a lengthy retelling of all the details of your life.

Crafting your life story is an ideal way to venture into the joys of retirement writing. Just think, unlike a novel, you don't need to come up with an intricate plot or create a cast of characters from your imagination.

Keep the project fun and, if needed, take breaks along the way.

OF COURSE, YOU'VE GOT A STORY TO TELL!

You may think your ordinary life is boring and simply not interesting enough to fill a book.

If that's the case, consider this:

- Every life is unique and special. No one else can pen the story you are about to write.
- As someone who has lived for several decades, you've witnessed dramatic changes and historical events.
- Everyone suffers adversities. You, no doubt, have a powerful story of perseverance to tell.
- Once you begin writing, you'll discover delightful, poignant, interesting, unique, and whimsical stories to tell about yourself and the people you love and know.
- Life is full of humorous and embarrassing moments that are entertaining. You've surely encountered funny situations and quirky people on your journey through life.

THE DIFFERENT TYPES OF LIFE STORIES

What's the difference between a family history, an autobiography, and a memoir? Although similar, there are differences. To explain briefly:

- A family history focuses primarily on your ancestors, briefly touching on your own life.

- An autobiography centers on your life while including a bit of family history.
- A memoir emphasizes pivotal events in your life that convey an important message.

How do you know for sure which one suits your needs best? The answers to the following questions will help you choose which type of book to write:

- Do you imagine writing a book where you are just one of many characters? Do you picture yourself as a historian rather than a central character? Do you enjoy researching and exploring forgotten people from the past? If that's the case, you're probably better off writing a family history.
- Is the primary goal of your book to share your life stories with children, grandchildren, and future descendants? Do you envision writing your book in chronological order with you as the primary character? An autobiography will be a good match.
- Will your book center on life lessons? Is there a prominent theme that runs through your life that connects your stories? Are you interested in trying to find a publisher for your life story or self-publishing your book to sell? A memoir is probably your best bet.

Now that you better understand your choices, let's discuss each type more thoroughly.

WRITE A FAMILY HISTORY

Family histories cover a long period of time – typically at least three generations. Your job is to bring these people to life with entertaining facts about their lives.

How do you get started?

- Create a detailed family tree. An old family Bible may list names and include dates of births and deaths.
- Write down everything you know about your ancestors. What do you remember about your great-grandparents, grandparents, and parents? What stories have been passed down from generation to generation?
- Interview living relatives who can share a wealth of information. Quoting personal family stories and memories will also add a personal touch.

- Look through old photos, letters, diaries, land deeds, postcards, military records, ship passenger arrival records, and school yearbooks. Look for old newspaper clippings with engagement, wedding, birth announcements, and obituaries.
- Thankfully, the Internet has made it easier to do some digging. Start with https://www.familysearch.org/ which offers the largest collection of genealogical records in the world. Looking through the archives is free or you can hire an accredited genealogist to help you. A couple of other sites you may want to check are https://www.ancestry.com/ and https://www.genealogy.com/.

Once you've completed these steps, you'll want to make your family history come to life. Long books that trudge through every event relentlessly are challenging to write and result in a boring read. Search for exciting or tragic events.

What problems or obstacles did your family members face? Is there a fascinating rags-to-riches tale or a war story of survival? Did a relative have to make an impossible choice or face a difficult challenge? Did anyone commit a major crime? Were any of your ancestors affected by natural disasters or historical events?

Instead of writing about every ancestor, focus on those with the most engaging stories. Begin with the most exciting part of their lives. Later, you can include flashbacks to explain how a person reached a critical point in life.

Here are some more tips to make your book an intriguing read:

- Add details about what life was like during different eras. Research fashion trends, architecture, transportation, local and world events, music, and hairstyles to add flavor. Include pop culture and technology references. If you're writing about a specific date, check weather reports.
- Inject humor with funny anecdotes whenever possible. Did an ancestor have an absurd character trait or habit? Did you find a journal with amusing tidbits you can include?
- Include your own story to give readers a sense of what formed and affected your personality and life. Think about valuable life lessons you've learned from your parents and grandparents. Did you carry on the family legacy or take your own unique path?
- To make your book more cohesive, search for a common thread that ties your stories together. Are there common generational beliefs, personality traits, talents, or attitudes? For example, were your ancestors famous for their rebellious ways or risk-taking? How did those behaviors play out over the generations and with what consequences?

- Photos, newspaper articles, letters, diary entries, maps, and other illustrations can add interest and break up your story for easier reading. Include detailed captions for any photos or images.
- Source citations can provide credibility to your research and leave a trail that others can follow to learn more if desired.

WRITE AN AUTOBIOGRAPHY

An autobiography is the inspiring story of an entire life, usually told chronologically. Autobiographies are written from the author's point of view, making them personal and intimate like a journal. Typically, the goal is to share and preserve memories for future generations.

An autobiography may include:

- family background and stories about your childhood
- your cultural heritage, traditions, and values
- people who influenced your life
- places you lived
- historical events you lived through
- turning points and emotional moments in your life
- travels
- personal achievements, career accomplishments, and unusual hobbies
- volunteer work
- regrets, mistakes, failures, personal struggles, and challenges you overcame
- life lessons learned

How to begin?

- Brainstorm. List the most critical moments, people, events, lessons, experiences, and places in your life. Keep a notebook handy to jot down ideas and memories as they arise. Or take notes on your cell phone.
- Need help remembering important events? If you kept diaries, lucky you! That's the perfect place to begin down memory lane. You can also jog your memory with photos, scrapbooks, letters, school records, yearbooks, programs, and invitations. Or listen to music from the era, especially songs that trigger memories of important moments in your life.

- Visit or phone family members and old friends and ask them to help you remember important events.
- Consider revisiting locations and settings from the past. Not only will this jog your memory but it will also help you add accurate and colorful descriptions later.
- Create an outline. Organize your book with the most captivating stories from your life.

Time to write your first draft. Here are some tips to keep in mind to make your autobiography a fascinating read:

- Although autobiographies are typically told in chronological order, don't start your story with boring details like how much you weighed at birth. Unless your birth was dramatic, consider beginning with an exciting event or life-changing moment. Then go back to your childhood stories that help explain what led you to that point. In other words, imitate novels that reel you in with thrilling action and intrigue then flash back to the beginning to fill in background information.
- Be a storyteller, not a reporter. For example, don't just list career accomplishments and places you've traveled. Explain how these experiences influenced and impacted your life.
- Make your autobiography read like a novel including action, conflict, drama, and suspense. Don't forget to add dialogue. Of course, you won't be able to remember exact words, but you can recreate a conversation based on a general sense of what happened and what was said.
- Stick to just a few personal stories and anecdotes from each part of your life that shaped you into who you are today. Leave out the boring parts. Save specific details for the truly significant events in your life.
- An autobiography shouldn't be like a college essay with formal words you rarely use. Pretend you're opening your heart to a trusted friend or family member. Write with an authentic voice. Are you funny, reflective, or spiritually minded? Let your personality shine through.
- Don't let your book become a huge brag fest without any mention of negative aspects of your life. Reveal yourself as a complete person with strengths and successes as well as flaws, weaknesses, and failures. That doesn't mean you must share explicit and intimate details. Just try to be as candid as possible. Perhaps you made poor choices that led you down paths you now regret. Others can learn from those mistakes.

- Be sure to include photos. If you're sharing a bit of family history as part of your background, add birth, marriage, and death records. If so inclined, share snippets from your journal, love letters, or newspaper articles.

Remember, unless you're a celebrity, an autobiography is usually harder to sell than a memoir. Most people write an autobiography to share their story with family and future descendants. To that end, an autobiography is certainly a worthwhile endeavor.

WRITE A MEMOIR

While family histories and autobiographies are often written for family and future descendants, memoirs are typically written for a wider audience.

These books focus on significant moments, meaningful transitions, and life-changing events that are tied together with a central theme. Memoirs require deep introspection and self-examination.

Matthew McConaughey's popular bestselling memoir *Greenlights* is a good example. The famous actor tied his stories together by comparing greenlights to signs life gave him to move forward and those he created for himself by overcoming challenges and obstacles. By sharing his philosophy, readers are helped to recognize "greenlights" in their lives and discover their own path.

With that in mind, if you plan to approach agents and publishers with a memoir, they'll expect your book to benefit readers in an impactful way. They are looking for:

- an evocative book that conveys an important lesson that helps readers improve their lives
- a relatable story that emotionally moves readers and fills them with hope
- a compelling book that educates, shares a universal truth or enlightens readers in some way
- a book that gives readers a glimpse into a different time or kind of world
- an inspiring story describing how to survive and triumph over tragedies and challenges

You may focus on your philosophy about life and share stories that run the gamut from a difficult childhood to a successful career like McConaughey.

Or you can narrow your focus and share life lessons learned from specific experiences such as:

- travels or adventures
- making difficult choices
- adjusting to a new life
- people that changed your life forever
- funny anecdotes that result from a character flaw
- pets that taught you valuable lessons

Consider how you can tell your story so readers can apply life lessons in their own lives. Even if they haven't had the same exact experience, readers should be able to identify with your story and benefit from it. Make readers feel optimistic that if they believe in themselves, they can make powerful changes in their lives too.

Keep in mind that a memoir should read much like a novel. I'd highly recommend reading at least a few quality memoirs to see how this is done. Here are just a few popular memoirs you may want to read – or read again – paying attention to how the author transformed their personal story into a compelling book:

- *The Glass House* by Jeannette Walls
- *Out of Africa* by Isak Dinesen
- *Eat, Pray, Love* by Elizabeth Gilbert
- *Tuesdays with Morrie* by Mitch Albom
- *Angela's Ashes* by Frank McCourt
- *I Know Why the Caged Bird Sings* by Maya Angelou
- *Wild* by Cheryl Strayed

You'll notice that many memoirs focus on emotional issues such as abandonment, betrayal, disease, poverty, loss, addiction, or fear with a message of hope.

Say you made a mistake in your youth that had tragic consequences. Your memoir could tell the story of how you moved forward to find inner peace. Or perhaps you were a victim of abuse, an orphan, or a recovered addict and your memoir reveals how you found happiness, success, or faith. (If reliving your story is too painful, consider this option carefully. You may want to be in therapy while writing about disturbing memories.)

When writers share stories about overcoming a crisis with perseverance and determination, readers are moved and inspired to face their own challenges.

However, you don't necessarily need a tragic or dramatic story to write a memoir. Joe Kita writes in a *Reader's Digest* article, "How to Write a Memoir" that although 99.9 percent of people lead average lives "every single one of them is trying to make some sense out of his or her existence, to find some meaning in the world, and therein lies the value and opportunity of a memoir."

Memoirs can even be lighthearted and funny. For example, Gerald Durrell's memoir *My Family and Other Animals* is about his family's life on the island of Corfu and is meant to make you laugh. *Me Talk Pretty One Day* by David Sedaris is a collection of humorous anecdotes about his new life in Paris.

If you need help finding a focus, ask yourself the following questions:

- What's the number one message your life has taught you?
- If you only had 15 minutes to tell someone who you are, what stories would you tell them? What do these stories have in common?
- What makes your life meaningful?
- What are the most significant and pivotal moments in your life?
- What life-altering decisions and choices did you make? Why did you make them?
- Was there a time when your lifelong-held beliefs were challenged?
- Who are the intriguing people who changed your life?
- When were you the most scared, confused, or on top of the world?
- Which past events still haunt you? What critical mistakes have you made?
- Were there funny events in your life that taught you important lessons?
- What did you learn from desperate struggles or painful conflicts?

Once you've given these questions careful thought, start listing significant events from your life. Search for stories with plenty of emotion. These are often the moments that reveal your true character.

Keep a notebook with you and jot down random ideas, dramatic events, remembered conversations from the past, funny stories, or an opening sentence that comes to mind.

If you feel stuck, enlist the help of your spouse or best friend to help you choose the meaningful and intriguing stories that made you who you are today and need to be told. Talk to your old classmates, friends, and family to help you remember and gain perspective on life events.

If you don't have a central theme yet, look through the significant events of your life and see if there is a connection between them. You might discover certain lessons or ideas that keep popping up throughout your life.

Can there be more than one theme that runs through a memoir? Yes. However, if your story has several themes, think about the overarching point and the message you want to share.

Next, narrow your focus and create a general outline. Take your list and search for relevant experiences and details connected to your theme. Be selective. Maybe you have an entertaining, quirky aunt. Or the strangest thing happened on the way to New York. Great, but if characters and events don't relate to your story, leave them out. You don't want to obscure your theme and bore your readers with irrelevant details.

Now, it's time to start writing. Simply begin with one story – the one that's most important to you. Stay focused on that one vignette. Be introspective and vulnerable. Think about how the event impacted your life and what you learned from the experience.

When you're finished, choose another story that stands out in your mind. Continue the process, sharing an anecdote that fits the point you're trying to make in each chapter. Take your time and, if needed, take breaks in between each story to reflect on its meaning.

As you write, here are a few tips to keep in mind:

- Start your memoir by grabbing your reader's attention with a gripping incident that captures the book's central theme as vividly as possible.
- Use all your senses and details to re-create a moment in time. Help your readers visualize scenes by using strong, memorable imagery and vivid language. Avoid phrases like "I felt" or "I saw." Instead, use physical reactions and body language to describe the moment.
- You want readers to be invested in and relate to your main character – that's you. Display your personality, humor, angst, and excitement. Write as if you're talking to your best friend. Be candid, honest, and vulnerable. Use dialogue with emotional impact.
- Bragging turns readers off. Remember, you are a multi-faceted person with both strengths and weaknesses. Don't paint yourself as flawless or a hero. Share your shortcomings, fragility, and failures along with your successes.
- Resist writing as a victim in an angry, bitter, resentful, or sarcastic tone with an agenda in mind. Also, avoid a condescending or preachy attitude.
- Make your memoir read like a gripping novel. Raise the stakes in your story. Increase emotional tension, conflict, suspense, and drama. Share moral dilemmas you faced, heart-breaking choices, and disappointing moments. Describe how impossible it seemed to succeed. If you overcame a tragedy or challenge, share all the times you tried to prevail but failed. Surprise your readers with twists and turns in your life.
- Showcase your personal growth. Reveal valuable lessons learned and ways you were able to change your life for the better. Describe how you found the courage to move forward and find happiness. Your ending should climax like a novel with a revelation, truism, or transformation related to your theme.
- After you've written your story add visual interest. Gather photos, journals, and other memorabilia that you want to include.

One warning: To write a good memoir, you must be a good storyteller. However, your memoir must be based on facts. Make sure your book doesn't contain fabrications and distortions like some best-selling memoirs in the past. Remember the backlash in 2003 when it was discovered that James Frey's book, *A Million Little Pieces*, was full of lies, exaggerations, and embellishments?

Of course, a bit of creative license is allowed. For instance, no one can remember conversations word for word. You'll need to do your best to recapture the essence of discussions when using dialogue. Or you may tell events out of order to add interest to your story.

But do your best to tell the truth. Strive for balance, objectivity, and accuracy. Write with a degree of detachment and reflection.

If your memory is fuzzy, some research and fact-checking is in order. Use public records when necessary. Memories can be vague, personal, and differ from the recollections of others. Interview family members and friends to consider their viewpoints and fill in gaps in your memory.

As a side note, seriously consider whether to include family secrets or embarrassing stories about your loved ones, especially if you plan to publish your book. This is a personal choice but, in my opinion, relationships are more important than publishing intimate stories others may find humiliating. I'd suggest talking to family and friends first to see how they feel about revealing private stories.

How long should your memoir be? If you plan to approach agents and traditional publishers, the typical length is about 75,000 words. If you're writing a legacy memoir that you plan to self-publish and is intended for a more limited audience, the length is up to you.

PART III: PUBLISH A BOOK

CHAPTER 9: CHOOSE THE RIGHT PUBLISHING PATH

Congratulations! You've finished your book. It's been edited and polished. Now you're ready to publish.

What's next?

That depends. Do you want to try and find an agent and a traditional publisher? Or do you plan to self-publish?

Or maybe you're not sure which path to take.

Your decision depends on your goals, the type of book you want to write, and if you're willing to put in the intensive time and effort to try and find an agent and a publishing house.

Whatever you choose, I'll give you the information you need. I've landed a literary agent, been published by a well-known traditional publishing house, formed a partnership to start an independent publishing company, and self-published books. I'll share all my tips and experience gained along the way.

Of course, there are advantages and disadvantages to both traditional and self-publishing. So, let's go over exactly what these options mean and what you'll want to consider before deciding which route to take.

WHAT IS A TRADITIONAL PUBLISHER?

Traditional publishing refers to the old-fashioned process of getting a book deal with a commercial publishing company.

Most writers try to find an agent to represent them first. Why? Most of the larger publishing houses (but not all) refuse to look at "unsolicited manuscripts" that an agent doesn't submit.

By the way, literary agents are worth their weight in gold if you can find one. They are experts in the publishing industry, have valuable contacts, and know which editors are most likely to buy your book. Agents also strive to get the best book deal, help negotiate a fair contract, and protect your author rights. On top of all that, a good agent will give you great advice during the editing process and provide much-needed encouragement.

In return for their services, the agent receives a percentage of money earned from the sale of your book – typically 15 percent. Agents should not ask for any money upfront. They work on commission, so to speak.

If you are unable or do not wish to retain an agent, you can directly approach publishers that accept unsolicited manuscripts. If a publisher is interested in your book, you will negotiate with the publishing house yourself. Warning: If you're asked to pay money to a publisher, then it is NOT a traditional book publisher. More on this later, but you're probably dealing with a vanity publisher, which you should avoid at all costs.

Once an agreement is made with the publishing company, a contract is signed. The book publisher then retains the rights to your manuscript. This means the publisher has the final say on every aspect of your book, from editorial content to cover design to setting the price.

You may receive an advance, usually between $5,000 to $10,000. However, this isn't always the case, especially with independent and smaller publishing houses.

Working with an in-house editor, you're expected to complete writing the book in an agreed-upon time frame. After editing and proofreading are finished, the publisher prints and sells the book through bookstores and online retailers.

You'll receive royalties or a percentage of the sale of books, but only after the advance is paid off in full through book sales. Many people are surprised that royalties usually range between 8 to 25 percent, with the lower end of that range being more typical. In addition, discounts, returns, marketing, and overhead costs are usually subtracted before royalties are dispersed.

Now that you know what traditionally published means, let's discuss the pros and cons.

ADVANTAGES OF TRADITIONAL PUBLISHING

- A traditional publisher pays for any upfront costs.
- You'll usually work with an established professional team, including editors, cover designers, and formatters, as part of the contract.
- If you're looking for prestige, literary acclaim, or validation by the publishing industry, it may be worth trying to find an agent and traditional publisher. Many literary prizes and major reviewers won't accept self-published books.
- Well-known publishing houses usually set up sales channels, which include bookstores, distributors, wholesalers, and their own catalogs
- If you envision your book in a brick-and-mortar bookstore, traditional publishing houses are designed to make this happen. Keep in mind, however, that books are typically in the bookstore for a month and only remain if they are perpetual sellers, which unfortunately doesn't happen often.
- Traditional publishers often budget funds to help market and promote your book. Just know that you'll still be encouraged to hire a book publicist and/or work aggressively to promote your book. In fact, agents and publishers often seek authors with a "platform" that includes a significant social media presence and an email list of potential readers.
- As a writer, you'll benefit from the reputation of a well-known New York publisher. Bookstores, readers, and the media will take you more seriously.

DISADVANTAGES OF TRADITIONAL PUBLISHING

- The odds of finding a literary agent to represent you and a commercial publishing house are formidable. Be prepared for a frustrating and often disappointing process.
- A traditional publisher owns the publishing rights to your book. Therefore, the publisher will make all the decisions regarding editing, the cover, price, and production. You will have no say or control in the matter. Once a book goes out of print, you cannot publish it on your own afterward.
- The publisher will take the bulk of the profit. If you have an agent, they also take a percentage.
- The road to publication is an excruciatingly long and arduous process. Finding an agent can take months or even years. Once that is achieved, your

agent will likely spend several months or more sending query letters and book proposals. If the agent is successful and you sign a contract with a publisher, it'll probably be at least another year before your book is published and launched.

In conclusion, you'll have to weigh the pros and cons before deciding. Despite the disadvantages, many writers dream of being published by a large reputable New York publishing house. And, yes, I was one of those people. If you don't want to go to the grave wondering what would have happened if only you pursued your goal with gusto, go for it. True, the statistics are daunting and, honestly, the chances of finding a traditional publisher your first time at bat are slim. But the feat is not impossible, even if you've never published a book before. I'm proof of that.

However, if you decide to go down this road, please take my advice. Expect a rollercoaster ride of emotions. Every published writer – including myself – experiences plenty of rejections on the journey to publication.

When I started writing professionally, the wide range of feelings I experienced, dependent on my successes or failures, were dizzying. When a well-known agent agreed to represent my young adult novel, I danced on tables. When the book didn't sell, my self-confidence took a dive. When I received three journalism awards and a book I co-wrote was published by McGraw Hill, I was on top of the world. When another novel was rejected, my dreams came crashing down. You get the picture.

And, keep in mind, I was more successful than many writers who never get traditionally published. Yet, it was still hard not to get swept away by my emotions. As a side note, you won't completely avoid these stressful highs and lows as an indie (independent, self-published) author. For example, if you put a lot of effort into marketing with little or no success, it can also be distressing.

So, here's my point. No matter what route you choose, don't put all your eggs in one basket. In other words, don't make your whole world about writing and publishing or you will go completely bonkers. There's a reason many famous writers who dedicated their entire lives to their art famously became alcoholics. Have a well-balanced life that includes time for your spirituality, loved ones, and other interests.

Remember, writing should be a satisfying experience on its own. Getting into print is just a bonus. Don't live and die by whether you get published by a traditional publishing house.

By the way, retaining an agent and publishing your book with a New York publishing house usually doesn't change your life all that much. I assumed that I finally "made it" once I was traditionally published. That wasn't exactly the case. Sure, this accomplishment boosted my confidence. It was a great credit that got my foot in the door sometimes. However, I still got plenty of rejections afterward, and, believe me, I didn't become rich and famous. I've heard similar experiences from other traditionally published authors.

If you're truly meant to be a writer, you'll retain your joy no matter what happens. You won't give up or allow setbacks to discourage you to the point of quitting. You won't let financial success, rave reviews, or selling thousands of books be the measure of your success as a writer and certainly not as a person.

If you decide to move forward and try and find an agent and a commercial publisher, be aware that you may need to take another path to your dreams, which we'll discuss next.

WHAT IS SELF-PUBLISHING?

Self-publishing refers to authors who publish their books without any help from an established publishing house.

That means if you choose this path, you're personally responsible for editing, publishing, formatting, designing a book cover, and marketing – or hiring professionals to do this work for you.

On the plus side, you'll retain all rights and have total control over the editorial content, cover, price, and production. You'll also keep the profits from book sales subtracting a small percentage that online retailers like Amazon require.

Some authors self-publish books as a hobby for their own satisfaction and pleasure. If you want to simply have fun, live out your dream of becoming an author, and have your book available to purchase - without all the headaches of trying to find an agent or a publishing house – this is the way to go.

Others create and publish their books as a business and are often referred to as indie authors or "authorprenuers" (a combination of author and entrepreneur). Interestingly, some famous authors that have gone this route include Mark Twain, Walt Whitman, Virginia Woolf, Edgar Allan Poe, and James Joyce. Even Stephen King started his career by self-publishing.

Other lesser-known authors also found success by self-publishing. Remember the book *Feed Me!* that taught parents how to make fresh baby food at home? I bought that book when my kids were young. Author Vicki Lansky submitted her book to 49 publishers to no avail before deciding to self-publish. The book went on to sell more than two million copies. Traditional publishers took note and eventually bought the rights.

As always, I'll keep it real. These examples of phenomenal success are the exception to the rule. Perhaps you'll only sell a few copies or maybe you'll sell a few hundred. Or if your content is exceptional, appeals to readers, and you learn how to successfully market and promote your book, your book may generate the attention it needs to become an Amazon bestseller. Only time will tell.

Sometimes writers choose this route because they're turned down by traditional publishers and don't have a choice. But there are plenty of other reasons to self-publish as listed below.

ADVANTAGES OF SELF-PUBLISHING

- Today, it's possible to self-publish without spending a penny if you're willing to edit, format, and design your book cover. Use a print-on-demand (POD) company like Amazon's KDP (Kindle Direct Publishing) and you won't pay for printing costs or to list your book with Amazon. You have nothing to lose except time spent, which is hopefully enjoyable.
- Self-publishing gives you full creative control and freedom over your book's content, cover design, and price.
- You won't have to spend months or years trying to convince an agent to represent you or a publishing house to look at your work – or suffer disappointment if rejected.
- Self-publishing allows you to showcase your work without deadlines or the pressure of making money. You are your own boss. You can finish and publish your book whenever you want. You can choose to actively promote your book or opt out of marketing and see what happens. Totally up to you.
- If you want to write a niche book, offbeat fiction, poetry, or autobiography that wouldn't interest a traditional publisher, self-publishing is a great option. You won't be restricted by genres and can publish whatever you want.
- Self-publishers can get a book published in a fraction of the time it takes traditional publishers. Usually, it's as easy as pushing a "Publish" button when you're finished and you're on your way.
- You are paid directly and usually monthly for your book sales by online retailers you choose to use. If you're ambitious and willing to work hard to market your book, higher royalties mean more money in your pocket.
- Self-published books that sell extremely well may be noticed by traditional publishers interested in buying the rights.
- While self-published titles are not typically found in brick-and-mortar bookstores, Amazon is a bookstore—albeit an online one – and dominates the market.

- Becoming a self-publisher and forming a company can provide tax breaks if certain requirements are met, allowing writers to deduct expenses related to writing and marketing.

DISADVANTAGES OF SELF-PUBLISHING

- Although the publishing industry is slowly changing, a stigma still exists regarding self-published books. These books are not typically considered for literary awards or covered by mainstream media. In other words, even if your book is on Amazon's Bestseller List, don't expect to see it on the *New York Times* Bestseller List. Self-published books are typically not displayed on the shelves at Barnes & Noble either.
- If you plan to make money from your book, keep in mind that the market is extremely competitive, so it's hard to get your book noticed. If you envision publishing one book, becoming famous, and retiring on the profits, you're likely to be disappointed. Chances are, you'll have to publish several books to gain traction. Even then, this is a hard market to crack.
- Remember, as a self-published author, you are 100 percent responsible for making your book a success. As with any new skill, publishing a book has a steep learning curve. If you want your book to be successful, you'll need to take time to learn how to write, publish, and market a book. However, if you want to write a book just for fun and your own satisfaction, this disadvantage may not concern you.

In conclusion, examine your goals and desires before making your decision. Whether you try and find a traditional publisher or self-publish, the next two chapters will discuss how to move forward.

WHAT A WRITER IN RETIREMENT HAS TO SAY...

SANDRA BENNETT

I think the major advantage of being traditionally published is that someone else pays the upfront costs. They believe in your story and help support you every step along the way, including marketing and distribution. A traditional publisher can get your books distributed into bookstores around the country, which you'll find much more difficult on your own. If you are lucky, they may even sell your book overseas and have it printed in other languages.

The major disadvantage is that you lose control of the publication. Depending on the publisher, you may have little say as to how your book is presented, including the design of your front cover. If you are given an advance payment, it must be paid out before any royalties are paid, and with the small percentage you are given, this may mean you never see any royalties or only a minor amount.

My first books went through an independent publishing company that had the books printed in China and listed them as eBooks on Amazon. This was okay, but I still felt I lost some control of how they planned and priced things.

I have since published completely on my own, using my contacts for graphic designer, editor, and formatter, and then sent the book to the printer myself. I have also used IngramSpark to do a reprint of a book that was originally traditionally published, but I had the rights returned to me.

As for the pros and cons, that's a difficult one. It depends on your aims and aspirations. Some people prefer traditional publishers as they have a 'better' reputation. You may feel more like a 'real' author if you have been accepted by a traditional publisher, instead of feeling like an imposter. But getting that contract is a long and hard journey for most of us and if we just want to see our books in the hands of children, like I do, then self-publishing is the preferred way to go.

* * *

CHAPTER 10:

FIND A TRADITIONAL PUBLISHER

Keep in mind before we get started: Things have changed since I accomplished the feat of finding an agent and traditional publisher - before social media became a juggernaut. These days you should take time to build an author's platform before approaching agents and publishers. That means having a social media presence, an established website, and a substantial email list. Some experts suggest you need about 15,000 followers to get a decent advance.

That being said, debut authors have been published without a massive number of followers. So, start building an authentic community of followers who are interested in you as a person and an author. But keep in mind that the quality of your work still counts. In the end, agents are more focused on the commercial appeal of your manuscript than on how many followers you have.

Traditional query letters are what I used and that's still a valid process for finding an agent. Nevertheless, there are other options available today. For instance, online pitch events at online writing conferences and Zoom pitch events allow authors to have limited time one-on-one with agents.

"Twitter pitch events" are another option. These events give writers an opportunity to pitch a manuscript during a specific time using an allowed character limit (typically 280 characters). Literary agents "like" pitches when they're interested in learning more and to request materials. There are several book pitch events on Twitter each year. Arguably, the best-known event is #PitMad (Pitch Madness). Other hashtags are more specific such as #AdPit (adult fiction/non-fiction), #YA (young adult), etc. You include the hashtag in your pitch.

To give you an example of a pitch, horror and fantasy author Morgan Dante gives the following sample in her article, "Pitching Your Book on Twitter" for *The Writing Cooperative*:

"In search of (character goal), (character name) finds herself in the midst of (main conflict) where she must face (escalating main conflict) or else (consequence if he fails)."

Even though more options are available today, one thing remains the same. You'll need a well-written and persuasive query letter to attract the attention of agents and publishers. Even if an agent or publisher is interested in one of your online pitches, you'll likely be asked to send a query letter, synopsis, and sample chapters. Thus, you should have these materials ready beforehand.

WRITE A QUERY LETTER

A query letter formally introduces yourself and pitches your proposed book.

In 300 to 500 words, you must get an agent or publishing house excited about reading your manuscript. This oh-so-important letter may be more significant than your novel or nonfiction book. Be sure to keep your query letter short and to the point. In its entirety, the letter should be one single-spaced page.

A great hook, a strong voice, and a clear premise is essential. The opening sentence should instantly grab the readers' attention, while the rest of the text should entice them to explore the manuscript further.

In general, keep your query letter short and simple. My successful query letters were not sent on fluorescent paper or typed in a funky font. I didn't start with a dumb joke or sound arrogant by saying "This book is sure to be a best seller."

However, agents receive hundreds of unsolicited submissions every month, so being creative – matching the voice of your story – may help you stand out. Award-winning author Carmela Dutra used this technique successfully after learning the names of agents' pets. The following is an example of one of her creative queries:

"My border and your Great Dane were talking (telepathically, of course, while my cat silently judged them) and they both convinced me to submit my hilarious cozy mystery to you. Dutra ended her query with: *Could Pippin, my Fool of a Tool Border Collie send Bruno the full manuscript?"*

Dutra's letter accomplished a few important things. The query demonstrated that she did her research about the agent(s) to learn more about them. It also helped them get a sense of who she is as an author and matched the quirky voice of her story. Her query letter garnished seven requests to send more material and agents praised her creativeness.

However, be careful if using this technique. This can work if you have the talent to pull it off and match the voice of your story. If not, use the standard outline as listed below.

THE BEGINNING

The introduction is your chance to hook the literary agent or publisher.

Don't start your letter with "To Whom It May Concern." Do your research to find agents' and editors' full names and use them in the salutation. This sounds more professional and lets them know your letter isn't mass-produced. Don't get off on the wrong foot by misspelling their name or using an incorrect professional title. Also, consider how they prefer to be addressed. Some agents prefer to be on a casual first-name basis; others require formal titles like Ms. or Mr. (last name). Keep an eye out for those who use specifically listed pronouns.

If you were lucky to meet an agent or editor in person at a writer's conference, pitched an idea successfully at an online event, received a "like" at a Twitter pitch event, or have some other connection, be sure and mention it right away.

If your proposed book is a novel, consider starting your letter with an intriguing one- or two-sentence pitch. I included the title, genre, and word count for my young adult novel:

In my 145-page young adult novel "Just Call Me Goody-Two-Shoes," Jade, a 15-year-old perfectionist, faces an older brother's addiction and falls for the guy her best friend is dating. She discovers life isn't always neat and orderly and choices aren't always simple.

As another option, you might start off with a simple sentence, and share the title, genre, and word count in the following sentences. Dutra, who recently succeeded in finding an agent for her cozy mystery comedy, used the following hook:

"Owning your own food truck is killer work, especially when murder is involved."

On the other hand, if you're writing nonfiction, a startling and attention-grabbing statement, personal experience, anecdote, or statistic can work well. Include the title, genre, and word count in the first paragraph. If you're considered a highly regarded authority in your field, briefly point that out as well. For example:

Through my years of experience in (industry), I have developed a proven method for (solving issue or problem) which I share in my book (book title).

Finally, show you've done your homework. Avoid writing: "I found your name in *Writer's Market* and see you represent romance novels." Instead, let them know you didn't just pull their name out of a hat. Familiarize yourself with the books an agent represents. Connect with them on social media to understand their personality. This can help you find common ground and personalize your letter. For example:

After reviewing your profile on MSWL, I believe my rom-com (heavy on the com) would be a perfect addition to your list.

Dutra found this to be an effective tactic. "Personalized query letters I sent out had a higher response rate than generic ones," she says. She gives the following example if you both share a love for comics (Dutra is a Dark Horse and DC fan):

"I read an article about your love for Marvel comics, especially [insert comic name]. It would be interesting to see a spin on X-Men where [input one-sentence summary). I believe my manuscript aligns nicely with what you're seeking."

Help them visualize how your book visually fits on a shelf with their other published books. Compare your book to a similar recent title that an agent represented or was published by the house you are querying. Mention your manuscript is written in the same style or has a parallel theme and then explain what sets your book apart.

THE MIDDLE

The next paragraphs should briefly summarize your book.

If your book is fiction, establish the setting and time period, discuss your main characters, and describe the basic plot line. Include conflicts and obstacles your character faces and heart-breaking choices that must be made. You don't need to reveal the ending; save that for your synopsis. Include a twist or an element that makes your book unique.

Nonfiction books are different. In addition to summarizing the subject of your manuscript, focus on how readers will benefit from your book. Explain how it will change lives. Include what proven methods, secrets, or life lessons will be revealed, who will want to buy your book (your target audience), and why it is essential reading in the current marketplace.

THE END

This is when you'll add your bio and blow your horn. List any publishing credits, writing awards, writing-related degrees, and memberships to well-known writing organizations. Include your professional background or personal life experience if it applies to the subject of your book.

Make note of any related media attention or ongoing gigs such as a podcast, blog, or magazine column that keep you in touch with your target audience. If you have an impressive author's platform that includes a substantial email list, followers on social media, or visitors to your blog, be sure and mention it.

If your manuscript is under consideration by any other agents, let them know. This can send a signal that your book has definite potential.

What if you don't have any credentials? Don't reveal you've wanted to be a writer since you were 12 and are taking it up during retirement. Don't apologize for a lack of experience or beg. Keep your bio short. Simply include a few basic facts, perhaps about your work history and personal achievements. Share an interesting tidbit about you that gives insight into the type of author you've become. A bit of charisma can help, so let some personality shine through. If your book is funny, inject humor into your letter.

End your query with a direct request to send a proposal, synopsis, or the entire manuscript.

BE PREPARED

Before beginning the querying process, be prepared in case an agent or publisher is interested in your work.

If you're submitting a novel or memoir, I'd recommend having a complete and edited manuscript before approaching agents and publishers. If they're interested, you could receive a request to see the entire book.

Even if you're writing a nonfiction book, consider finishing your manuscript first. You don't want to feel rushed or stressed if a publisher accepts your proposal and you have a deadline to meet. Odds are that the finished manuscript won't be your best work.

After you have some experience, writing a query letter and proposal before completing a nonfiction book makes sense. Why write an entire book if there's no interest in it?

For example, when I began mailing query letters for my first nonfiction book, a book proposal and sample chapters were already written, but not a complete manuscript. However, by this time I had years of experience as a freelance writer and newspaper reporter. As a result, I was more confident in my work and accustomed to deadlines.

Since agents and publishers may ask for a synopsis for a novel or a book proposal for a nonfiction book (see the next sections for more information on how to write these documents), it makes sense to prepare these in advance as well.

WRITE A SYNOPSIS

If you've written a novel, agents and publishers will probably ask for a synopsis – or a summary – of your book.

The synopsis should include:

- your book's entire narrative arc from beginning to end
- important characters
- the protagonist's motivation
- major plot turns
- conflicts and obstacles
- the crisis or climax
- the resolution
- the life-changing effect on your main character
- the ending

When writing a synopsis, don't make the mistake of simply writing, "This happens..." and "Then this happens..." Instead of a mechanical, boring explanation of your storyline, your synopsis should include the characters' emotions and motivations.

Write in your own unique voice and make it clear what it is that makes your story compelling. Remember, you don't need to include every plot line, minor character, back story, and poetic description.

Synopses are usually written in the third person and present tense. The only exception is if you've written a memoir, in which case, first person may be more appropriate.

As a rule, agents and publishers expect about one to three single-spaced pages. However, the length of a synopsis varies and some may want a more in-depth synopsis. Check submission guidelines for specifications.

PREPARE A BOOK PROPOSAL

Agents and editors usually want to see a book proposal for a nonfiction book before looking at a complete manuscript.

Unlike a synopsis, a proposal focuses more on marketability than creative storytelling skills. Of course, your writing should be respectable, but agents and publishers aren't expecting a literary masterpiece from a nonfiction book.

The exception to this rule is narrative nonfiction (sometimes referred to as creative or literary nonfiction) such as a memoir, a biographical story about a person, or a book centered on real-life events. Think *Into the Wild* by Jon Krakauer or *In Cold Blood* by Truman Capote. In this case, your proposal must show your ability to artfully weave a story and display strong journalistic skills.

If, however, you're writing a self-help, health, business, self-improvement, or how-to book, publishers are generally more interested in the salability of your book. Why will readers pay for the advice your book provides? The profitability of your idea along with your platform often matters as much as the writing, if not more so. Your credibility as a professional and relevant background also plays an important part in gaining readers' confidence and trust.

Writing a good book proposal takes time and, while length varies, most are between 15 to 50 pages double-spaced, not including sample chapters.

The standard sections of a book proposal are detailed below:

1. Cover Page: Include the book's title, subtitle, and your name. Make it easy for the agent or publisher to contact you by including your address, phone number, email, and the URL of your author's website if you have one.
2. Overview: Catch the attention of a publisher or agent with a fascinating idea, great quote, compelling anecdote, or shocking statistic. Describe the idea behind your book with a concise, unforgettable, sales-oriented hook that conveys your book's appeal. Include general information as well. For example, is your manuscript an inspirational self-help book or a technical how-to book? Will the book be humorous, serious, or down-to-earth? How many pages will be in your book?
3. Reader Benefits: Explain how your book will fulfill a need and how readers will benefit. Be specific. For example, "After purchasing my book, readers will be able to... (list benefits, perhaps in bullet form)."
4. Target Audience: Identify a market of readers who will be compelled to spend money on the information in your book. Again, be specific. Resist the urge to boast that everyone is a potential reader. Editors and agents will think you didn't do your homework. Who exactly will buy your book and

why? What are their demographics (sex, age, education, and financial status)? What are their desires and fears? How does your book address an urgent need? List groups who may buy books in large volumes such as book clubs, associations, and specialty stores.

5. Competitive Book Analysis: Note 5-10 similar and competing book titles. Explain why your book is different and needed. For each competitor, list the title, subtitle, author, publisher, ISBN, year of publication, page count, and price. Most importantly, briefly summarize the competitor's approach compared to your book. Don't criticize the other books. Instead, show the unique angle you're taking that separates your book from others. Are you taking an unexpected humorous slant on a serious and dry topic? Do you have a different perspective on a subject due to personal experience? Is your book more up-to-date or comprehensive? Do you have a viewpoint that differs from common belief? By the way, don't claim your book has no competitors. If that's the case, publishers will assume your book is so specialized it won't sell.
6. Author Bio: Explain how your background, expertise, and experience give you the perfect platform to attract your target audience. Include any previous publications, awards and recognition, reviews from major periodicals, sales history of previous books, media appearances, interviews, and speaking engagements. Add an author photo, links to author sites and social media pages, and contact information. If you don't have any publishing experience, look for other assets that might help sell books. That may include your personal experiences as they relate to the book, connections to experts, a substantial email list and social media following, or previous success in marketing yourself and your work.
7. Detailed Marketing Plan: This section is critically important. What can you do to market and promote the book? The first book I co-authored was published in 1998 before social media took off. Our marketing plans included seminars, speaking events, and newspaper and magazine articles. These marketing techniques still work, but today you'll also need to explain how you plan to promote your book online. In other words, publishers want to know how many people you can influence to buy your book directly and easily via email, social media, or a blog. If you have a large number of followers or email subscribers, be sure and include numbers. If applicable, include any plans to hire a PR or book launch firm and how much you are willing to budget for marketing.
8. Chapter-by-Chapter Overview: Provide a brief outline that lists each chapter by number and name with a short one- or two-sentence description.

9. Sample Chapters: Include a few polished sample chapters from your manuscript. Which chapters to submit is up to you. You can include your first three chapters or the chapters you consider the most impressive.
10. The status of your book: Publishers will want to know if your book is completed. If not, when do you estimate the book will be finished?
11. Potential Endorsements: List names and titles of people of note who could provide advance praise/blurbs.

This list may seem overwhelming but take it one step at a time and you'll get through it.

SEND OUT QUERIES

As mentioned earlier, you'll probably want to try to retain an agent before querying publishing houses. The number of reputable publishing houses that accept a query from a non-agented author is minimal. Keep in mind, if you query traditional publishers before retaining an agent, this can hurt your chances since agents cannot re-query these publishers. This makes it less likely an agent will be willing to work with you.

So, how did I find an agent for my first novel? I bought a copy of *Writer's Market*, made a list of agents that specialized in young adult fiction and sent query letters. My efforts paid off. One well-established literary agent who represented the famous young adult author Gary Paulsen agreed to represent me.

Aside from *Writers Market*, a few other resources you may want to check out include PublishersMarketplace.com, AgentQuery.com, QueryTracker.net, ManuscriptWish List.com (or the hashtag #MSWL for Twitter), and the Association of American Literary Agents (AAL) Database.

I can't stress this enough. Whichever option you choose, do your homework before querying and beginning the submission process. Use the agent's name in your letter and be sure to spell it correctly. Make sure the agents you query accept the kind of book you're writing.

When you begin sending queries, here are some things to keep in mind:

- Don't send your full manuscript when you first contact an agent. Instead, send a one-page query letter, which almost all agents accept unless their guidelines state otherwise. If they aren't accepting query letters, they're probably not accepting new clients at this time.

- Read and follow an agent's specific guidelines when sending your query letter. Most prefer you submit a query through their work email, submissions email, or an online form. Although mailing query letters and submissions are extremely rare anymore, if you do so, include a self-addressed stamped envelope (SASE).
- As mentioned earlier, finish and polish your manuscript and book proposal before approaching agents. Make sure your query letter, book proposal, and sample chapters are free from grammar or spelling errors.
- Try to find an agent with experience and success in representing the type of novel or nonfiction book that you wrote. Most agents will list current clients on their website. Don't be afraid to contact established agents who are often searching for gems. On the flip side, don't automatically rule out new agents trying to build a roster of clients either. If you're a new and unpublished author, you may not interest an established agent. A new and "hungry" agent who has previous experience in the publishing world, perhaps as an editor, can also work.
- Proceed with caution, especially if participating in online pitching events. Be wary if you can't find any online mention or reference to an agent. Check to see if agents are members of the Association of American Literary Agents (AALA) or, at minimum, state on their website that they adhere to the strict code of conduct set forth by AALA. Also, steer clear of "agents" who charge upfront reading fees. Professional agents get paid only when they sell your work, typically 15 percent on your advance and royalties.

Keep track of your submissions with a Google Docs spreadsheet, in a Word document, or Query Tracker. Can you send out multiple query letters to different agents at once? Sure. If you do so, consider sending query letters in batches, perhaps 10 at a time. This allows you to correct any mistakes or adjust your letter based on feedback.

If an agent doesn't respond within the response time listed (the publishing business can be painfully slow, so double the time before giving up), consider it a rejection. Do not badger the agent with follow-up queries, phone calls, or try to visit in person. Don't wallow in misery either. Simply go on to the next agent on your list.

If you're lucky, an agent will express interest in seeing more. Send exactly what the agent requests – in my case, that meant a synopsis and sample chapters – but it can vary. Many agents want to see a full manuscript.

Remember, you'll need perseverance, dedication, and persistence if you choose this route. Dutra spent three years querying three different projects. She sent 266 queries for her cozy murder mystery and received 198 rejections along with 27 combined full and partial requests to see more material. The end results? Dutra signed with her dream agent. A true example that persistence can pay off.

This is a good time to develop a thick skin. Pay attention when an agent or an editor takes the time to point out flaws instead of sending a standard rejection letter. These professionals aren't always right but don't automatically assume they're wrong, especially if more than one mentions a particular flaw.

Are you required to have an agent before trying to find a traditional publisher? The simple answer is no. You can approach publishing houses yourself using that same copy of *Writer's Market* and sending query letters to appropriate publishers. I did so successfully after being turned down by agents with my first nonfiction book. Many of the tips above apply if you choose this path. However, as stated before, most reputable publishers do not accept queries from non-agented authors. I'd strongly suggest trying to find an agent first.

Keep in mind that just because you retain an agent doesn't mean your book is guaranteed to be accepted by a publisher. My first novel came ever-so-close to being published by a few well-known publishing houses but, sadly, in the end, did not sell. Don't throw up your arms in despair if this happens to you. You have other options, which we'll discuss in the next chapter.

CHAPTER 11:

SELF-PUBLISH A BOOK

Print-on-demand (POD) technology has rocked the self-publishing world with good reason. It's never been easier or cheaper to self-publish a book.

If you choose a reputable POD company like Amazon's KDP (Kindle Direct Publishing), no money is required upfront. eBooks are automatically sent out to devices and apps after the books are ordered. Paperbacks and hardcovers are printed and shipped only after they're ordered as well – which means you won't need to inventory books in your garage or make constant runs to the post office to ship books.

Amazon or other online retailers take a small percentage – and subtract printing costs in the case of paperbacks and hardcovers – but you keep most of the proceeds. Books can easily be purchased at a reduced author's rate if you schedule an event or book signing.

Be aware that there's a vast difference between self-publishing with reputable online retailers versus unethical vanity or subsidy publishers. Read this chapter carefully before making any decisions and understand all your options. Do not be lured in immediately by companies out to scam naïve first-time authors with ads like "We Want to Read Your Book." Buyer beware!

KEEP IT SIMPLE WITH KDP

Amazon's KDP is perfect for beginners. As mentioned earlier, if you're willing to do the editing and formatting yourself, publishing and listing your book on Amazon won't cost a dime. No risk or investment is involved. In other words, you have nothing to lose besides your time and effort.

How does it work?

You simply set up an account, upload your files, input some basic information, and format your book using Amazon's free tools. When you're finished, you submit your book for publication. After it's reviewed, your book will be published and released on Amazon within 24 to 48 hours.

Amazon takes a relatively small cut for each copy sold. You can earn up to 70% of the royalty for sales of eBooks and up to 60% on paperbacks and hardcovers after subtracting printing costs.

PROS AND CONS

Here are some advantages of using KDP:

- You can publish your book as an eBook, paperback, and hardcover.
- KDP provides automated tools, free guides, and tutorials for converting and uploading your files and listing your work for sale. Downloadable, printable guides are also available to help you enter your information. You don't have to be a technical genius to accomplish this feat. I'm technically challenged and was able to upload my book to KDP. However, if you can afford it and don't want the hassle of learning the ropes, you have the option of hiring someone to do this work for you.
- You have all the control. That means you decide on the content and set your own list price. You choose your cover with either a glossy or matte finish. If desired, KDP offers a free Cover Creator tool that allows you to design and customize your cover with various layouts and fonts. You also choose the book size, fonts, and formats.
- You can edit or make changes, even after publication, at any time without any fees.
- Royalties are paid monthly. Tracking book orders and royalties is simple. Monthly statements are straightforward and easy to understand.
- You can test the waters, create an online presence, build a personal brand, gain readers, and learn how to market and promote your book without investing any money.

- If you need help, KDP provides a list of editorial, book cover creation, and formatting services where you can get free quotes for services.

Here are a few disadvantages:

- Formatting your book is much more difficult if you want to include illustrations and photos.
- There are no upfront costs, but that means you do all the editing, cover design, and marketing yourself. If you're willing to spend money, however, you can hire someone to do it for you. Reedsy, Fivvr, and Upwork are a few reputable platforms you can check out. Before hiring any professional, be sure to check their portfolio, client reviews, and experience. It's also advisable to have clear communication about your expectations, timelines, and budget. As a side note, if you're not happy with the book cover choices KDP offers, Canva provides a variety of templates, graphics, and tools to help create visually appealing covers.
- If your book is under 100 pages, KDP does not include the title on the spine of your book.
- Because so many people self-publish on KDP, the competition is fierce. People won't likely stumble upon your book while shopping on Amazon. If you want your book to make money and stand out, you'll need to hustle to get reviews and spend substantial time marketing and promoting your book.

If you're retired, a first-time author, and want to keep things simple, I'd suggest you self-publish with Amazon's KDP. Sell your books through their online retail store and call it a day. Amazon store is the world's largest bookseller and most of your book sales will likely take place there. Viola! You're done.

This option is also great if you want to publish specialty books. You may want to write a book of poetry simply for the love of language and to nurture your creative soul. If you sell a few books – great! Or perhaps you're interested in publishing a family history to share with relatives and friends. You can do so without investing any money or worrying about making a profit.

If you choose to self-publish with KDP, you must make a few decisions regarding their options. Let's discuss those choices.

FREE ISBN (INTERNATIONAL STANDARD BOOK NUMBER)

What is an ISBN? If you want to publish a printed edition of your book, this 13-digit number is essential. It provides the basis for identifying books globally in the book industry and is required by most retailers. (An ISBN is not required for eBooks, however.)

KDP offers a free ISBN for paperback and hardcover books. Great, right? That depends.

If you simply want to become an author, publish a book, and have it listed only with Amazon, go ahead, and use their free ISBN. Just be aware that if you use their ISBN, you're giving Amazon exclusive rights to your book. If you have ambitious plans for your book, this limits your options. How?

- If you print books with another POD company like IngramSpark for wider distribution, they won't accept an ISBN from KDP.
- Brick-and-mortar stores like Barnes and Noble and libraries won't accept an ISBN from KDP either.
- If your book sells well and a traditional publisher becomes interested in purchasing rights to your book, they wouldn't be able to reprint your book.
- BookBub, one of the largest book promotion venues, no longer considers promoting books that are exclusive to the Amazon platform. Books must be available in different venues.

If you want to retain full rights to your book and keep your options open (which we'll discuss more fully in the next section), you can easily purchase your own ISBN as an author or self-publisher through Bowker. At the time of this writing, a single option is available starting at $125, or a block of 10 costs $295 for U.S. citizens.

There are a couple of reasons to consider the second, more expensive option. If you plan to sell your books outside Amazon, companies like IngramSpark require separate ISBNs for each format: eBooks, paperbacks, and hardcovers. In addition, the single option numbers are easily recognized by industry professionals as belonging to a one-book publisher and less likely to be taken seriously.

By purchasing your own ISBN through Bowker, your book will be included in their *Books in Print* database which is consulted by publishers, retailers, and libraries.

FREE BAR CODE (THE BOOKLAND EAN SCANNING SYMBOL)

A barcode is a visual representation of the ISBN that allows retailers and distributors to track inventory and sales quickly and efficiently.

KDP offers a free barcode identifier. If desired, it is printed on the back cover of your book automatically during the production process at no cost. If you plan to give Amazon exclusive rights, this is a convenient way to go.

However, if you plan to market your book outside of Amazon, barcodes can be purchased through Bowker and downloaded to your computer. Make sure the barcode matches the ISBN of your book. Once you have the barcode image file, insert it into the designated area on the back cover of your book. Make sure to leave enough white space around the barcode for better scanning. Remember, it's crucial to follow KDP's guidelines and ensure that the barcode is placed in a way that doesn't interfere with other important elements on the back cover. Be sure to check the box indicating your cover already has a barcode.

KDP SELECT

KDP offers the option of enrolling your eBook in KDP Select, which means you grant exclusive selling rights to Amazon for at least 90 days. This is not a requirement, but if you check this box, you'll get some extra benefits such as:

- KDP Select makes your book available for free to subscribers of Kindle Unlimited (KU) and the Kindle Owners Lending Library for Amazon Prime members. This is an easy way for your book to get more exposure, which as a new author you desperately need. You even get paid – although not a lot – earning a small share of a monthly fund.
- Amazon lists KDP Select deals that can help promote your book, find an audience, and hopefully get some valuable reviews. Kindle Countdown Deals allows you to offer your eBook for free to all Amazon customers for five days during each 90-day enrollment period. As another choice, you can discount your book for seven days.
- The enrollment period is for only 90 days. So, it's easy to opt out later if desired.

Before you enroll in KDP Select, there are a couple of cons:

- If you click that little box, Amazon demands a strict 100% exclusivity during your enrollment period. This means you can't sell your book to other retailers or use a distributor while enrolled. Keep in mind that many authors receive very few sales through other channels since Amazon rules the publishing world, so this might not require much of a sacrifice.
- You also cannot sell your book on your website or offer it free to new subscribers to your blog or newsletter. In addition, you cannot offer more than 10 percent of your book's content anywhere, including your website, blog, or social media.

EXPANDED DISTRIBUTION

KDP also offers a service called "Expanded Distribution" to help self-published authors reach more readers through bookstores, online retailers, libraries, and academic institutions outside of Amazon.

It's free to enroll printed editions of your book. All you do is check a box. Don't have too high of expectations, however. Although your book will be available, this is no guarantee it will land on the shelves of a store, library, or school. Typically, serious marketing on your part is needed to accomplish this feat.

If you're keeping things simple and only using Amazon's KDP to publish and sell your book, I'd check the box on the chance that a bookseller, library, or school may be interested and purchase your book. On the other hand, if you want to keep your options open, don't check the box.

This may all seem a bit confusing, but you basically have three choices:

- You reason that Amazon is a mammoth that dominates the book market. You don't want to put the extensive time and effort necessary to explore all your other options. So, you decide to give Amazon exclusive rights, use their free ISBN and barcode, and enjoy the benefits of KDP Select and Expanded Distribution. If you're a first-time author, this can be a good option.
- You choose to keep your options open. Therefore, you decide not to enroll in KDP Select and purchase your own ISBN and barcode. In this case, do not sign up for Expanded Distribution.
- You decide to enroll your eBook with KDP Select for at least 90 days for valuable exposure. You purchase your own ISBN and barcode to keep your options open later. After the 90-day period ends, you opt out and do as you please. Just keep in mind that KDP Select will automatically renew for another 90 days unless you take action to opt out. If you pull out during a 90-day period of exclusivity, you are still obligated to keep that title exclusive for the remainder of the 90 days. We'll discuss a popular option for distributing print books to other retailers and other distribution options for eBooks next.

INGRAMSPARK

If you don't give Amazon exclusivity and are willing to put in extra time and effort, you can explore other retailers to distribute your book. This is sometimes referred to in the Indie world as "going wide."

Maybe you don't want to miss out on possible sales from people who shop on Kobo, iBooks, Barnes & Noble, and other retailers. You're interested in marketing your book to physical bookstores, schools, and libraries. You want to explore the international market. If this describes you, IngramSpark (IS) is an excellent option as a one-stop shop, providing both POD and distribution services. Let's consider some pros and cons.

Here are some advantages:

- IS's global distribution network via Ingram is unmatched by other POD services. This is where IS knocks it out of the park. In addition to major retailers like Barnes & Noble, you'll have access to over 40,000 independent bookstores, online stores, chain stores, eBook retailers, libraries, and universities in more than 150 countries. However, this doesn't guarantee that your book will be on the shelves of physical bookstores and libraries. That requires intense marketing and promotional efforts on your part.
- IS offers authors a book returns option. If you opt-in, your book has a better chance of being stocked by brick-and-mortar bookstores, who are otherwise reluctant to sell self-published titles. This is a big advantage since physical bookstores will not typically accept books published by Amazon's KDP which are non-refundable.
- At the time of this writing, IS no longer charges set-up fees (previously $49). Books can now be uploaded for free.

There are a few disadvantages:

- Formatting your book is more complicated and frustrating than KDP with a steep learning curve. Download their guide and read carefully before moving forward.
- Royalties are less than KDP. You'll earn 60% of the list price for eBooks and 45% of your list price for print books minus the printing cost. (You can keep a higher percentage, but this will deter IS's partners from buying your book.)

- As of July 1, 2023, IS charges a 1 percent "market access" fee—1 percent of your book's list price—to distribute your book for you.
- If you check the box offering a book returns option, be aware that this is a double-edged sword. Booksellers buy independently published books on a trial basis. If a bookstore can't sell your books, they will be returned, which can be costly. Although you can click a box that requests returned books be shipped back to you, you'll pay the wholesale price of the book plus shipping and handling fees. The quality of returned books is not guaranteed. Some authors choose the more cost-effective option of having returned books shipped back to Ingram and destroyed to avoid the shipping costs. Others opt out of the book returns option altogether. Up to you.

Many indie authors use a hybrid approach, utilizing KDP for Amazon sales and IS for all other retailers. In my opinion, although somewhat complicated, this is a smart choice. Most of your book sales will likely come from Amazon. Using KDP ensures you get the highest royalties from those sales to maximize your profits. If you don't give Amazon exclusivity by purchasing your own ISBN and don't check the Expanded Distribution box, you can then use IS to produce a POD edition of your books. This will support book sales outside of Amazon and give you access to their global distribution network. You'll use the same ISBN for both Amazon and IS.

IS will distribute your book to Amazon for you, but you'll receive less royalties and books may be delayed causing Amazon to list your book as "out of stock" temporarily. For this reason, I recommend using KDP, and listing your book with Amazon yourself. If you take this route, do not sign IS's optional Amazon Agreement.

Many experts agree that it doesn't make sense to use IS for eBooks. So, let's discuss your other choices if you want to go wide with your eBooks.

DISTRIBUTION OPTIONS FOR EBOOKS

Basically, you have two choices if you want to offer your eBooks to retailers outside of Amazon. Again, make sure you aren't enrolled in KDP Select before proceeding.

- If you want to save money, you could use KDP and then distribute your book to Apple, Kobo, Nook, Barnes & Noble, and other online retailers by using their do-it-yourself portals. This method won't cost you a dime. Just be warned, while it is typically free to list your book with online stores, this can be a complicated and tedious process. You must sign up with different retailers, upload your book, and provide automatic payment information to each online store. Each retailer will pay you royalties directly, which also means extra bookkeeping.

- If you don't want all this headache, consider using aggregators like Draft2Digital for your eBooks. They serve as middlemen to make your eBook available to 30-plus online retailers as well as distributors. No payment is required upfront. Instead, a percentage of your sales, usually about 15%, will be taken from your profits. Many authors feel this small percentage is a fair trade for less hassle and centralized accounting and payment services. Will you sell a lot of books through an aggregator service? Probably not. As mentioned before, most of your eBooks will probably be sold through Amazon. But this is a good option if you want to reach other markets without the headache of doing it yourself.

Don't be fooled by expensive self-publishing packages that claim to distribute your eBook to thousands of outlets. You can do this free or inexpensively yourself.

OTHER SELF-PUBLISHING COMPANIES

Of course, KDP and IngramSpark aren't the only games in town. There are other reputable self-publishing companies.

B&N PRESS (BARNES & NOBLE PRESS)

B&N Press offers POD services. Users can easily upload their book and make it available for purchase on BN.com, on Nook devices, and in stores. With no delivery fees or production costs, B&N Press is free to use from start to finish. Exclusivity is not required.

B&N Press provides "qualified authors" the opportunity to apply for signings and events at Barnes & Noble bookstores. Keep in mind, that being accepted is by no means guaranteed. Also, using their POD services does not guarantee that your books will be in their physical stores.

BOOKBABY

If you have lots of money to spend and don't want to edit, format, or market your book, BookBaby, a full-service self-publishing company, is happy to help you every step of the way. For a substantial price, of course.

They offer POD services, formatting, editing services, cover design, publishing, proofreading, help converting your files to an eBook, distribution to eBook and print markets, and social media promotion. Their goal is to make everything easy for you, but all those extra services come at a hefty price. And if you discover a typo or want to make any edits after the publication of your book, there are additional charges. You can see how this quickly adds up.

LULU

Lulu is another option as one of the oldest self-publishing platforms. Lulu has no upfront set-up costs. Pricing varies widely, depending on the services and packages you select. Printing costs are considerably higher than KDP and IS, especially for hardcover books and books with a premium color interior. However, most authors seem satisfied with the production quality. The company also specializes in printing workbooks, art books, comic books, and cookbooks.

Lulu may be a good choice if you have extra money and don't want to deal with the steep learning curve at IS. You may not mind the higher prices if you want to publish a small batch of books, perhaps a personal memoir or family history with photos, to share with your friends and family only.

Publishing experts tend to agree that it makes no sense to publish and distribute an eBook through Lulu. On top of distribution fees, you'll pay "hosting fees" to Lulu for eBooks listed on their own bookstore. You're better off formatting your book with KDP and using an eBook-friendly aggregator like Draft2Digital.

These are just a few of the more well-known companies. There are plenty of other options, but please be careful. Not all are reputable. Read the section in this chapter on vanity and subsidy self-publishing companies before making a final decision.

STEER CLEAR OF VANITY AND SUBSIDY PUBLISHERS

Please be wary of unethical vanity presses such as AuthorHouse, Xlibris, iUniverse, and Trafford. Sure, their ads sound tempting: "Manuscripts Wanted," "We Want to Read Your Book," or "First-Time Authors Wanted."

Don't be fooled. These publishing predators aren't looking for quality work – they just want your money – and lots of it. These vanity publishers may label themselves as POD or self-publishing companies but are in the business of selling overpriced services and packages and preying on naïve first-time authors.

Unlike KDP and other credible companies, after you contact them, the high-pressure selling begins and can last for weeks or months. Packages range from several hundred to several thousand dollars, with over-inflated markups for editorial guidance and promotional services that don't work. Many of these companies provide poor-quality books and rake in profits. Forget about promised royalties; it would take a miracle just to break even and recoup your expenses.

Aware that the term "vanity publishers" may carry a stigma, these companies have gotten sneaky. Sometimes they use the label "subsidy publishers," "assisted publishing services," and "hybrid publishers." To flatter new authors, these companies claim to be more selective about the quality of writing they accept. Some profess to combine aspects of traditional publishing with self-publishing, offering to split the publishing distribution, warehouse, and marketing costs along with royalties. For a first-time author, this may seem like a great idea.

Don't be fooled. These companies want to look innovative but they're still playing the same old game – charging writers a ton of money to publish their books. True to form, these publishers ask for an exorbitant and overpriced amount of money upfront for publishing, editing, design, and marketing - usually thousands of dollars – claiming they are paying for a portion when you're really footing the bill.

Another deceptive tactic used is "small presses" that identify themselves as traditional publishers. When you submit a manuscript, they use a bait and switch to try and lure you into using their other "services." They'll say something along the lines: "Sorry your work doesn't match our editorial needs at this time, but would you be interested in our hybrid publishing services?"

To give you an example, author Carmela Dutra received positive feedback on her pitch from an editor during an online event and she agreed to a phone call.

"After specific questions, the truth was revealed," Dutra says. "They offered me hybrid publishing services and estimated my upfront cost would be – and this is supposed to be 'splitting the costs with them' - $8,000 to $13,000. She attempted to justify it by claiming they were distributed by Simon and Schuster, but I would need to pay extra for that option. In addition, extra expenses would be incurred for any additional needs, such as editing or cover art."

"If I hadn't done my due diligence on hybrids, the woman's persuasive way of wording things might have lured me into her trap," she adds. "It's a sad reality that authors pay these fees, hoping for great results, but often end up disappointed."

Don't allow these unsavory businesses to trick you into thinking they are traditional publishing houses or actual small presses. Remember, legitimate publishers and small presses invest their own money and resources to print and market books. They don't ask for any money upfront; they pay you, not the other way around.

If you aren't sure if a specific publishing company is authentic, Alli (Alliance of Independent Authors) lists the best and worst self-publishing services at https://selfpublishingadvice.org/best-self-publishing-services/.

AUDIOBOOKS

You may want to consider broadening your audience base with an audiobook. However, before moving forward, weigh the potential benefits against the costs and effort involved in audiobook production. Also, consider if you have the resources and strategies to promote an audiobook effectively.

Creating an audiobook can be expensive if you hire a professional narrator and pay for studio time and audio production services. The good news is that new technology has made the cost of producing an audiobook more manageable for indie authors. Authors and narrators often work together on a royalty-splitting basis, lowering the upfront cost to the writer.

Can you narrate your own audiobook? Sure. This saves money but requires suitable recording equipment and vocal skills. Costs can vary between $150 to $500 depending on the tools you choose to purchase. Be aware that this option takes time, effort, and quite a bit of patience.

Currently, the most popular digital platform for producing and distributing audiobooks is Amazon's ACX (Audiobook Creation Exchange), which uses Audible as its distributor to Amazon and iTunes, the two biggest retailers of audiobooks. Of course, other platforms are available that you may want to check out, such as Findaway Voices. Check the terms and conditions of distribution platforms to ensure they align with your goals.

PREPARE FOR PUBLICATION

How much you put into preparation depends, once again, on your goals. Consider these additional steps if you're serious about selling books:

ESTABLISH YOUR OWN PUBLISHING COMPANY

Why should you consider establishing your own publishing imprint - or a name for your publishing company? You can simply publish books under your own name. Just remember, there continues to be a stigma toward self-published books. This attitude is slowly changing but still influences some book retailers, readers, and the media. Why make it blatantly clear you are self-publishing your book?

So, if you plan on publishing more than one book and are serious about marketing, consider creating a unique name for your own publishing company. This name will be displayed by retailers and distribution channels and listed on your book's copyright page and assigned to your ISBN.

Choosing a company name can be a fun and creative process. However, the name should be professional and reflect your brand. For example, a name like "Passion Press" is suitable if you plan on writing romance novels but not if you plan on publishing technical books.

Before claiming the name as your own, make sure it's not trademarked, already in use in the publishing world, or used in your local community. You can do a quick Google search or check Literary Marketplace under publishers.

You will need to file a "Doing Business As" (DBA) name, sometimes called a "Trade Name Registration" or "Fictitious Name." This is a simple and inexpensive process. You won't be able to cash a check made out to your business name unless you have filed for a DBA. When you receive a certified copy of the statement, keep it in a safe place since you'll need it to open bank accounts.

GET A LIBRARY CONGRESS NUMBER

This is optional, but if you hope to sell your book to libraries, which is a great market, you'll need a Library of Congress catalog card number (LCCN), which should appear on the copyright page of your book. This must be done before the publication of your book. Be aware that the process can take several weeks.

Attaining a number is free and easy to apply for online. Visit https://www.loc.gov/programs/preassigned-control-number/ to obtain an account number and password. Fill out and submit the application form which typically includes details about the book such as the title, author, publisher, publication date, ISBN, format, etc. When your book is published, you will need to mail them a copy.

COPYRIGHT YOUR BOOK

Many new writers don't understand this, but U.S. copyright law automatically protects your self-published work from the moment you start typing. By placing the copyright symbol (©) on your work, you inform others that you know your rights.

However, official registration is necessary before you have the power to act in court against someone who is stealing, copying, or profiting from your work. Although this rarely happens, if you don't want to take any chances, register your work with the U.S. Copyright Office and create a public record of your authorship.

Luckily, registering a copyright is inexpensive and easy to do. Follow the instructions and complete the form, make a payment, and download your manuscript.

By the way, contrary to popular belief, mailing yourself a copy of your manuscript in a sealed envelope with a date stamp does not legally copyright your work and won't hold up in a court of law.

SEARCH FOR BOOK ENDORSEMENTS

Experts on your book's subject or even celebrities might endorse your book. These "advanced comments" with written permission can be used on your book's cover or front matter and promotional materials.

Blurbs from celebrities don't come easy. However, you don't have anything to lose if you want to try. Make a list of candidates that may be interested in your book. Find out how to contact them through the Internet or listings in *Who's Who*. Contact information can be found easily on sites such as IMDbPro. A monthly membership costs $19.99 at the time of this writing and may be canceled at any time. They offer a free month's trial.

Don't aim all your efforts at famous people, however. Send requests to lesser-known people who may be happy to help and gain free publicity. Contact other authors in your genre or prominent experts or associations connected to your subject matter.

Asking for book endorsements may lead to other opportunities, such as bulk book sales, reviews, or speaking engagements – even if a person declines to write an endorsement. For example, one author I contacted for an endorsement, agreed to feature my book on a website she co-founded for authors who write about dementia, AlzAuthors.com.

Prepare a cover letter with a powerful overview of your book, a bio, and why you feel the person will find the material interesting. Let them know it would be an honor if they read your book and provide a short comment which would be included on the book's cover or front pages. Ask if you can send them a copy. Sometimes, celebrities will agree to write a blurb for a hefty price. This is your call, but I personally refuse to pay for an endorsement.

SEND BOOK OUT TO REVIEWERS BEFORE PUBLICATION

If you're ambitious and plan to market your book to sell, don't rush to publish. In fact, you may want to wait at least six months after your book is finished. Some well-known reviewers will only look at your book if it's submitted months before publication.

See the next chapter for a list of book reviewers who review self-published books free of charge.

WHAT WRITERS IN RETIREMENT HAVE TO SAY...

BARRY SILVERSTEIN

I have used Amazon's Kindle Direct Publishing (KDP), IngramSpark, and Smashwords (recently acquired by Draft2Digital). I also recently used ACX (Audible).

I find KDP to be the easiest and most cost-effective to work with but also the most restrictive in terms of distribution because it is operated by Amazon. IngramSpark is more challenging to work with and more expensive than KDP, but the quality seems a bit higher and the distribution is superior.

Draft2Digital is easy once you learn how to meet the production requirements; it is a good platform that pays high royalties and offers wide eBook distribution but typically does not include Amazon.

With ACX, I experimented with narrating my own audiobook. I self-produced it using Apple's GarageBand and uploaded it to ACX without any problems.

I have found that publishing under a company name (GuideWords Publishing) provides legitimacy and credibility to a self-published author. That alone has allowed me to be taken more seriously.

* * *

CAT MICHAELS

I've used several platforms, and each has its pros and cons.

I highly recommend using Amazon for print and digital for beginners. Get your feet wet first and then go wide with your books. I stayed in KDP's exclusive program for 90 days and then went wider. On the downside, I don't use their expanded distribution because IngramSpark does it best. My local brick-and-mortar bookstores hate Amazon and will not stock any of my Amazon books (Ingram to the rescue again).

IngramSpark is THE place for producing hardcover books if your goal is to get books into schools and libraries. However, Ingram has several hoops to jump through, and I didn't find their formatting or required book submission process user-friendly.

I loved Apple for creating The Magical Aquarium, an interactive e-fantasy for young readers for iPad and iPhone in the iTunes store. I added video, sounds, photo carousels, and the works. It even won a Best Digital Book award. Con: However, I couldn't get much sales traction with Apple's iBooks or iTunes.

Aggregators like Smashwords (recently acquired by Draft2Digital) and BookBaby distribute your book across multiple platforms, like Amazon, Barnes and Noble, Kobo, and Apple. One-stop shopping here saves you time. However, you must be comfortable creating/juggling between multiple POD sites and with different format requirements.

Lulu had great customer service and quality. Especially excellent if you want to publish a print book with distribution limited to a few copies for friends and family. I published a dandy family history, just for my folks, through Lulu. I wouldn't recommend Lulu, however, for eBooks (Lulu reps admitted as much to me at a seminar I attended at their headquarters near me in Raleigh, North Carolina).

Many authors use Atticus (PC) or Vellum (Mac) to format their print and eBooks. I used Vellum for my eBooks and will use it for both print and eBook for my beachy romances.

* * *

ROSIE RUSSELL

I started with Blurb and moved on to Createspace - which merged with Amazon and is now KDP. I've also used IngramSpark since they offer hardcovers which are readily available for bookstores and libraries.

One will have to do their research on the publishing platforms they choose. Some are free to sign up to enter your book, but some have fees. (Important note: If you're approached by a company offering to publish your book for money, it's best not to sign up.) Join author groups and ask others what has helped them or what things to walk away from.

CHAPTER 12: MARKET AND PROMOTE A BOOK

Maybe you hate the idea of marketing your book. If so, you have options. In fact, you don't have to promote your book at all and can skip this chapter if you'd like.

The exception to this rule is if your book was traditionally published. Although many publishing houses help with promotion, you're expected to actively market your book as well. In your book proposal, you should have listed all the ways you planned on accomplishing this feat. I'd recommend living up to your word.

However, if you self-published your book, whether you want to promote your book is your decision. Your choice will depend on your objectives and personality.

Here are a few of your options:

- Maybe you don't want to spend time or money promoting your book. Then don't. Publish your book, list it on Amazon, and see what happens. If you can be happy with whatever results – even if you only sell a few copies – you'll save yourself a lot of time, energy, and frustration. Instead of obsessing over how many books you're selling or worrying about how much money you're earning, you can focus on the joy of writing. Be content that you accomplished your goal of becoming an author and continue enjoying your retirement years. Nothing wrong with that!
- Perhaps you want to dabble a bit in marketing but don't want to spend a ton of time, energy, and money doing so. That works too. Learn about some

ways to promote your book that you find appealing. Experiment, and see what works best for you. Engage in a few promotional activities – some are free if you prefer – that you enjoy and call it a day.

- On the opposite end of the spectrum, you may have some entrepreneurial skills. You plan on publishing several books and want to take a stab at becoming an author-publisher as an encore career. You're willing and eager to learn everything you can about marketing your books and spend some money on advertising. Then go for it!

In the end, everyone is different. Marketing books is my least favorite thing about being an author. But my father loved it. He couldn't wait to be interviewed by the media, speak at public events, and hobnob at book signings.

So, let's discuss some of your marketing options. Remember that some methods may sound fun and even a bit glamorous, but won't sell many books. On the other hand, more intensive marketing techniques may seem tedious but are more successful.

We'll start with a few marketing techniques that many new writers fantasize about when they picture life as an author.

GET BOOK REVIEWS

Do you dream of book reviews praising your novel and you as an author? Nothing wrong with that. Keep in mind, however, that reviews are more than just ego boosters.

Book reviews are an essential and powerful tool to help build your reputation as an author and promote your book.

Here are just a few of the benefits:

- Good reviews influence readers' decisions to buy.
- The more positive reviews a book receives, the better it ranks on Amazon, which gives your book more visibility.
- Book reviews open doors to marketing opportunities like BookBub, which helps boost sales.
- Quotes from book reviews can be used on social media and paid advertising.

These benefits apply if you've written a quality book. If not, then garnishing bad reviews will work against you. That being said, let's review some different kinds of book reviews.

NEWSPAPERS AND MAGAZINES

In the past, newspapers and magazines provided the only opportunity to get book reviews. You have other choices these days, but these traditional publications are still influential. Especially if you somehow hit the jackpot and score a review in publications like *The New York Times*. Unfortunately, these reviews are next to impossible to get if you're self-published or just starting out.

No need to throw up your arms in despair though. If your book is tied to a current event, you can try pitching a newsworthy story to get the media's attention. After I approached *The Seattle Times* while living in Washington State, my father and I were featured in an article about our book on steel framing. Since many experts felt recent devastating floods in the Pacific Northwest were caused by clear cuts of mountainsides, an editor thought readers would be interested in learning about an environmental alternative to wood.

If you have an interesting story connected to your book, a newspaper might publish a feature story about you and your book. Feature pieces can be effective marketing tools since readers feel more connected to you and may be more likely to buy your book. You can also try contacting your hometown newspaper or alumni magazine from a college you attended.

BOOK TRADE PUBLICATIONS

Editorial reviews by book trade publications like *Publishers Weekly, Foreword Reviews, Kirkus Reviews*, and *Library Journal* can influence booksellers, librarians, and book reviewers.

Once again, getting reviews in these publications is difficult, especially if you're a self-published author. If you're willing to pay for reviews, fee-for-review services like Kirkus Indie Reviews and Publishers Weekly's BookLife are available. These reviews are included in the "Editorial Description" section on your Amazon page. How much these paid reviews pay off in book sales is debatable. And please be wary of disreputable review services.

Don't despair if you're unable to get reviews from prestigious trade publications and don't want to spend money on paid reviews. I've listed some reputable sites that review self-published books free of charge and, in my opinion, are certainly worth a try:

- Readers' Favorite is a great site for free reviews. They review published and unpublished (ARC and manuscripts) books in any of their 140+ genres. Your review will be posted on their site with a featured Review Page and other trade and social media sites.

- Midwest Book Review welcomes – and even gives priority to – small presses and self-published authors.
- Fore Word Reviews, another respectable publication, offers beautifully written, objective reviews of indie books for librarians, booksellers, and book lovers.
- City Book Review, the parent company for their brands San Francisco, Manhattan, Tulsa, and Seattle Book Reviews, and Kids' BookBuzz are well-respected publications that will review your book for free if it is submitted 90 days before the publication date. They review about 40 percent of their submissions, so there's no guarantee. But you have nothing to lose, and the form on their submissions page is easy to use.
- Book Reporter primarily reviews fiction books and will review self-published titles. They must be available with wide distribution offline as well as online. Typically, they review books with recommendations from publishing colleagues so are more difficult to get than some of the other reviewers I've mentioned.

BOOK BLOGGERS

Reviews by book bloggers with significant followers can create book buzz with their fans.

How do you find book bloggers? Here are a few ways:

- Sites like https://blog.reedsy.com/book-review-blogs/ and https://kindlepreneur.com/book-review-blogs/ conveniently list book bloggers by genre.
- Do a Google search for "book review bloggers."
- Check Twitter, Instagram, and Facebook with hashtags like #bookblogger, #bookstagram, #bookstagrammer, and #bookreview.
- Search YouTube for BookTubers, where video bloggers share their thoughts about books they're reading.

Keep in mind that some book bloggers will not review unsolicited books or self-published authors. Read the blogger's review policy carefully. Some blogs have a form to fill out, while others prefer an email. Don't waste your time – or the book bloggers' time - by contacting blogs that don't review books in your genre.

Once you have a list of book bloggers you plan to approach, you'll need to pitch the reviewers. Here are some tips:

- Personalize your pitch by using names.

- Briefly introduce yourself and explain why you think they'll be interested in the type of book you wrote.
- Include your book's title, publisher, release date, and genre in the first paragraph.
- Provide a brief summary and an image of your book cover.
- Include a link to your website if you have one.
- Mention that you hope they can provide a review and include information on how they can obtain their ARC (advance review copy) along with a link. Sites like BookFunnel make this easier.
- Respectfully follow up if you don't hear back. Many book bloggers are buried with pitches, so don't keep hounding them. This can get you blacklisted.
- Always be polite and thank book bloggers for their time.

CUSTOMER REVIEWS ON AMAZON AND OTHER ONLINE SITES

Finally, you'll want to obtain reviews by customers on online book sites like Amazon and Goodreads that readers post.

Getting these reviews is harder work than you may think. There are rules. Many new authors plan to ask family members and friends to start posting reviews. Unfortunately, this is against Amazon's policy. If Amazon detects that you're connected to reviewers in any way, they'll immediately remove the reviews. Don't consider creating a false name or personality and write reviews for your own book either, which is strictly prohibited.

That's not all. You're not allowed to pay for customer reviews. You cannot offer free books or any gift in exchange for a review. Trading positive book reviews with other authors is also against the rules, so don't head to Facebook or Twitter to find review swaps. If you get caught breaking these rules, you risk account suspension or closure.

So, what can you do? You are allowed to send out advance review copies (ARCs), typically in a PDF file, and encourage people to review your book when it's released. These ARCs are common in traditional publishing and are still considered a good business practice in the industry. However, any free copies you give away cannot have any strings attached.

Where can you find people willing to review your book?

- Beta readers may be willing to write a review if you remind them when your book is published. Avoid begging: "If you loved my book, please leave a review so I can sell more books." It's better to say: "Reviews are always appreciated. I'd love to hear your honest opinion."

- If you have an email list for a newsletter or blog, or social media followers, offer your subscribers an advanced copy and encourage them to write an honest review if they enjoy the book.
- You can set up a "launch team." Put together a list of people in your network and send them an ARC about a month before your book is released. Let them know you're excited to announce that your new book (title) launches (date). Remind them that early reviews are the single most important factor in determining if a book succeeds, and an honest review would be appreciated. Send a reminder when your book is released and include links to Amazon and Goodreads.
- This may seem counterproductive, but if you're starting out, offering your book for free can help get your book into readers' hands and may result in more reviews. Amazon's KDP Select allows you to use free eBook campaigns when you launch your book and periodically after that. Goodreads giveaways are another option. Promotional companies like Freebooksy and Fussy Librarian can help promote your book during these free periods so you can get more downloads.
- Use the back of your book to thank your readers and encourage them to write an honest review if they enjoyed reading it. Remind your readers that their views will not only impact other people's purchasing decisions but that their opinion matters to you as well.

Plan your book review campaign four to six months before your publication date. Mass media, book trade publications, and book bloggers often request submissions at least a few months before publication. On the other hand, customer reviews on Amazon will not be accepted until the publication of your book.

A good goal if you're serious about selling books is to garnish at least 10 customer reviews and three editorial reviews as soon as possible after your book is published. The more, the better. If you can get at least 50 good reviews, your book will likely be viewed as reputable and should continue to generate reviews.

Remember that when you ask for reviews, you risk bad one-star reviews from people who don't like your book. Whatever you do, don't comment on these negative reviews. However, if it is a personal attack against you, ask Amazon to remove the review.

HOST A BOOK LAUNCH PARTY

Maybe you envision a grand book launch party like you see in the movies. Keeping it real here. Unless you're a famous author, don't count on a traditional publisher hosting one for you.

But that doesn't mean you can't have one – even if you're a new self-published author.

You may want to bask in the glory of finishing and publishing your book with some of your loved ones. Then go ahead and throw a party for family, friends, and acquaintances. Host the party in your home for a more intimate setting. Pop a bottle of champagne and celebrate the fact that you've accomplished your goal.

If you do so, enjoy your party instead of viewing it as an effective marketing strategy. If you sell some books, that's great, but pressuring your loved ones to buy your book isn't likely to go well.

So, try and make it fun. Print posters with your book cover to display. Use party decorations that relate to the theme of your book. Make a short speech thanking those who supported your writing journey. Read a short passage from your book. Share a funny story about writing your book to amuse guests.

Supply goody bags printed with the name of your book – that just happens to be the right size to fit any book purchases – and fill them with fun prizes and a few promotional items. If you have the money, you may want to give away your books while encouraging guests to leave an honest book review if they enjoy your writing.

What if you're feeling more ambitious? If that's the case, invite more guests. Search your email lists and social media contacts. Consider having the party at a bookstore or another paid venue.

Whatever you decide, take photos to post on your author's website and social media.

Maybe an in-person party doesn't sound appealing. That's okay. These days, you have other options.

Have a live virtual launch party. Use a social media site like Facebook, Instagram Live, YouTube Live, Zoom, or Twitter Chat. Announce the event well ahead of time on your feed. Post reminders and notify your followers when the live stream begins.

Plan enough activities to keep things interesting. Here are a few ideas to consider:

- Have a friend host your party and interview you.
- Dress up as a character in your book and have a live reading.
- Make a character's favorite drink and share the recipe.

- If your book is nonfiction, make your live event like a workshop and invite attendees to participate.
- Create contests and offer giveaways.
- Use the chat feature to answer viewers' questions.
- Of course, remind attendees where they can purchase your book.

If going live makes you nervous, you have one more option. On the day of your "virtual launch party," instead of going live, simply create posts on a social media platform of your choice – perhaps once every hour or two. Once again, be sure to announce the time of your event in advance so hopefully, you can attract visitors.

What should you post?

- Offer giveaways and free prizes. An Amazon gift card is easy to send.
- Post related memes.
- Share any good reviews you've garnished for your book.
- Post a short quiz and offer a small prize to those who answer correctly.
- Offer free copies of your books to those who win a raffle.
- Post a quote from your book.
- Answer any questions and chat with visitors in the comment section.
- Of course, post a link so visitors can purchase your book if desired.

I tried this last option while promoting my book on caring for a parent with dementia. Did I sell hundreds of books? No. Not unexpected since my book appeals primarily to caregivers and is geared toward a specific audience.

I did sell several books that day, but the time I spent preparing for the virtual launch party and posting throughout the day didn't pay off in dollars. Some authors, however, have better success depending on their fan base and the subject of their books. If you're not overly concerned about how many books are sold, you may simply enjoy the experience of interacting with friends, family, and fans in this way.

ARRANGE BOOK SIGNINGS

Many authors dream about a book signing at a large bookstore like Barnes & Noble. If that's your dream, go for it. Personally, I found getting book signings to be challenging to negotiate. I had to "hard sell" our book publishing company and blow my own horn to book a few signings at their stores.

Author Carmela Dutra has found success arranging book signings in brick-and-mortar bookstores by asking to talk with their book-buying manager. "Many are happy to work with local authors and usually willing to order between 20 to 50 books," she says. "Offer to sign any unsold books which prevent them from returning unsold merchandise," Dutra adds.

If you're unable to arrange a book signing at a large store, don't despair. Try to get your book into a local bookstore and offer to do a book signing. These stores may be open to accepting your books on consignment.

Book festivals, libraries, schools, book clubs, and writing groups sometimes look for speakers and book readings and may host a book signing afterward. I've done a few of these as well. Many book festivals rent booths for book signings if you're not invited to be a speaker.

If you're able to arrange a book signing, come prepared. Print a large "Author Signing Today" sign, a poster of your book cover, and an author photo. Order plenty of books ahead of time. Bring pens, business cards, flyers, and free giveaways to attract visitors. Be sure to send a thank-you card afterward to whoever hosts the signing.

Be aware that book signings aren't always fun. Unless you're well-known, you can easily find yourself stuck at a table stacked behind a pile of books with hardly anyone stopping by. Personally, while it was rewarding to meet a few enthusiastic buyers at book signings, most of the time I felt like a salesperson trying to peddle my books. Since I tend to be an introvert, these events turned out to be stressful for me.

However, you may be different. If this is your dream and you enjoy this type of thing, give book signings a try. As an added benefit, photos at book signings make you look more professional. Post pictures on your author's website and social media sites.

SET UP MEDIA INTERVIEWS

If you're bold, you may want to shoot for the moon and try to book appearances in national newspapers, magazines, and TV and radio shows. You have nothing to lose. Remember that you'll have a better chance, however, if you try to develop a relationship with local media.

When you're pitching for an interview:

- Find an interesting angle or even something controversial about your book that will hook reporters.

- Explain specifically how your book will benefit their readers or viewers.
- Time the announcement of your new book with a relevant news event, movie, or trade show.
- Keep an eye out for trendy stories related to your book and volunteer to be featured as an expert.
- If you've written a memoir – perhaps about battling cancer, prejudice, or depression – offer to bring attention to the issue, providing a voice for people who are often ignored.

TRY ONLINE MARKETING

Do you hate large groups and making small talk like me? If so, live events like book festivals, speaking engagements, book signings, interviews, or attending networking events may not be your cup of tea.

Online marketing is another option.

Social media can help you get the word out about your book and potentially help you find book buyers and future fans. And if you ever want to sell a book to a traditional publishing house, they like to see several thousand actively involved followers.

There are plenty of free and organic ways to build an author platform:

- Use Amazon Author Central, which is free. Include your photo, bio, blog posts, and videos.
- Create an author's Facebook, Twitter, and/or Instagram page and post at least once a day. Interact with people who leave comments.
- Explore various social media outlets that may be a good fit. For example, if you write about fashion or crafts, Pinterest may work well. On the other hand, if you write books offering business tips, LinkedIn may be your ticket.
- Make YouTube videos or if you're trendy, try TikTok.

Gaining followers and selling books online takes time, persistence, and patience before seeing results. However, this type of promotion won't cost you a dime.

Social media sites also offer paid advertising. You don't have to spend a lot of money to experiment. Start small to see what works best for you. For example, you can set up an ad on Facebook for as little as $5. Most platforms allow you to set daily or total limits on spending as well as dictate the amount of time an ad will run. Canva and Book Brush can help you design appealing ads.

Amazon ads are another option. Amazon states on its site, for best results, "target complementary and popular keywords, interests, and products, including similar books and authors." Amazon ads can be easily accessed through KDP or Author Central.

A few words of warning when using social media to promote your book:

- Don't buy followers which will likely be spam followers or bots anyway. Grow your numbers organically, which will attract readers who are genuinely interested in your book.
- Don't use social media platforms to constantly barrage people to buy your book. This will backfire and drive people away. Many authors use the 80/20 rule. About 80% of your posts should entertain (funny and inspirational quotes, memes, or viewpoint questions) or provide information (links to relevant articles). The other 20% of your posts can include links to your books, book reviews, quotes from your book, and periodic updates about your writing life.
- Use social media judicially since it can become a huge time waster. Set time limits, perhaps 30 minutes a day when you'll share content, reply to messages and comments, and network. Also, limit your social media exposure to only a couple of popular platforms that bring the most results. For myself, I get the most response from Facebook since that's where a lot of boomers hang out. Experiment and see what works best for you.

USE A BOOK PROMOTIONAL SERVICE

New sites and services are popping up for authors all the time, but at the top of this list is BookBub. The site is a free service for readers who get a daily email with books either offered for free or deeply discounted. They provide a premium promotional service to authors utilizing their significant email lists for advertising. You can check out the different kinds of ads offered at BookBub Ads.

The coveted "Featured Deal" campaigns are pricey and challenging to attain. A small percentage of books are selected, but if your book is lucky enough to be chosen, pop a champagne bottle. If selected, your book will be sent to millions of readers actively searching for a new book. Although pricey, an author usually gets more than their money back in increased sales and visibility.

Although it's free to apply, there are hoops to jump through:

- You must have a professionally edited book with a professionally designed cover.
- You need a substantial number of both editorial and authentic customer reviews. I'd recommend having 50-plus reviews before applying.
- Your book must be available from multiple retailers. This is when it pays to use a distributor like IngramSpark as explained in Chapter 11.
- Blurbs from well-known authors and celebrities, as well as winning literary awards, helps.
- You will be required to make sure your book is deeply discounted if accepted.

If your book is not selected, don't despair. BookBub Ads are also available. The ads appear at the bottom of the Featured Deal emails. Not as prestigious, but these ads still generate clicks and sales. These ads target fans of similar authors, which means that you won't waste money paying for advertising to readers who aren't interested in your genre. Unlike "Featured Deals" campaigns, you're not required to discount your book to place ads; nonetheless, if you're running a short-term campaign, a lowered price will help drive sales. A quick trial costing $10 or $20 can deliver valuable data about which ads resonate with readers. You can easily track the results and adjust your campaign if necessary.

If nothing else, claim your author profile for free and build followers there. Add BookBub to your website with a link, and whenever you release a new book, your followers on BookBub are notified. Once your author account is approved, you can apply for an advertising account.

Buck Books is another popular site that promotes books priced at 99 cents or for free. You can sign up to be promoted in their regular daily deals broadcast along with some other authors. Or apply for a once-a-week solo broadcast that features only you and your book. Although competitive, if rejected, you may still be eligible for a regular daily deals broadcast. To be considered, your book must have a professionally designed cover, well-written sales copy, and at least 10 reviews.

There are tons of book promotion companies out there. Some are free, but many offer paid advertising. Most require that you offer steeply discounted or free books during the advertising period. ManyBooks, Hello Books, BookDoggy, Ebook Betty, Book Gorilla, Freebooksy, BargainBooksy, Free Kindle Books and Tips, BookAngel and the Fussy Librarians are just some that you may want to check out.

OTHER PRODUCTIVE MARKETING STRATEGIES

In addition to some of the promotional activities I've listed above, if you're ambitious, try other intensive and concentrated types of marketing as well. Although these strategies may take a lot of time and effort, if you're serious about selling books, you'll probably want to include some, if not all, of the following:

- learn to write compelling sales copy
- choose the right categories and keywords when listing your book with Amazon
- start an email list and send out regular newsletters
- create an author's website (see Part V for tips)
- collaborate with other authors to cross-promote
- set up speaking appearances at libraries, bookstores, book clubs, seminars, conventions, etc.
- write articles for magazines on your subject or guest blog on popular sites

LOOK FOR ADDITIONAL INCOME OPPORTUNITIES

If you've written a nonfiction book, experiment with other income opportunities that can stem from becoming an author.

Here are some ideas:

- teach an online or video course (you can either host it on your own site or use one of the popular platforms such as Udemy, Thinkific, or Teachable)
- teach in person with adult college courses or workshops
- package your knowledge into a PDF and sell "guides" directly from your website or on social media sites
- host seminars, webinars, or live online coaching programs
- apply for paid speaking engagements
- start a consulting or coaching business
- become an affiliate or sell ad space on a blog related to your book or on your YouTube channel
- sell merchandise such as T-shirts or mugs connected to your book

BE REASONABLE WITH EXPECTATIONS

Describing how to take advantage of all these marketing strategies is a book by itself. If you're serious about marketing, research books, writing magazines, articles on the Internet, podcasts, and other sources for more information.

Remember, there are no guarantees in this business. Selling books isn't easy. Anything can happen. You might diligently utilize all these suggestions and sell under 100 books. Perhaps you'll make just enough money to supplement your Social Security checks. Or maybe you'll get lucky and hit the jackpot. Be prepared for anything and enjoy the ride!

One word of warning: Some writers self-publish and think if they just spend enough money, they can make their book a best seller. You can easily spend hundreds or thousands of dollars to no avail.

Be careful of PR firms, marketing educational programs, or paid reviewers who target and try to scam new authors. Paying hundreds or even thousands of dollars for advertisements in newspapers or magazines, book reviews, or a public relations company hardly ever works.

Take it from *USA Today* bestselling author Charlotte Byrd who has sold over two million books. "A lot of PR companies aimed at indie authors aren't very effective and I'd rather spend that money on Facebook advertising," she says. "I've found Facebook and Amazon ads to be invaluable. I target authors that are similar to my books and drive sales to the first book in the series. I also publish books with cliffhangers and three to six-book series."

This is your decision, but I wouldn't allow fantasies and ambitions to destroy your retirement plans and suck all the joy out of writing.

WHAT WRITERS IN RETIREMENT HAVE TO SAY...

ROSIE RUSSELL

Word of mouth, social media posts, and book launches have helped book sales. I've done a few craft fairs but am still looking for book fairs to sign up for.

Selling in person has given me the best results.

* * *

BARRY SILVERSTEIN

Promoting books as a small, independent publisher is very challenging. My strategy for marketing has been to make heavy use of free and inexpensive channels. I write and distribute a low-cost press release, print a sales sheet for each book, and offer/distribute ARCs (Advance Review Copies) to appropriate book reviewers, bloggers, book review publications, and friends.

The most effective thing that I have done is target boomer-oriented blogs, newsletters, and publications. This is how I have obtained book reviews and have gotten book excerpts published. I have also written articles based on my books for specific publications. I promote my books through my blog and via LinkedIn, Twitter, and Facebook. I think that positive reviews from select publications have helped.

Asking beta readers and friends to post positive reviews and promote books via word of mouth is one of the more effective ways to do book promotion.

I have done a small amount of targeted advertising via Facebook, Amazon, and Google and have not found it to directly result in sales.

For me, blogging and writing books is really an avocation. I enjoy writing and am happy when someone reads my blog or buys my books and enjoys them. I'm not doing it to make a substantial profit.

* * *

SANDRA BENNETT

Promotion is one of the hardest parts of being an author. I am always looking for new opportunities. Social media can be helpful in gaining awareness, but I'm not sure that it has been all that successful in translating into sales. However, the more you put yourself out there, the more people will find you.

I try to do school visits when I can, although these can be difficult to get. I also try to get involved in events, markets, conferences etc., anywhere that you can get to meet people in person. Book Fairs and markets can be good, but you need to consider the costs associated with having a stall. Sometimes the fees can outweigh the sales. Outdoor markets are also not always great for books, depending on the weather, this can be great or a disaster. Often people at markets are looking for bargains, so be prepared to discount heavily.

One of the best marketing strategies for me has been to think outside the box in terms of where to market my books. Instead of looking at bookstores only, what other types of places might consider selling your book? One of my books is a fiction children's chapter books based on an adventure with Australian dinosaurs, so I have developed a fantastic relationship with the National Dinosaur Museum who often invite me to do book readings whenever they have on a special event.

PART IV: START AN ENCORE CAREER AS A FREELANCE WRITER

CHAPTER 13:

PROS AND CONS

So, exactly what is a freelance writer? This term refers to a professional writer who offers services to clients and publications. Some clients pay hourly; others pay an agreed-upon amount for each project.

A freelancer may:

- write articles for print and online magazines
- ghostwrite an eBook
- write blogs
- give book reviews
- write website content
- edit
- provide copywriting
- write press releases
- provide social media writing for businesses

You can try to sell short stories, but that's a tall order these days. If you want to earn money as a freelancer, most likely you'll write nonfiction which is more in demand and pays better.

As a professional freelance writer, I've written thousands of articles, blogs, and press releases published in national and regional print and online magazines, newspapers, blogs, and websites. I'm happy to share how I achieved those goals. This section will teach you how to write articles that sell, find freelance gigs on the Internet, query magazines and newspapers, and pitch to online magazines and blogs.

Before we discuss how to get started as a freelance writer, let's review some advantages and disadvantages of this business. While freelancing certainly has its allure and is sometimes glamorized, this career choice has some drawbacks, especially if you're dependent on the income.

To help you decide if freelance writing is right for you, let's discuss the good, the bad, and the ugly of this career.

THE ADVANTAGES OF FREELANCING

Here's what I love about freelancing:

- You can make a living pursuing your passion and indulging your creative side.
- Freelancing gives you flexibility. You keep your independence and are your own boss. That means you set your schedule and choose how much you want to work. In addition, you select which clients you want to work for and assignments that interest you.
- Working for various clients allows you to explore different types of writing, find your voice, and uncover new writing techniques.
- Since most writing assignments are completed via the Internet or emailed, you can live wherever you want. If that means in a bungalow somewhere overlooking the ocean – so be it!
- You can work at home in your pajamas. This is one of my favorite things about freelancing.

If your goal is to eventually become an author, there are even more benefits. Writing articles for blogs, print and online magazines, newspapers, and websites is a great way to start your career. Freelancing opened doors for me and pumped up my bio while trying to find agents and traditional publishers for my books.

If you freelance before becoming an author, you can:

- earn a bit of money while establishing yourself as a professional writer
- collect "clips" or published works to display on an author's website or impress traditional publishers
- gather writing credits that make the media and readers take you more seriously
- build your writer platform and visibility

- improve your writing skills

THE DISADVANTAGES OF FREELANCING

What's the downside? Here are a few disadvantages to keep in mind:

- Starting a career as a freelance writer isn't easy. Rejections are part of the bargain and inevitable. Discouragement and frustration can easily set in.
- Often, you'll work for pennies to get your foot in the door. Just to be clear, there are certainly easier ways to make money. This isn't the ticket to becoming rich. If you want to eventually write full-time and make a decent living to support yourself, you'll probably work harder than you did at your old 9-to-5 job. I certainly did!
- There is no job security. Work is sporadic, and income is not consistent. Freelancers rarely receive benefits.
- If you're an extrovert, working alone at home may not appeal to you.
- Deadlines can be stressful.
- No one is there to keep you going if you feel like giving up, want to be lazy, or are distracted. Self-discipline is needed to succeed.

Keep in mind that some of the disadvantages listed above may not affect you if you don't plan on making a living from freelance writing.

Is freelance writing worth the effort? Only you can answer that question.

Personally, I'm grateful that I've been able to make a living doing something I love. How many people can say that? I wouldn't change a thing.

WARNING: DON'T QUIT YOUR DAY JOB TOO SOON

If you have a pension, social security income, or enough retirement savings to live on and earning a bit of money will simply add to your fun money, then you don't have much to lose by trying out this occupation.

However, if your goal is to earn a living as a full-time freelance writer, remember that building your career takes time. Be sure you have regular well-paying writing gigs before giving up your day job.

Unfortunately, I learned this lesson the hard way. After my first short story for teens was sold to a literary magazine, I sold an article written for a college magazine article writing class to a regional parenting magazine. Then, a short piece for *Woman's World* followed – my first national publication! I was on the moon. I continued to sell my work in the year that followed – another short story and several more articles to different regional magazines.

With my confidence boosted, I decided to become a full-time freelance writer and quit my job.

Let's just say, it didn't go so well.

Writing as a hobby was different; it was a thrill just to see my byline and earn a few bucks. But as a business, writing was frustrating. Editors didn't always answer my queries. Smaller magazines paid on publication, not acceptance, which often meant waiting months or even a year for payment. A few editors held articles for possible publication for months and then sent a standard rejection letter.

By jumping the gun too soon, I was forced to temp as a receptionist at a hotel chain to make ends meet. A job I absolutely detested. Some days were spent crying in frustration, and I swore off writing – not for the first or last time. Of course, when you're addicted to writing, you always come back. Eventually, I achieved the goal of becoming a full-time freelance writer. But it took *years*.

Admittedly, becoming a freelancer is easier now than when I first started over 30 years ago. In the early 1980s, you sold your work to publishers of print magazines or newspapers. Not a lot of options. The Internet has opened a whole new world of opportunities for freelance writing.

Even so, many professional writers and authors have a source of backup income or a part- or full-time job so they can live out their dreams. If you want to write full-time and need an income, set goals with a timeline. Have a good backup strategy if things don't go according to plan – because they probably won't. Be sure and talk to your partner. You're going to need his or her support. Be honest and realistic.

CHAPTER 14:

WRITE PROFESSIONAL ARTICLES

Okay, so you've decided to become a freelancer, and are now ready to start writing. Where do you begin?

KNOWLEDGE IS POWER

To increase your chances of success, you need to produce quality work from the start and build a good reputation.

So, take classes if needed. Brush up on your writing and grammar skills. Read books, magazines, and online articles about freelance writing. If you plan to freelance online, learn about keywords and basic SEO (search engine optimization).

Be aware that there are different basic article styles, including:

- *How-to or self-help articles* help readers solve a problem or answer a question. This type of popular article describes steps, methods, or tips to help the reader accomplish something specific.
- *Lifestyle articles* usually focus on health, relationships, food, interior design, gardening, travel, hobbies, or recreation.

- *Essays* revolve around one subject you feel passionate about and present your viewpoint.
- *Inspirational articles* are meant to touch reader's hearts and make a difference in their lives. These articles often center on overcoming difficulties, struggles, and challenges while remaining positive and even triumphant.
- *Interview or profile articles* typically focus on a celebrity or successful person. These articles can be a simple Q&A focusing on one aspect of a person's life with a brief introduction and list of questions and answers. Or these articles can be a more detailed personality profile with an in-depth look at a person's childhood, significant life events, accomplishments, and quirks. In the latter case, the article is based on an extensive interview with the subject along with interviews with others who can provide different perspectives and anecdotes.
- *Humorous articles* are always in demand. Talented humorists often use everyday situations readers easily relate to that make them smile or laugh.
- *Travel articles* can be added to the list above. Because this type of writing is often of special interest to retirees, I've dedicated an entire section (Section VI) to this genre.

CHOOSE A TOPIC

If you plan on using freelance writing sites (see Chapter 15 for a list of popular options), clients will usually post the types of articles they're seeking including the subject.

On the other hand, if you want to write for online and print magazines or blogs, you'll need to pitch your own ideas, hoping to catch an editor's interest. Hopefully, you have some ideas in mind. If not, where can you find inspiration for articles? As described in Chapter 4, the answer is everywhere.

Here are a few suggestions to get you started:

- Search your background and experiences for ideas. To give you a few examples, in the past, I taught an after-school journalism class to elementary school children and produced a small school newspaper. This led to an article teaching kids how to make their own neighborhood or family newspaper which was published in a popular children's magazine. After starting a desktop publishing business in the 80s, I penned a how-to article published in a business magazine. More recently, after going through menopause, I wrote a series of humorous articles on the subject for an online magazine.

- What problems have you faced, and what unique solutions worked for you? When my kids were young, their first pet died. I wasn't sure how to help them through their grief. This led to my first published article for a regional parenting magazine, "When a Pet Dies."
- Talk to friends and relatives. Have they survived a devastating ordeal? Is someone you know doing something unusual? For instance, my father patented a building system for steel-framed homes, which led to six magazine articles.
- Along the same lines, interesting conversations at a family gathering or party may trigger ideas. What are people currently talking about, or what problems are they facing? What questions do they have on the subject?
- Of course, the Internet provides a wealth of ideas at your fingertips. Try exploring what terms are popular on Google Trends in categories that interest you. Or use Google Alerts. Choose a subject that interests you, type in a keyword, and you'll get emails when articles on your subject appear. For example, I have emails sent to me under the categories "baby boomer" and "over 50" to keep me up-to-date on what interests this age group for my blog, *Baby Boomer Bliss.*
- Don't limit yourself to what you know. You don't necessarily have to be an expert to cover a topic. Subjects that fascinate you can make great articles. Do the necessary research and interview experts. When my kids were young, they were interested in insects. Did you know that some ants herd, raise, and milk caterpillars? Neither did I until one of my boys told me about it. I'm no entomologist, but I researched this interesting subject and wrote an article published in a children's magazine.
- Browse through a copy of *Writer's Market* to get an idea of what magazines are looking for right now.
- Leading stories in newspapers and magazines as well as current topics on social media or podcasts can also give you an idea of what's currently of interest to readers. Think about how you can tweak a national story to make it local to appeal to a regional publication. How does an issue affect your community? Your local newspaper or regional magazine may be interested. Alternatively, look at local news stories from your regional newspaper or magazine. Can you find ways to make it a national story? For example, I read an inspiring story about a young boy trying to change a law regarding smoking to protect children in a newspaper published by a local children's

museum. After interviewing him, I queried a popular national children's magazine that later published my article.

- Think of a new angle on a familiar topic. Browse magazine or blog titles and try changing one word for a different spin.
- Some articles are simply based on your point of view. How does your opinion on a subject you're passionate about differ from others? I wrote an article for a popular online magazine sharing some surprising emotions I experienced when my mother died from Lewy Body dementia and my caregiving days ended abruptly. As the famous Nora Ephron, a former freelance journalist who held editorial positions at *New York* magazine and *Esquire*, advised: "Find a subject on which you have something interesting, surprising, or perverse to say."
- Find the unusual in the mundane. Andy Rooney wrote about everything from bathtubs to eyeglasses in a humorous way, making him famous.

RESEARCH AND INTERVIEW EXPERTS

Once you have an idea, you must back up your article with research, statistics, quotes, and anecdotes.

You may want to review Chapter 7 which explains where you can begin researching. Books, magazine articles, and the Internet are all good places to start.

Use free online services such as Profnet and HARO that help connect writers with experts. You can also find experts to interview at universities, associations, professional organizations, consulting firms, and social media.

BEGIN WITH A STRONG OPENING PARAGRAPH

The first sentence and paragraph are the most important parts of your article. You'll want to hook the reader's attention immediately and make them curious to learn more.

You might use an intriguing question, a thought-provoking fact, a provocative quote from someone you interviewed, a funny anecdote, or a startling statistic to start.

Be sure to use imagery, details, and sensory information to engage with the reader and make an emotional impact.

CREATE THE MAIN BODY

Now, it's time to provide specifics.

Each paragraph should have a central idea and build logically on the one before it with a seamless flow. Weave in facts, statistics, and quotes from experts or reliable sources. Add any applicable personal experiences and anecdotes from people you interviewed.

If you have an extraordinary comprehension of the subject, share your viewpoint with readers.

WRITE THE CONCLUSION

Your conclusion should summarize all your thoughts and evidence. Be sure to answer the question your article raised in its opening paragraph by the time you reach the end.

Although conclusions must be strong and thought-provoking, keep them short and concise. Three sentences should be plenty.

If you're writing for an online publication, consider inviting the reader's opinion. Editors often want to encourage comments and debates on social media platforms, comment pages, and discussion forums.

CREATE AN ENTICING TITLE

An informative and captivating title conveys what your article is about, who will read it, and questions the article will answer.

If you're writing for an online publication, the title must also be "search-friendly." Choosing keywords that people type into search engines when looking for information on a subject is essential.

You can be more creative if you're writing for a print publication. In that case, you want a catchy title that grabs readers' attention. Playing with words, including a pun, or using humor can help your title stand out. Study past magazines to get an idea of an editor's preferred style.

One warning: After all your hard work, an editor may change your title. Don't take it personally. This happens quite often.

FACT CHECK

Make sure you get your facts straight. Your reputation as a reliable writer is at stake.

Verify statistics, facts, quotations, and dates using multiple sources. Make sure the names of experts are spelled correctly and their titles are accurate.

If an editor buys an article and finds it's misleading or inaccurate, you'll probably never sell another article to that publication. And remember, editors talk to each other.

EDIT

Get your red pencil ready and start polishing your article. Make sure your lead is attention-grabbing and that the structure flows together seamlessly. Ensure your article is targeted for your intended audience. Remove unnecessary words or phrases and get rid of clichés. Rephrase sentences to make them shorter and clearer. Proofread for spelling and grammar errors.

Tailor the length of your article to match the editor's requirements. If your article falls short of the mandatory word count, don't pad it with redundant or unnecessary words. Go back to your research and find more facts to add. If the article is too long, edit mercilessly.

Put your article aside for at least a few days, then re-edit as many times as necessary.

CHAPTER 15:

SELL YOUR ARTICLES

There are a few ways to go when trying to sell your writing services.

FREELANCE WRITING SITES

Fortunately, plenty of freelance writing sites connect writers with clients. This is one of the easiest ways to search for jobs, especially when you're starting out.

Sites you may want to check out – some require fees while others are free – include:

- Upwork
- Contena
- ProBlogger
- FlexJobs
- Contently
- Freelance Writing Jobs
- Freelance
- ConstantContent
- BloggingPro
- FreelanceWriter
- TextBroker
- Mediabistro

- Writer Access
- Guru.

I've personally used Upwork for years. It's a great place to start and is free to sign up. Upwork, like most freelance sites, takes a percentage of freelancer earnings; a flat fee of 10% is deducted from your payments. Upwork posts thousands of writing jobs including many entry-level jobs that do not require any writing experience.

On the downside, you can easily find yourself working high-demand jobs for peanuts at first. Nonetheless, these sites can get you started, and as you gain writing credits, you can charge more later. Be prepared to spend plenty of time scrolling through their offerings to find decent jobs.

You'll need to write a killer cover letter since the competition can be high on these sites. Your job is to convince a potential client that you are the best person to write the proposed article.

Upwork makes the following recommendations:

- Start with a warm and professional greeting. This person is considering hiring you – so your opening should encourage them to think of you as someone they'd like to work with.
- Get to the point. Let the employer know why you're contacting them and what skills you have that make you the right person for this position.
- Let potential clients know where they can find more information about your work experience. Blow your horn about any writing experience you may have, along with links to any published works and your author's website or blog if you have one. If you don't have any writing samples, include relevant work experience, educational background, expertise, or life experience that makes you a good fit. Stress that you are reliable, productive, and dependable. Let a bit of your personality shine through. Be confident, honest, and enthusiastic.

Content platforms are another option. Here are a few you may want to check out:

- Medium allows you to write about a wide variety of topics and make a little money to boot. When your best stories are read by Medium members, a portion of their membership dues will be shared with you. You'll find tons of semi-retired and retired writers there.
- HubPages allows writers to publish articles, known as "Hubs," on a variety of topics. It provides a revenue-sharing model for authors.
- Newsbreak offers eligibility for monetization after you meet certain minimum requirements.

- Substack claims on their website that when a reader pays for a subscription an average of 86% of the money goes to the writer.

Social media can also be useful. LinkedIn can be a good place to start looking for freelance writing jobs. Follow hashtags on Twitter like #writingjobs, #freelancewriting, and #contentmarketing, and opportunities will start filling your feed. If you're serious, pitch to multiple publications and websites. Try to apply for writing jobs each day.

PRINT MAGAZINES OR NEWSPAPERS

Although many magazines and newspapers are struggling these days, this traditional type of freelancing still exists. Seeing your byline in a print magazine is a thrill, but you'll most likely need some writing credits before approaching this competitive market. Start with online or smaller magazines and work your way up.

If you plan to approach print magazines, you must learn how to write query letters – which are basically sales pitches. Your goal is to persuade an editor or client that your article idea is of interest to their readers and that you're the best person to write it.

As a side note, you'll probably want to have an article written and polished before sending query letters. This won't be necessary after you've learned the ropes and are an experienced writer. Once you get to that point, query letters can save you time and effort. You won't spend hours or days writing an article on a subject that no one is interested in reading.

When you're ready, get out your *Writer's Market* for a list of magazines that may accept your work. This book includes contact information and writer's guidelines.

Some popular magazines you see on newsstands are created for the general population, but most have a specific or niche audience in mind. Trade and regional magazines are usually easier to break into as a beginner.

Here are some tips to remember:

- Do your homework. I can't emphasize this enough. Sending the wrong type of article ideas to editors will only irritate them and can ruin future chances. Read past magazines to get an idea of what audience they're trying to reach and become familiar with the tone, style, and average length of articles. You can also search for submission guidelines on a magazine's website for more details. Don't address the letter to "Dear Sir," "To Whom It May Concern," or even "Editor-in-Chief." Find the appropriate editor to send your pitch to and spell the name correctly. Magazine staff changes frequently, so double-check the name for each query.

- You probably have about 30 seconds to get a busy editor's attention. The subject line in your email should be a short, catchy headline summarizing your article while begging to be opened. Make your first sentence count. If you've written your article already, you can use your opening sentence as your first line. Write with confidence. Whatever you do, do not start your letter, "Although I've never been published before, I have a great idea..."
- Keep your email or letter short and sweet. For an email pitch, you want to stay around two to three paragraphs or one page if you're writing a letter. Get to the point. Briefly tell the editor what your article is about and how it will benefit their readers. Tailor your query to a publication's needs and explain your story's value. What makes your article unique, fascinating, timely, or significant? Why are you the best one to write the story? How will their readers relate to the story?
- Mention key sources for your stories and experts you plan to interview.
- Include an estimate of a word count based on requirements or the average length of articles in the publication.
- If you're a published writer, include clips or links to writing samples. If that's not the case, let the editor know if you have an educational background, expertise, or life experience pertaining to the proposed article.
- What if you don't have any qualifications? Don't draw attention to the fact, and never beg. Editors don't want to hear how you've wanted to become a writer since childhood and are trying to realize your dream in retirement. Include a sentence or two about yourself and insert a bit of personality and charm. You may need to demonstrate your writing skills by sending the completed piece.
- Include contact information. Give editors an email and phone number so they can reach you if they have questions.
- Your email or letter must be professionally written and error-free.

When you've sent a query or article off, don't sit around waiting for a reply. Make a note of the submission details in your records, forget about it, and get to work on the next piece.

Plan on writing tons of query letters with ideas for articles you think will appeal to a magazine's audience. Be prepared for plenty of rejections. This business requires persistence.

If you haven't heard from the editor in a few weeks, follow up with a polite letter or email. After three months, assume it's a rejection and move on to your next pitch.

Don't take it personally or badger the editor. Always remain respectful. Don't burn bridges.

Keep in mind that the more ideas you send out, the more likely you are to sell some of your articles. If you want to succeed, don't give up easily. Pitching becomes easier once you get your foot in the door at a publication.

ONLINE MAGAZINES, BLOGS, AND WEBSITES

Online publications are usually more lucrative than solely concentrating on print magazines or newspapers.

Thankfully, endless online magazines publish articles, features, and news pieces, not to mention all the blogs and websites covering every topic under the sun.

If you're directly pitching an article to an online magazine, blog, or website, search for a "Write for Us" or "Submission Guidelines" tab. You may need to scroll to the bottom of the page. If you still can't find the contact person, try the "About Us" or "Our Team" page.

The same tips given for querying print magazines and newspapers apply.

BUSINESSES

If you have a specific area of expertise, in addition to checking freelance writing sites, scour well-known niche job boards such as CareerBuilder, Indeed, and SimplyHired.

If you have advertising experience, copywriting can open doors for you. Many companies offer part-time work for content marketing, copywriting, and copyediting. Businesses often need blog content, advertising copy, white papers, landing pages, website content, press releases, newsletters, and social media content.

BOOK REVIEW SITES

If you love to read, this may sound too good to be true, but some sites will pay you to write book reviews.

Although this is certainly not a way to get rich, it's still a way to receive free books and receive some compensation for doing what you love.

There are plenty of sites to choose from, but here's a list of some you may want to check out:

- Kirkus Media is searching for people who will review English and Spanish-language self-published titles. Reviews are about 350 words with a two-week deadline. You should gain some experience before approaching this well-known book reviewer. When you're ready, send your resume along with writing samples.
- Online Book Club pays $5 to $60 per review. The books are free and, after your first approved review, you are eligible to get paid for your reviews.
- Reedsy.com allows you to choose the types of books you want to review. Once you've established yourself as a book reviewer, you can connect with authors who contact you directly for a review.
- The U.S. Review of Books hires freelancers to review books. Reviews are about 300 words and are due two to three weeks after receiving an assignment. Reviewers are paid monthly.
- BookBrowse accepts applications for book reviewers. Once accepted, you can browse through titles to see which books interest you. Reviewers tend to write about one review a month and receive a byline and a modest payment.
- Upwork can connect you with people who are looking for freelance book reviewers. Check out their listings, which may be a one-time gig or ongoing.

How do you write a book review? Here's a basic outline to follow:

- Provide a basic plot summary. If you're reviewing a fiction book, reveal the genre and theme, explain the story, and briefly describe the primary characters and main conflict. No spoilers – do not reveal the ending. Writing a review for a non-fiction book is different. In this case, you want to describe the problems or issues the book is tackling and how the author addresses them. Was the book clear, effective, and concise? Mention the authors' names and qualifications, experience, or expertise as they relate to the book's topic.
- Give your evaluation. What worked well for you, and what didn't? In addition to your own opinion and reactions to the book, provide an objective critique describing the strengths and weaknesses of the work. Include examples from the book to validate your points.

- Offer a recommendation: Would you recommend this book to others? Briefly explain why or why not. What kind of audience do you think this book will attract, and what kind of readers won't enjoy it? You might mention other similar book titles and how the book compares.

If this interests you, I'd highly recommend reading other book reviews to help you understand the basics of writing one. There are many samples on the Internet.

CHAPTER 16:

AVOID SCAMMERS

Beware of ads designed to lure you in with decent wages while claiming no writing experience is necessary. There are tons of scammers trying to take advantage of people by offering "work at home" writing jobs.

For example, I recently saw an online ad: "Seeking Freelance Writers Now! $35 to $45 an Hour. No Experience Necessary." This is one of those things that's too good to be true. You'll only receive this kind of pay when you have considerable experience.

Remember that when you first start freelancing, you'll need to begin small until you gain some writing credits. This means your income will be nothing to brag about. There are no shortcuts to working your way up. However, some people get impatient or desperate, which makes them vulnerable to con artists.

COMMON SCAMS

Aside from unrealistic offers, what else should you look out for?

- Some swindlers offer fake writing jobs on job boards to get personal information for scamming purposes. Craigslist seems to be notorious for this, but you can find these types of false offers all over the Internet.
- A "client" may offer a 30% up-front payment for a writing project and promise to pay the rest upon completion via a direct transfer to your bank

account. Anxious to get your writing career off the ground, you agree and provide the information for the transfer. Congratulations, you just handed over everything a scammer needs to clear out your account.

- A client or fellow "freelancer" may contact you and claim to have the ability to help you make thousands of dollars by adding some kind of technical wizardry to your existing Upwork account (or another freelance site). All you need to do is give them access to your account, and you'll split the profits. If you agree, your new "partner" has access to your bank and ID information. Once again, you gave a scammer the information needed to steal your money.
- A "client" may ask for an original, custom sample of your work, for which you won't be paid. You write and submit the article, and it's "rejected." You, and all the other un-hired applicants, have supplied the "client" with free work. This one is tricky because this may be a legitimate request if you're just starting and could possibly lead to more work. Just be careful. This is a personal decision, but I never worked for free even when I was first starting out.

HOW TO AVOID SCAMS

There are a few ways to protect yourself:

- Use common sense. If you come across a job posting that is simply too good to be true, beware!
- Never pay to work. Also, be careful when you're required to pay money upfront to gain access to resources, coaching, training, and exclusive jobs. Legitimate freelance writer platforms, like Upwork, usually have free sign-ups with a limited number of free proposals. You'll have the option to pay a fee for the opportunity to post more proposals, but this shouldn't be mandatory.
- Be wary when a client contacts you through a freelance site and asks to discuss work by contacting you personally off the site. This is usually against a freelance site's policies and could be a red flag. Also, do not start work before a contract is in place.
- Before you sign up with a freelance site, check their policy regarding payment protection. Do not give out any personal or bank information to an

individual. If you're not using a freelance site, consider using an online payment processing platform like PayPal or Zelle for payments.

- Be sure to research any company with red flags. Google the name and look for reviews. Type in the name of the company and the word "scam" and see what pops up. Check the Better Business Bureau. Only accept work from employers who have a verified work history and good ratings on freelance sites.

CHAPTER 17:

BUILD A PORTFOLIO

Most editors or potential clients will request "clips" or writing samples of published pieces to get a sense of your voice and expertise. When you're just starting out, this is easier said than done. So, what can you do?

START SMALL

In my case, I started with smaller print magazines, including literary and regional magazines, and slowly worked my way up. I didn't earn much money initially, but gathered credentials along the way.

This strategy can still work, but today, you have other options as well:

- You can accept low-paying gigs that don't require any experience on freelance writing sites to fill out your portfolio.
- If you're willing to work for free, you can send articles to niche article sites, respectable non-profit agencies, or blogs that accept articles as guest posts.
- Perhaps you're aware of small or local businesses that want to expand their online presence. You might offer to write low-cost blog posts or web content. Get testimonials from your clients if you take this route.

VOLUNTEER

Volunteer work can help as well. For example, if you're involved with a charitable organization, perhaps you can volunteer to write newsletters or blogs.

As mentioned earlier, I volunteered to produce a children's newspaper at an elementary school. Children's magazines seemed to be impressed by this fact. This led to several of my articles being published in well-known children's magazines and eventually, an offer to be an editor at one.

LAUNCH YOUR OWN BLOG

You can launch your own blog (see Section 5) so you'll have something to show potential clients and improve your writing skills at the same time.

CHAPTER 18:

DECIDE WHETHER TO NICHE OR NOT

Some freelance writers specialize in one type of writing – sometimes called a niche. They choose a topic they have expertise in, like personal finance or technology. Or they focus on a subject they feel passionate about and narrow their list of writing projects and clients to match.

Then there are freelancers who experiment with a wide variety of genres, sometimes referred to as generalists.

To niche or not to niche, that is the question. In the end, what you choose to do will depend on your goals and interests.

WHY BECOME A GENERALIST?

When starting out, you'll probably be a generalist. Gaining experience and writing credits are your priorities at this point, so why limit yourself to one specific topic? Likely, you'll take whatever you can to get established – and you should.

This is a great way to grow as a writer, spread your wings, and try various writing projects.

If you get bored easily and want to write about what fascinates and excites you, you may choose to stay a generalist.

WHY FIND A NICHE?

On the other hand, once you become established, you may want to develop a niche. Why?

If you want to make a decent living from writing, you'll probably make more money by becoming an expert in one field. Prospective clients are often willing to pay more for writers who understand their industry and audience.

In addition, you may feel more comfortable and confident writing about subjects you're familiar with and working with specific, regular clients.

HAVE MORE THAN ONE NICHE

As another option, if you're like me, you may develop a niche but change it over the years as your interests change.

For example, I started out writing fiction for young adults in my 20s. While raising my kids, I primarily wrote for parenting and children's magazines. Now in my 60s, I tend to write primarily for the over-50 crowd.

If you keep your options open, you'll discover which type of freelancing jobs you love and which you hate. You'll work with different clients and learn how to market yourself to various industries. This will help you decide which niche works best for you if you choose to take that path.

PART V: BECOME A BLOGGER AND/OR CREATE AN AUTHOR'S WEBSITE

CHAPTER 19:

WHY BECOME A BLOGGER?

The good news is that anyone can become a blogger – and for free.

You can start a free account with a platform like WordPress.com or Blogger.com and be on your way. If you plan to earn money from your blog, there are other options that cost some money but are worth considering, which we'll discuss later.

Blogs started basically as online journals. Some people still use blogs this way. However, blogging has evolved. Today, blogs tend to be based on a topic or niche and target a specific audience with the goal of making money. As a result, the competition is fierce. If you plan to become rich or famous by writing a blog, the chances are slim to none.

That's why you may want to start to blog for other reasons. Like what?

There are some practical reasons for starting a blog:

- If you want to be a freelance writer or an author, blogging can provide writing samples when you're just starting.
- Writing a blog can help establish you as an expert and authority on a specific subject. This may help sell books, drum up business, or lead to speaking engagements.
- If you have an author's website, you may choose to have a blog as part of your site to bring in more visitors.
- Eventually, you may earn some extra income.

While there's nothing wrong with any of those goals, there are certainly other reasons to blog. Initially, I started my blog in 2013 as a platform for a book I wanted to write to help baby boomers find happiness. The irony is that I have yet to finish that book. Other book ideas, including this one, took priority. But I'm still blogging and loving it.

Admittedly, it took a while to find joy in blogging. It's extremely easy to get frustrated when you're beginning.

First, there's a learning curve. As a technically challenged person, I had to learn how to use WordPress.

Lots of research followed to educate myself on how to promote my blog to attract readers. By the way, this is no easy feat. Like most bloggers, I quickly became obsessed – and depressed – with the numbers. I found myself constantly checking how many visitors, subscribers, and commenters I had on any given day. Turns out that building up a readership for a blog takes a *lot* of time, effort, and patience.

In fact, if you're starting a blog to earn a living, don't count on it. There are no guarantees you'll be able to monetize your blog. And don't believe all the hype from people selling online courses that try to convince you blogging is a great way to make easy, passive income. Make no mistake, writing and promoting a blog is a ton of work. There's nothing passive about it.

Nonetheless, as time passed, I realized blogging doesn't have to be about making money, gathering a huge following, chasing fame, or selling books. My blog provided more than an author platform, and it wasn't all about the numbers.

Writing a blog can serve a different and more profound purpose. I would even say that it's changed how I look at and live my life. That's why, if you're thinking about starting a blog, I'd recommend it. That is if you're blogging for the right reasons. Let's go over some of the benefits.

A CREATIVE OUTLET

Blogging can be a wonderful creative endeavor that expresses your ideas, thoughts, and feelings. A blog allows you to stretch as a writer, explore, experiment, and try new things whenever the muse hits.

I love this aspect of blogging. Most of the time, I loved my career as a freelance writer, but not always. Sometimes, I wrote articles that bored me to tears to make a living. Other times, I worked late into the night to meet tight deadlines as my brain desperately begged to call it quits.

My blog is my baby. I have total control and freedom. That means I can write about subjects I'm interested in and feel passionate about – and hopefully, my visitors will enjoy reading. Although I blog regularly, I write when I choose. And believe me, that's not at dawn or midnight. That is luxurious.

A WAY TO CONNECT WITH PEOPLE

You may think that writing – and blogging – is an isolating experience, but that doesn't need to be the case.

Writing a blog provides opportunities to connect with readers when they leave comments. If you promote your blog on social media, you can – and should - interact with your followers.

You'll probably get to know other bloggers as well. Many Facebook groups are dedicated to bloggers. You may think other bloggers are your competition, but you'll quickly learn it helps to support each other.

A CATHARTIC EXPERIENCE

Blogging is a wonderful creative release. When I write, I become so focused that my problems fade away, giving me an escape from my troubles for a while. Putting my thoughts and feelings into writing has brought comfort and helped me relive happy moments.

I've written about exciting times like my trip to South Africa when I went on safari and shark-cage diving. I shared empowering challenges like running my first Spartan Race (an arduous obstacle course) after turning 60. I've written about simple pleasures like playing in the snow with my grandchildren. When I need a smile, I read these happy blogs and enjoy the memories.

Of course, life isn't always blissful. My blog has certainly seen me through some ups and downs. I poured my heart out while caregiving for my mother, who suffered from Lewy Body dementia and wrote about her eventual death. When my mother-in-law died from ovarian cancer, and my son went through a painful divorce and custody battle the same year, I shared my angst. (Ironically, shortly after I started writing a blog about happiness, I had one of the worst years of my life.) Sharing these experiences has helped me heal. In addition, I hope to help other readers going through similar situations.

A PATH TO CLARITY

As you write about your life, blogging helps you think about what's important and determine if you're headed in the right direction.

That's certainly been the case for me. Blogging provides a sort of filter since I can't write about every event, idea, thought, and feeling that enters my mind. My blogs have helped me understand what is most meaningful to me.

I've discovered along the way that sometimes it's the simplest moments that make me the happiest.

AN INSPIRATION FOR OTHERS

Yes, blogging can help you in many ways. But the huge bonus is that blogging can also change other people's lives.

Writing a blog provides a fantastic opportunity to inspire and touch other people's lives in a positive way. Some readers have left comments letting me know that I have, in some small way, inspired them or provided valuable information, and that always brings me such joy.

Have I talked you into blogging? If so, you're probably wondering where to begin.

CHAPTER 20:

GETTING STARTED

Maybe you're fired up and ready to write your first blog. However, there are a few choices you need to make before you start writing.

CHOOSE A TOPIC

You can simply blog about your thoughts and your life. If blogging is a hobby and outlet for you, enjoy!

If you want to find an audience or monetize your blog, however, it helps to have a general topic in mind. Even so, blogging should still be fun. So, pick a subject that interests and excites you.

To help you narrow choices, ask yourself:

1. What are your goals for your blog? Are you trying to sell books, start a business, or establish yourself as an expert?
2. What's one topic you could talk about forever? What fascinates you? Are you obsessed with writing, travel, fashion, photography, fitness, business start-ups, or something else?
3. Will this subject interest a lot of other people?
4. Are you knowledgeable about this topic? Do you have personal experience with the subject that allows you to write with an authentic voice?

5. Do you have a solution to a problem and feel compelled to share it to help others? Can you help others reach a specific goal?
6. Do you have a sense of purpose and a unique voice about your subject?
7. Can your topic be divided into several different categories?

After carefully considering these questions and choosing your subject, try to find a unique angle to stand out. Niche blogs help you build loyal followers. For example, there are many baby boomer blogs, but mine is focused on helping boomers find happiness as they age. Thus, the title is *Baby Boomer Bliss*.

PICK A PLATFORM

If you're new to blogging, you may not have heard about WordPress. It's by far one of the biggest blogging platforms in the world, with a gazillion ways to design and layout your blog. This is the platform I use and would recommend.

There is a learning curve, but even though I'm technically challenged and don't understand coding, I figured it out. You can hire a webmaster to help you set up your site if desired.

Of course, WordPress is not your only choice. Choices abound, including Blogger, SquareSpace, Weebly, Wix, and others.

Before you sign up with your chosen platform, you'll need to make an important decision.

A FREE-HOSTED OR SELF-HOSTED SITE?

What's the difference between a free-hosted and a self-hosted site? Which is better? Let's discuss both options to help you decide which path to follow.

FREE HOSTED SITES

Free blogging platforms like WordPress.com or Blogger.com offer to host your website at no cost. Many provide free domain names (your URL or web address) if desired.

You won't choose your extension (for example, .com, .org, or .net). Instead, you'll have the platform's name tacked to the end of your chosen name. For instance, yourauthorname.wordpress.com. (See the next section for tips on how to select your domain name.)

The files and software used to build your website have a place on the Internet with a URL address. You'll control the content, but your site belongs to the free blogging platform.

These services are usually user-friendly and easy to set up but have some limitations, such as:

- Although monthly fees are not required, if you want to fully customize your site, you'll pay additional fees for extra templates and more design options.
- Functionality will be limited, particularly when it comes to e-commerce or monetization.
- Usually, you have a limited selection of plugins and storage.
- You may not be able to get in-depth analytics about the number of visitors or how people find your site.

In summary, a free site can be a good option if you want to blog as a hobby and don't plan on trying to earn money on your site. This is the way to go if you want to keep things free and simple.

SELF-HOSTED SITES

Self-hosting platforms, like WordPress.org, are free software you download and install as your web host. You pay for a unique domain name and a hosting company.

Domain names are available from providers like GoDaddy, Bluehost, and HostGator. The fees for domain names typically range from $2 to $20 per year. Many domain providers also offer hosting services and include a free domain name for signing up. This is a good option if you want to keep everything under one umbrella.

Hosting providers typically offer one-click installation of WordPress and 24/7 support. Some hosting companies cost as little as $4–7 monthly. However, many of these companies have a steeply discounted sign-on price to attract customers and then increase that price once the initial contract is up.

Self-hosting is best for established authors or anyone who wants to monetize their site. Advantages of a self-hosted platform include:

- the ability to fully customize your site design by choosing fonts, colors, page templates, headers, footers, etc., which can be important for long-term author branding
- an email address connected to your domain name

- freedom to add functions to earn money from your site (e.g., advertising, e-commerce, membership, or paywall areas)
- more effective integration of email newsletter sign-up tools
- insight into your website traffic and what marketing efforts are working

Keep in mind that this isn't a permanent decision. Although it's a bit of a headache, you can start with a free hosted platform and change to a self-hosting platform later. If you choose this route, you may want to start with WordPress' free platform for an easier transition from free hosting to self-hosting.

CHOOSE A DOMAIN NAME

As mentioned earlier, a domain name is simply your URL or web address. For example, JulieGorges.com, my author website, is a domain that I pay an annual fee to own. That's true for my blog, BabyBoomerBliss.net, as well.

So, how do you choose a domain name?

If you blog as a hobby, you might opt to use your own name, a nickname, or get creative. Perhaps a humorous name appeals to you and fits your personality. In other words, you can use anything that strikes your fancy.

On the other hand, if you plan to monetize your blog or use your blog to promote your books or a business, you'll want to choose a domain name more carefully. In that case, keep these tips in mind:

- Make it an easy name to remember, spell, and pronounce.
- Shorter is usually better.
- Don't use numbers or hyphens.
- Be sure to choose keywords related to the topic of your blog.

If you're serious about a writing career, you could create an author website and have a blog as part of it. In that case, you'll want to use your author's name as the URL. If [yourauthorname].com is already taken, try using a middle initial or adding "author," "writer," or "books" after your name.

A .com address will probably perform better and earn more respect. However, if you want a specific name that is already taken, you can use .net, .org, or another extension. As noted earlier, if you choose a free hosted blogging platform, you won't be able to choose your extension.

CHAPTER 21:

BUILD YOUR SITE

Once you've made the above decisions and taken the appropriate steps, you can begin creating and designing your author's website or blog.

CHOOSE A THEME

Your theme includes the layout, colors, fonts, and more. Find a design template that matches your style and needs with the desired number of columns, sidebars, headers, and footers.

If you opt for a free hosted site, you'll be limited in your choice of themes. The good news is that you'll be presented with well-tested and popular designs. On the other hand, if you decide on a self-hosted WordPress site, the themes are seemingly limitless. Most are free, but premium themes are also available.

Keep in mind that themes can be created by anyone with little testing. Always check ratings and reviews. Take note of how many people have downloaded and used the theme, which means it's more likely any bugs have been worked out. Try to find user-friendly themes that allow you to customize your site – especially the header image – without knowing any code.

You may be tempted to go wild with fonts and colors, but if you want your site to look professional, build your site with an easy-to-read and simple design. As a rule, stick to no more than three colors and three fonts. Don't be afraid of white space, which can enhance your design and make your site look up-to-date.

Be warned, all the theme choices can be overwhelming and even paralyzing. The important thing is to get started. Remember, you don't have to launch the perfect site all at once. Start small, build your technical skills, and improve your online presence over time. Your brand will evolve, and you can always update your theme later.

DECIDE ON MENU ITEMS

Now, it's time to determine what pages you want on your site.

A menu is much like a table of contents. It provides links that help visitors navigate between different pages and sections of a website.

Don't go overboard with too many pages. Studies have shown that visitors' eyes tend to glaze over if there are more than five menu items. If you need more than that, consider drop-down menus or sub-menus, to include additional information. With these layers, visitors can investigate as much as they want or just skim the surface.

Also, don't get too clever with the names of menu items or pages, which can confuse or frustrate visitors. Be straightforward and label your pages clearly.

What menu items should you include? It depends on your goals and the type of blog you've chosen. To give you an example, your site may contain the following pages:

HOME

If you're simply writing a blog, your blogs serve as your homepage. On the other hand, if you're including a blog as part of an author's website, your blog will be one of your menu items.

Remember, your home page is where readers first land when they visit your site. This is where you'll include important "calls to action." Encourage readers to purchase your latest book, sign up for your blog or newsletter, and follow you on social media links. You might also include a brief introduction of yourself.

If your blog serves as the home page, you can include these calls to action in the header, sidebar, or footer.

ABOUT ME

If visitors click on this page, they want to know more about you – but don't overdo it. This is not the place to plaster a huge photo of yourself and write endlessly about every detail of your life. Keep your bio brief and let your personality shine.

If the purpose of your blog is to promote yourself as an author or freelance writer, briefly list any writing credentials and achievements. This is where to include a professional author photo or a casual photo if you prefer.

If you're blogging about a specific topic, readers will want to understand how reading your blog will benefit them personally. What inspired you to start your blog? What will they get out of your posts? If applicable, you might include tidbits about your life that pertain to your blog.

LIST OF BOOKS/ONLINE COURSES/PUBLICATIONS

This is where you blow your horn and share links if applicable.

If you're an author, include a list of your published books with detailed information and purchasing links. If you're a freelance writer, share a list of your published articles and links to samples of your work. If you offer online courses, list them with links if appropriate. If you're promoting a business, you may want to add a "Shopping" page that lists your products.

BLOG

If you're blogging as part of your author's website, this page is dedicated to your posts. As an author, you could write on topics related to your books or share writing advice.

CONTACT FORM

Unless you're not interested in new opportunities, make it clear how you can be contacted. Contact forms are available for this purpose. Unless it's a spam or trolling situation, try to answer your readers' questions, feedback, and views.

CREATE CATEGORIES IF NEEDED

In addition to menu items, most blogging platforms give you a category option to organize your content.

If you're writing a blog as a hobby, sharing your thoughts and feelings along with snippets of your life as a type of online journal, you probably don't need categories.

However, if you're writing on a specific topic that has many different aspects, categories can help readers navigate to posts on specific subjects they're interested in.

To give you an idea of what I mean, the categories I use for Baby Boomer Bliss include Happiness, Travel & Leisure, Humor, Relationships, Health & Fitness, Money, Boomer Interviews, and Nostalgia.

SELECT PLUG-INS AND WIDGETS

Plug-ins and widgets are tools and features you want to add. There are tons to choose from, but it's best to be selective.

Widgets, typically seen in sidebars, may include a subscribe button, social icons, and/or a list of your most popular posts.

Important plug-ins to consider are SEO (search engine optimization) tools to help search engines find your blog, an anti-spam plug-in, a contact form, a backup plug-in, and sharing tools that allow readers to share and bookmark your posts.

An analytics program is also useful. It allows you to see how much traffic comes to your blog, search terms used to find your blog, and which pages people visit.

A WordPress.org blog comes with many of these essentials.

CHAPTER 22:

WRITE YOUR BLOGS

You probably thought you'd never get to this point, but it's finally time to start writing your blogs.

The following are some tips to remember if you want to attract readers.

CRAFT A QUALITY HEADLINE

Your blog title determines whether people will click through to read your post or scroll right past it.

Here are a few things to keep in mind when writing headlines:

- Know your audience. What are their interests, problems, goals, fears, and challenges?
- Persuasive adjectives like ultimate, new, simple, fast, essential, smart, creative, surprising, easy, hidden, or valuable can lure readers in and make them eager to learn more.
- "How to" and "list" headlines (10 Ways to...) also work well.
- Use sensory words that resonate with your readers and their personal experiences. Appeal to their emotions, desires, and curiosity.

Be specific so readers will feel like your post was written just for them. You want them to think, "Yeah, that's me. That's exactly how I feel."

For example, take the headline, "How to Save for Retirement." This subject will interest boomers, but it's too broad. Plus, this title will have tons of competition from well-known blogs, making it harder to get noticed.

What are your options?

- Use a title that tons of boomers will find relatable. Such as: "How to Save for Retirement When You're Living Paycheck to Paycheck," "10 Simple Ways to Save for Retirement When Starting Late," or "How to Combat Rising Medical Costs in Retirement."
- Make your readers feel like they'll learn something new. For example: "Overlooked Ways to Save for Retirement," "Are You Saving for Retirement the Right Way?" or "10 Things You Didn't Know About Saving for Retirement."
- Introduce a risk or threat your reader will want to avoid at all costs. What is the worst-case scenario if they don't solve their problem? For instance: "How to Avoid the Top 4 Retirement Mistakes" (I actually used this title for a guest blog), "5 Ways to Make Sure You Don't Outlive Your Savings," or "10 Surprising Myths About Saving for Retirement."

Just make sure your headline doesn't make empty promises with hyperbole and exaggerated statements. Be honest and deliver on your promises for solutions.

MAKE THAT FIRST PARAGRAPH COUNT

Attention spans are extremely short these days, so start your blog with a punch. You must make your first paragraph irresistible.

There are a few ways to accomplish this feat.

- Use a question. For example, using the same subject matter discussed earlier on saving for retirement, you might ask: Are you worried you'll run out of money during retirement? Are you concerned you'll be unable to pay for soaring healthcare costs? Do you have too much debt going into retirement? Then, reassure your readers you can help them avoid those consequences by giving them valuable information.
- Use a startling fact or statistic. For example, you might point out that according to the Insured Retirement Institute, the average Social Security check is $14,000 a year. That's not nearly enough for a comfortable

retirement. Or share the statistic that 45% of boomers have zero savings for retirement, according to a CNBC article.

- Use an anecdote. If you had a problem or experience that you solved or overcame successfully, share it with your readers so they'll feel a sense of comradery with you. Have you found a way to save for retirement successfully? If not, do you know someone who started saving for retirement late but found a unique way to accomplish their goals?
- Use an inspirational or funny quote. For instance: "I'm going to retire and live off my savings. What I'll do the second day, I have no idea." ~Author unknown

WRITE YOUR BLOG POSTS

So, now it's time to make sure your blog posts deliver what you promised in those eye-catching headlines and attention-grabbing first sentences.

Here are some tips to keep in mind:

- Don't hold back any knowledge or expertise you may have on the subject. Fully work through the problem with your readers. Give them solid solutions and powerful advice. Don't just tell readers what to do. Explain how to do it.
- Make your blog unique. See if you can add a one-of-a-kind perspective, experience, or twist to your articles. Something readers aren't anticipating. What do you know that most people don't? What common beliefs are you challenging? How can you shed new light on an age-old problem? What methods do you use that most people aren't familiar with?
- Avoid sounding too academic or stiff – and therefore boring. Be conversational. Go by the classic rule from George Orwell's essay *Politics and the English Language*: "Never use a long word when a short one will do." Let your personality shine through. Use humor when appropriate.
- Make your blog easy to read with short or fragmented sentences. Use short paragraphs no more than one to three sentences and subheadings with only a few paragraphs underneath. Bullets can be used to break up the text.
- Be firm. Avoid weak words like might, maybe, possibly, probably, and perhaps.
- Use anecdotes, examples, and metaphors to clarify points.

- Close with a motivational and inspirational bang. Give your readers a good old-fashioned pep talk. Tell them what they're capable of accomplishing and what their life will be like once they've followed your advice.
- Add visuals – photos and illustrations – to attract attention.
- Edit ruthlessly. Eliminate any needless words, sentences, or paragraphs. Make sure your blog doesn't have any spelling or grammar errors.

CHAPTER 23:

DRIVE TRAFFIC TO YOUR BLOG

Do you want to simply have fun with your blog or enjoy writing as an art form? Perhaps you aren't concerned with how many people visit your blog. If that's the case, you can skip this chapter.

However, if you want to use your blog to reach a broad audience, sell books, promote your business, or make a little money, you'll need to learn about SEO (search engine optimization) and promotion strategies.

Why?

The truth is that you may follow all the advice in the previous chapter and write a wonderful, engaging, and informative blog. Then, you confidently sit back and wait for visitors and comments. Crickets. Your blog is a ghost town.

What went wrong?

Unfortunately, writing a great blog is usually not enough to substantially increase traffic. Simply put, if people can't find your blog online, even if it's spectacular, no one will read it. That's where SEO can help.

I'll share some basic suggestions with you in this chapter, but let me stress there is no quick, easy answer to the question, "How do I drive traffic to my blog?" You'll have to experiment to find what works best for you personally. And be warned, gaining an audience usually takes lots of time and effort.

If you're serious about ranking high on Google to get more traffic, there are scores of books and Internet sites to educate you. I'd suggest learning as much as possible. In the meantime, here are some tips to get you started.

POST REGULARLY

Both search engines and visitors like to see fresh, quality content. The more content you have, the more chances you have for ranking for various keywords. This results in more organic traffic for your blog.

How often should you post a blog? Opinions vary, and much depends on how much time you want to invest in writing. *Writer's Market* suggests at least once a week for starters. Some experts suggest three times a week, daily, or even multiple times a day.

My general advice: If you're serious about increasing traffic to your blog, post frequently, but don't sacrifice quantity for quality.

USE KEYWORDS

What are keywords? This term refers to words and phrases people type into search engines to find what they're looking for online.

You'll want to include keywords in your blog titles, URLs, meta descriptions (a summary of your blog's content that appears under your page title in search engine result pages), introductions, subheadings, photo captions, and alternative texts. Then, sprinkle keywords throughout your blog. This will help people searching for information online find your blog if it matches their needs.

Keywords can be one word or a two-word phrase. However, more often, keywords are three- to five-word phrases, sometimes called "long-tail keywords." For example, the single word "dating" is a keyword. "Dating tips" is a keyword phrase. "Dating Tips for Boomers" is a long-tail keyword.

Long-tail keywords are usually your best bet. Why? If you use the popular keyword "dating," you'll compete with major dating websites. More specific long-tail keywords are less competitive and often work better.

As a bonus, if you use precise phrases focused on a niche, people typing those keywords into search engines will likely be more interested in the subject matter. As a result, readers may be more motivated to subscribe to your blog, sign up for a newsletter, or buy your book.

Be aware that choosing the right keywords can be tricky. Thankfully, tools are available to help you. There are keyword tool websites you can check out, such as UberSuggest, Google Adwords Keyword Planner, Keyword Tool, SEMrush, or Soovle. A word of caution when using these tools. It's easy to spend hours researching and analyzing results. Remember to stay focused, do some research, and then get back to writing your blog.

This may surprise you, but search engines themselves can be helpful. Google search for a keyword related to your niche. You'll notice auto suggestions pop up as you type. For example, if you type in "dating tips," you'll see underneath dating tips for shy guys, men, seniors, women, introverts, single moms, and beginners.

These suggestions help you find specific keyword phrases that will likely be more successful than a broad term.

You can also check under "People Also Ask" and "Related Searches" for closely related keyword phrases. For instance, using "dating tips" again, Google shows you questions like "What are the five rules of dating?" and phrases like "dating tips funny." Pop over to Yahoo, and you'll see the question: "How do I become better at dating?" Under "Searches Related to Dating," you'll see "long-distance dating tips," "dating tips for older people," and "safe dating tips."

These variations of your key phrases come directly from search engines, which means they're popular keyword phrases you may want to try. Not to mention, these suggestions can give you plenty of ideas for your blogs.

As an example of how keywords can help traffic, one of my most popular blogs on *Baby Boomer Bliss* is titled "5 Ways to Become a Happy-Go-Lucky Person." The keyword "happy-go-lucky" is used multiple times in the right places. Now, I think this blog is fun and designed to improve readers' lives by learning to lighten up with specific ways to do so. However, I also believe using a three-word keyword phrase several times in the right places helps people find this blog.

A word of warning: Don't get carried away. Using too many keywords or keyword phrases - sometimes called "keyword stuffing"—could hurt your blog's rankings and is disapproved by search engines. Write about your topic and use keywords in a natural and organic way. In other words, don't force keywords where they don't belong.

PICTURES ARE POWERFUL

Pictures and illustrations lure readers in by adding an interesting visual element. Photos also break up large blocks of text, making your blog easier to read.

But that's not all.

Blog posts with appropriate images perform better in search engines. As a bonus, blogs on social media that contain images get shared more, which can help drive more traffic to your site.

Consider these statistics from Search Engine Journal:

- Blog articles containing images receive 94% more views.
- Tweets containing images are retweeted 150% more.
- Facebook posts with images receive three times more engagement.

Photos and images are also a great place to add your keywords, both in the caption and alternative text. Although readers won't see the text you add to alternative text areas, search engines will take note.

Where can you find photos and illustrations? Of course, you can test the waters with your own photography. But what if photography isn't in your skill set?

Fortunately, many websites offer copyright-free pictures and illustrations for a reasonable price or even for free. Unsplash, Pixabay, Burst, and Pexels are just a few sites you may want to check out. Be sure to check the licenses on these types of websites to make sure you're using copyright-free images that do not require permission or crediting the artist.

Canva is another fun option. This site allows you to create your own unique images for blog posts. Using your own photos or stock photos available on their site, you can add text and other elements.

LEARN ABOUT LINKS

Links can help get your site noticed in search engines. There are basically two types of links: internal links and external links.

Let's discuss internal links, first. These links on your website link to other pages on your site. Of course, your menu will link to other pages, but you can also place internal links directly in your blog articles. These are called hyperlinks (look for a symbol that looks like a paperclip to insert these links).

Here are a few ideas to help you add internal links to your blog:

- Add hyperlinks in your blogs to other articles you've written in the past on a similar topic. For example, one of my blogs was about losing pandemic pounds. I inserted a hyperlink to a previous blog I wrote on stress eating. This can increase your page views and help your blog's ranking.
- You can create internal links to the most popular or newest posts on your website using plugins, so they'll appear in the sidebar on all your pages and posts. In addition, some WordPress themes – like the one I have on Baby Boomer Bliss – automatically add related posts to the end of each blog.

- At the end of the year, write a blog listing your top 10 most popular blogs and include links to those articles.

Now we'll move on to external links, which is when one website refers to another site with a link. There are essentially two types of external links.

"Outbound links" send a reader from your blog to a different website. Bloggers often use these types of external links to back up statistics, verify facts, or point readers to valuable content unavailable in their blogs. This is a professional way to cite and credit your sources, which is the right thing to do anyway. Make sure to provide links to only relevant and reputable websites to help your rankings.

Even more important are "inbound links," often referred to as "backlinks." These are hyperlinks from someone else's website that point to your blog. Many experts believe these external links are the best way to obtain higher rankings.

Why? These backlinks are at the core of Google's page rank algorithm, which evaluates the quality and quantity of links to determine your blog's importance and authority. In other words, Google views backlinks from other trusted, authoritative websites as votes of popularity and ranks your site accordingly.

As you can imagine, generating worthy backlinks isn't easy. That's why some bloggers turn to ads promising "high-quality backlinks" for a price. A word of warning: Buying backlinks is against Google's Webmaster Guidelines. If you're caught, their penalties can destroy your search engine rankings.

For those willing to take the risk, high-quality backlinks from reputable sources are often expensive. You may be tempted to buy low-quality backlinks that are more affordable. But these kinds of links are usually from substandard websites. Having lots of low-quality, spammy links is worse than not having any links at all.

My advice? Steer clear and gain backlinks in legitimate ways. Here are some suggestions to get you started:

- Make your content link-worthy with original ideas and valuable content. In other words, make sure to write content people want to share.
- Write guest blogs that include a link back to your site. This can be worthwhile if the blogger has authority and a large following.
- Freelance writing can help bring traffic to your blog, and you can even get paid. One of my most significant boosts in traffic came from writing an article for *Next Avenue* – for which I was well compensated – and included a link back to my blog.
- Become an expert. Question and answer sites, like Quora, allow you to include links to your blog. However, don't just post your links which looks spammy. Take time to write detailed answers, then include links to blog posts that fit the subject matter.

- Sites like HARO (Help a Reporter Out) connect journalists and bloggers with experts they need to support their articles. You can sign up to receive emails and respond to requests matching your expertise. This may lead to interviews and a quote in an article that includes a link to your blog.
- Claim your blog in free blog directories, catalogs, and aggregators. This is a somewhat effective tactic, but don't waste a lot of time listing your blogs in all the directories. Choose a few quality directories and call it a day. Blogarama, AllTop, BlogCatalog, OnTopList, Technorati, and BlogLovin' are some you may want to check out.
- You can write and submit articles to article directories, which often allow you to include links to your blog in the resource box. However, this tactic isn't as effective as in the past. Google and other search engines have become more sophisticated, and tend to prioritize high-quality, original content over content that is duplicated across multiple sites. There are hundreds of directories to choose from; personally, I use EzineArticles. HubPages and GoArticles are a couple others you may want to check out. Medium, while not a traditional article directory, is a platform where writers can publish articles and reach a wide audience.
- Comment on popular forums and blogs related to your blog theme. Many blogs allow you to leave your name and a link with your comment. Some forums have a signature area where you can include a link to your blog.
- Become part of a blogging group. My group occasionally has "blog hops." Members agree to post a blog about a topic that's broad enough to allow the articles to be unique. Everybody includes links to the other members' blogs at the end of the articles. In addition, sometimes, we interview other members and write a blog including a link to their site.

INSTALL AN SEO PLUGIN

If the term search engine optimization (SEO) gives you a headache – like it does me – then you'll probably want to use an SEO plugin to simplify matters.

Of course, there are plenty of options and many have free plans available. Two of the most popular SEO plugins are Yoast SEO and The All in One SEO Pack for WordPress.

Technical matters, such as sitemaps, are automatically generated by installing the plugin and following the steps provided. In addition, many of these plugins analyze your blog to determine how it scores based on SEO ranking factors. This may include how many times a keyword phrase is used, the length of your text, or if any external and internal links were added. If the score is low, you can adjust your article accordingly.

Keep in mind that although these plugins are helpful, by themselves, these tools will not drive tons of traffic to your blog. You'll still have to work at promoting your blog in other ways.

GET SUBSCRIBERS

Be sure to have a subscribe button on your blog. Consider offering a free eBook or another incentive to tempt readers to subscribe.

Subscribers can provide that initial surge of traffic to new blog posts you publish. This can lead to inbound links as they check out other blogs you've written. As a bonus, they may share your blog on their social media sites. All of this helps your blog rank in search engines, translating into sustainable organic search traffic growth over time.

SHARE CONTENT ON SOCIAL MEDIA

Social media marketing can help spread awareness about your content and increase traffic to your blog. Of course, you'll need to try and increase followers on your social media sites for this to work. The more likes and comments you get, the more people see your social media posts.

A word of warning: You can waste a lot of time on social media, so experiment and note which social media sites bring the most visitors. Then, focus on one or two. For example, my target audience is boomers who typically hang around Facebook. Aside from organic search traffic, most of my visitors come from this source. So, that is where I focus most my efforts.

A few more tips:

- Plugins are available that will automatically post your blogs to all your social media sites, saving you tons of time. HootSuite is another option.
- Don't just share your new blogs. Share older blogs too, especially when articles are timely.
- Make sharing easy for your readers with share buttons.
- Start a Facebook fan page for your blog.

- Make sure your profiles on Facebook, Twitter, LinkedIn, etc. have links to your site.

INCLUDE INTERVIEWS

Interview celebrities, influencers, other popular bloggers, authors, or motivational speakers. Typically, they'll want their followers to know about the interview, which can drive traffic to your blog.

If they include a link to your interview on their websites, you can gain some of those essential backlinks as a bonus.

One of my most popular blogs is an interview with the 60s heartthrob Bobby Rydell (before he sadly passed away). Rydell's publicists posted the interview on their social media sites several times, bringing in record numbers of visitors to my blog.

USE MARKETING STRATEGIES

Remember all those marketing strategies you used when promoting your book? You can use many of the same methods to market your blog.

For example:

- Look for speaking engagements, and be sure to mention your blog.
- Join groups interested in your topic and become involved by volunteering or taking on leadership roles.
- Write articles for online and print publications that include a link to your blog.
- Begin pitching to the media.

ENGAGE WITH READERS

If anyone comments on your website content, make sure you respond. They'll be more willing to share your blog with others.

You can promote comments by asking a question related to your blog or encourage readers to share their own experiences at the end of the post.

CHAPTER 24:
MONETIZE YOUR BLOG

Once you build up your audience, you may want to earn money from your blog. The more popular your site and content become, the more you can earn. There are no hard and fast rules on how much traffic you need to make money from your site. However, I'd recommend at least 50 page views each day or a total of 1,500 per month before going through the time and effort of trying to monetize your blog.

What are some of your options when you're ready?

ADS

Offer advertising space on your site. You can directly contact businesses or, easier yet, use an ad network like Google AdSense to sell ad space for you.

AdSense is popular since it's free and easy to use. The network matches ads to your site based on your content and visitors. Advertisers pay you whenever a user clicks on an ad. Other alternatives to AdSense you may want to check out include Media.net and PropellerAds.

Tip: Try not to clutter your blog with too many ads, which can be a turn-off to visitors.

AFFILIATE MARKETING

Earn commissions using an affiliate link to promote a product or service from a retailer or advertiser. You earn money each time someone clicks the link on your site and buys the product. Some affiliates also pay commissions for leads, free-trial sign-ups, clicks to a website, or downloads for an app.

You can approach businesses directly or use free affiliate marketplaces like ShareASale and FlexOffers, to help you connect with advertisers.

Amazon Associates is arguably the biggest player in the affiliate world. In this case, when visitors click on a link on your blog, visit Amazon, and make a purchase – even if it's not the product you're promoting – you receive a small commission.

Note: You must be transparent and always disclose your affiliate relationships on your blog.

MEMBERSHIP

Ask members to sponsor you monthly with donations.

In exchange, you can offer members special, exclusive content, access to a community forum where fans can interact with you, discounts on books or online courses, and other perks.

An easy way to do so is with a membership service. One of the most popular is Patreon. With this service, you can set membership tiers with increasing benefits for each tier.

SPONSORED BLOGS

You can charge a business an agreed-upon price to write about their product on your blog with a positive review.

Tip: Only recommend quality products so you don't lose your readers' trust.

OFFER PRODUCTS

Create an online store and sell physical or digital products on your blog.

Free and paid WordPress ecommerce plugins can add a store component to your site.

ONLINE COURSES

Create self-guided teaching resources such as videos or downloadable eBooks to earn extra income.

Be aware that developing an online curriculum requires significant time and effort. You'll need a large, engaged audience to make this endeavor worthwhile.

You can host your online course on WordPress. Or use a third-party platform like Udemy, SkillShare, or Thinkific. These platforms usually charge a monthly fee or a percentage of sales.

FREELANCE WRITING SERVICES

If you become a freelance writer (see Section 4), you can advertise your services on your blog.

WHAT WRITERS IN RETIREMENT HAVE TO SAY...

SANDRA BENNETT

Blogging can be fun, interesting, and entertaining. And it's another avenue to get your name out there.

However, you need to give your audience a reason to want to read it. Think about who your target audience is and what they need, then give that to them in your blog. Don't make it all about you or over salesy. Also, try not to make each blog too lengthy, or people won't read it.

You may not get too many people commenting, but you can encourage this by asking questions.

* * *

BARRY SILVERSTEIN

If you want to start a blog, be aware of the following:

- Your blog should have a reason for existing. You need a brand and theme that can be sustained over time.
- Pick a blogging platform that is easy to use, offers design options, and can work for both desktop and mobile viewing.
- Be prepared to make a significant time commitment. To be effective and relevant, a blog needs to be updated on a frequent basis.
- Get your blog listed in as many blogging directories as possible (it's usually free to do so).

* * *

ROSIE RUSSELL

If you're not comfortable blogging alone at first, I'd suggest joining a few other author friends to get started. Everyone can pick a topic and share their thoughts, feelings, and experiences on the subject.

Once you're comfortable with writing and being "out there," you can branch out more on your own.

Blogging is a lot of work, but it's also a lot of fun. It's a great way to stay active in writing. When working with others, it also helps one be accountable for keeping it up.

You have powerful words and ideas that can transform readers' lives. Those ideas are worth fighting for.

PART VI: BECOME A TRAVEL WRITER

CHAPTER 25:

GETTING STARTED

Travel writing combines a yen for adventure with a love for writing.

By becoming a travel writer, you can:

- share your joy of traveling with others
- take readers to faraway thrilling locations they may never visit
- spark a desire in readers to explore and experience new adventures for themselves
- help readers gain an appreciation for different cultures

All of this makes travel writing a rewarding endeavor. However, if you're new to this genre, you probably have a lot of questions, such as:

- How does travel writing differ from other forms of writing?
- Do you write about the people, the architecture, the food, the sights, the history, or the sounds?
- How do you take your experiences and turn them into a book, article, or blog?
- What are your publishing options?
- What types of travel articles and books are publishers and magazine editors looking for these days?

This chapter will address all those questions. But before you start writing, let's discuss a few ways to increase your chances of becoming a successful travel writer.

STUDY THE GENRE

You'll be more productive if you learn about the trade before you start writing and try to get published. I'll share some more information in this section to get you started, but if you're serious about travel writing, don't stop there. Learn all you can about this genre. How?

Here are a few ways:

- Read books, articles, and blogs about the art of travel writing. Consider attending workshops and conferences for travel writers where you can learn about the industry.
- Read travel memoirs, articles, and blog posts written by experts to inspire and educate you on the various types of travel writing. Lots of authors have written travel narratives at some point in their careers. Try travel chronicles from classic writers like Ernest Hemingway, John Steinbeck, Mark Twain, and Henry James – for both pleasure and education.
- Practice is a necessary part of learning any new craft. Do your research on travel writing and then start sharing your travel experiences, tips, photos, and videos on social media to get a feel for travel writing. As a bonus, this will help establish yourself as a travel expert.
- Create a travel blog. Experiment with different types of articles. Showcase your writing, photos, and videos. Share upcoming travel plans. Include a brief bio, any writing credits, links to social media, and an opportunity to subscribe to your blog or newsletter. (See the previous section for more information on how to start a blog.)

SOME GENERAL ADVICE

Here are some other basic guidelines to keep in mind:

- When you're getting started, remember that travel writing usually uses a first-person viewpoint (using words like I, me, we, our, mine) written in the past tense.
- Use tantalizing descriptions that make your story both entertaining and enlightening. You want readers to see, feel, and taste what you're describing. Details matter, as well as your unique perspective, emotions, and reactions.

- Be conversational, relatable, amusing, honest, self-deprecating, engaging, clever, and vulnerable while remaining informative.
- Make sure your article or book provides essential value. That may mean sharing hidden jewels, valuable tips, life lessons, or a unique cultural insight.
- Use lots of sensory details.
- Check your facts. Use reliable sources.
- Use subheadings, short paragraphs, and bullets to make your article or book easier to read.

TYPES OF TRAVEL ARTICLES AND BOOKS

Suppose you plan to submit your travel writing to editors and publishers. In that case, it helps to have a general idea of the different kinds of popular travel articles and books, which I've included below.

Keep in mind that travel articles and books sometimes overlap several categories. In addition, travel writing is continually growing and changing. For instance, stories about adventure trekking may go out of style and be replaced by articles on luxury travel. So, stay on top of current trends.

With that in mind, here's a list of typical travel articles and books:

- Destination Articles

  Perhaps the most popular type of travel writing, these pieces briefly cover various aspects of a city or country. Articles can include points of interest, architecture, natural scenery, history, trendy spots, fascinating facts, and cost-saving tips.

- How-To Articles

  Topics can range widely– from tips on how to pack a suitcase to bartering advice to ways of overcoming language barriers. While expert advice provides the foundation, personal anecdotes, especially at the beginning of the article, will add flavor. Humor is an asset.

- Special-interest articles

  Instead of taking a reader on a typical tour of a place, these articles focus on a specific topic. If you're passionate about an outdoor activity, wild about a specific type of adventure, or enthusiastic about ecotourism or heritage tours, you may be able to corner a niche. Many writers tailor these articles to smaller specialty magazines or websites, which can be a good way to get started.

- Round-ups

  After researching information on several different places, these articles are grouped together with a common theme. For example, "10 Best Road Trips in the U.S.," "The World's 10 Most Romantic Spots," or "Top 20 Beaches in the French Riviera." I've written these types of articles for Canadian national home and lifestyle magazines without visiting each place in person. Keep in mind, however, that you need to be skilled at researching and then writing brief, enticing descriptions about each destination.

- Historical, Holiday, and Special Events Articles

  These articles are tied to an anniversary, special event, holiday, or historical event. Writers are expected to write about a destination before the event takes place, which means you need to pitch these stories well in advance. Of course, significant global events, like the Olympics, fashion weeks, and film festivals lend themselves to this type of travel writing. However, don't overlook smaller regional events, which may be a good way to break into travel writing.

- Personal Essays

  Essays often revolve around a theme that gives readers a personal perspective that is thoughtful, deep, and reflective. These articles require exemplary writing skills, insight, a strong voice, and a solid point of view. Publishers are on the lookout for funny essays as well. Suppose you can write about misadventures, universal human mistakes, and/or people who say or do inappropriate things (including yourself) in a humorous way. In that case, you may have a chance of getting your foot in the door.

- Itineraries

These types of articles reveal the exact schedule a writer follows on a trip – either city-by-city or sight-by-sight. They're meant for the traveler taking a similar trip who wants a template. An itinerary post typically includes recommendations of hotels, restaurants, and camping sites. If you're lucky, you may be able to work out a deal for some free meals or accommodations.

- Journey articles

The destination is less important than the experience of the journey and life lessons learned along the way in these articles. Some advice and beneficial facts may be included, but the focus is a strong narrative story, stirring prose, detailed description, and perhaps some humor. Cross-country railway journeys, scenic drives, adventurous hikes, cargo ship voyages, bicycle tours, or sailing adventures can lend themselves to journey articles.

- Copywriting

Copywriting includes articles, emails, traveling brochures, press releases, and advertisements for businesses involved in the travel industry. Maybe this type of travel writing sounds boring, but that's not necessarily true. Remember, your job is to creatively weave a story that sells a travel experience. This can involve colorful descriptions that make adventures come alive. Often more lucrative than other types of travel writing, clients may include travel agencies, hotels, inns, vacation rentals, restaurants, cruise lines, and bed & breakfasts.

- Guidebooks

Guidebooks are straightforward, informative, and fact-filled. This is a competitive market, with *Lonely Planet* and *Fodor's* leading the pack with guidebooks that are read by millions of travelers worldwide. The best travel guide writing combines detailed information, exhaustive research, and stringent fact-checking with beautifully crafted, free-flowing prose that provokes itchy feet.

- Travel Memoirs

A travel memoir is a genre all its own. It's not a guidebook or how-to book. These books combine reminisces and reflections to reveal how a journey changed and transformed the author. Travel memoirs like Cheryl Strayed's bestselling *Wild* have become popular and even adapted into Hollywood blockbusters. You'll need an extraordinary personal story for your memoir to compete in today's market. Of course, you can always write a travel journal for your own pleasure or self-publish a travel memoir.

- Nature Writing

Nature articles and books may include field guides based on scientific facts, fiction or poetry about nature, or personal essays about discovery, solitude, adventure, or escape. While this type of article or book is usually based on science, it is often written in the first person and includes personal observations and reflections about nature.

CHAPTER 26:

MAKE YOUR TRAVEL WRITING STAND OUT

Remember, your goal is to transport readers to a specific time and place. If you want to make a mark in this competitive genre, you must hook your readers, provide lots of details, and have a strong and unique voice. Here are some tips to help you accomplish these feats.

BE OBSERVANT AND TAKE NOTES

Record your thoughts in the moment. Pocket notebooks easily fit into backpacks, purses, and, yes, even most pockets. Or, if you prefer, use your phone to keep brief notes.

Why is this important? If you wait to write everything down after you go home, many facts, details, and nuances will be lost. Even hours later, small but important moments may be forgotten.

Of course, you'll take general notes about the places you visit and events that take place, but what are some other things you should include in your notes?

- Jot down sounds, scents, tastes, and textures to help readers feel like they're right there with you.

- Since the best travel stories usually involve interactions with locals you've met, note any interesting people and conversations. Quote people accurately and identify them. Include how and where you met them. If they tell you something alarming or enlightening, be sure and write it down.
- Describe your emotions. Take note of moments that affected you the most and why.
- Of course, you'll detail all your extraordinary experiences. But don't forget to write down what went horribly wrong.

While taking notes, allow your thoughts and feelings to flow freely without pausing to self-edit. Don't worry about proper spelling, punctuation, or a poetic way to describe the scenery. You can edit and refine it later.

FIND A FOCUS

Travel stories are more gripping when they focus on a specific topic. Find something that gives your article or book direction and purpose.

Ask yourself, what is the point of your piece?

For example, is the objective of your trip to understand a culture better? If that's the case, keep the following tips in mind:

- Do some research before you leave.
- Try and learn some words in the local language.
- Travel widely and visit local villages.
- Use public transportation.
- Observe and respect local culture.
- Focus on meeting new people, learning about their traditions and viewpoints, trying new foods, and visiting historical sights and museums.
- Take note of cultural differences. What did you learn that surprised you the most? How did learning about a new culture and a different way of life contribute to your personal growth?
- What about your background or past experiences gave you a unique perspective?

Is the point of your trip to cross off an item on a bucket list like shark cage diving, seeing the Northern Lights, sailing the Greek islands, or climbing Kilimanjaro? Ask yourself:

- Why is achieving your goal so important to you?
- Is your bucket list item tied to a passion you've had all your life?
- Did achieving your goal change you in a positive way?
- Was your goal to overcome a fear? If so, how did the experience empower you?
- Did you make sacrifices or overcome setbacks to achieve your objective? Was it worth it?

Are you traveling to find yourself by revisiting your homeland? Then you'll want to do the following:

- Search records before you leave.
- Find relatives as well as street addresses, schools, cemeteries, and other landmarks that connect you to your past.
- Share what you learned about your cultural identity. Did you feel more connected to your ancestors? What elements, values, and traditions will you incorporate into your own life and pass along to your children and grandchildren?
- Was your trip a life-changing experience? How so?
- If you spent your childhood years in your homeland, how do you view your country now as an adult compared to when you were a kid?

No matter your goal, focus on the emotional takeaway from your trip. What life lesson did you learn from your experiences and bring home with you? How did your travels change you? What sight, person, or event affected you the most? How did you push yourself outside your comfort zone? Who did you talk to during your travels that changed your perspective?

If you plan to write a travel memoir, you can dive even deeper with honest and intimate storytelling. Reflect on your travels and contemplate your story's overarching theme. What's the moral, life lesson, or point of your story? Elizabeth Gilbert's famous travel memoir *Eat Pray Love* about her journey of self-discovery is a good example of this type of writing.

HOOK YOUR READERS

Your lead or hook in your first paragraph must grab your reader's attention immediately. Make an emotional impact. You must shock, intrigue, touch, or amuse your readers so they'll keep reading.

Don't start with your boring trip to the airport. Begin with the most exciting, funny, or painful event that affected you the most. You can fill in the details about how you found yourself in a precarious or enlightening situation later.

Another option is to leave readers with an intriguing question or statement that makes them want to know more. Here are a few examples of some great hooks:

- "The first time I blew off steam internationally was not born of carpe diam. It was born of deep despair." - *What I Was Doing While You Were Breeding: A Memoir* by Kristin Newman
- "I lost my arm on my last trip home." - *Kindred* written by Octavia Butler
- "I am about to buy a house in a foreign country." - *Under the Tuscan Sun*, by Frances Mayes
- "I suppose I should have warned Rand." Geraldine DeRuiter's article, "Pranzo in Italy" in Everywherest

After reading those lines, who isn't curious to learn more? If using this technique, don't meander for pages or keep your readers guessing about the theme of your story for too long. Get to the point.

USE FICTION WRITING TECHNIQUES

Travel writing is much more than simply listing things you saw and did on a trip. Here are a few fiction writing techniques to create a scene and paint a picture that can be used in nonfiction pieces as well:

- A travel article or book should have an exciting plot like any good novel. I don't mean a monotonous litany of "this happened" and "that happened." What's at stake? What challenges did you or others face? How did your trip change you or others? Once you know your "plot," you can gather experiences that fit the story and leave out the rest.
- Include interesting "characters." Did you meet a quirky stranger? Were your traveling companions quite the characters? What did they look like?

Did they have a particular manner of speaking, walking, or laughing? A distinctive feature?

- Don't forget to add dialogue. This is where those notes I suggested taking earlier in the chapter come in handy. You'll be able to refer to conversations and describe characters more accurately.
- Of course, the setting is particularly crucial when writing a travel story. Use plenty of sensory details. Steer away from overused cliches like "stunning," "bustling markets," "off the beaten path," "breathtaking," "cultural melting pots," or "crystal blue waters." Find your own unique way to describe the scene around you.
- Add plenty of suspense, humor, and drama.
- Just like a novel, end with a revelation, discovery, lesson, or personal transformation.

NURTURE A NICHE

Develop a niche to separate yourself from the crowd. Hone your expertise in your area of choice and own it.

Ask yourself questions to help you find your specialty. For example:

- Is there a related subject you're passionate about, like food? Do you love to learn about unusual fruits and vegetables and collect recipes from around the world?
- Are you avid about practicing healthy habits and enhancing your well-being even while traveling? Do you frequent yoga and meditation retreats, spas, detox boot camps, and mineral hot springs?
- Are you passionate about a specific kind of adventure, like jungle tourism or ecotourism?
- Do you enjoy volunteering while visiting exotic countries? Are you zealous about conservation expeditions?
- Is there something about you that is unique? Are you a single woman traveler over 80 with a disability? Are you a grandparent raising grandchildren who loves to travel with them? Are you a working nomad?

Once you find your niche, post about it on social media sites, write blogs, and comment on other popular blogs and online forums. Share your knowledge and passion with authority and style.

Over time you may become a go-to authority on the subject, widen your readership, cultivate connections with potential readers and other travel bloggers, and attract media attention.

CHAPTER 27:
PUBLISHING OPTIONS

Travel writing is a competitive field, but if this is your passion, don't let that stop you. The more you write, the more confident you'll become in sharing your unique perspective and point of view as well as your expertise. Take your time to learn the ropes and write in an authentic way, and you'll increase your chances of being successful.

Here's a list of some publishing options you may want to consider.

PRINT MAGAZINES

Let's keep it real. Before you begin dreaming about being paid to vacation in exotic places by well-known travel magazines, be aware that the competition for these types of gigs is intense. The prestigious magazine assignments usually go to writers with plenty of experience and extraordinary photography skills.

Try starting small with lesser-known or regional publications that may be more receptive. Study small pieces that appear in the front of a magazine and pitch a story or two to that section's editor. Your goal is to build a relationship with an editor that will hopefully lead to regular assignments later.

Always check submission guidelines. These are usually available online or check *Writer's Market*. Publications may accept only queries, or they may welcome articles "on spec" (pre-written articles). When editorial guidelines state that the publication wants family-oriented destination articles, regional weekend getaways, or humorous first-person essays, give them what they want.

NEWSPAPERS

Travel sections in major publications such as *The New York Times* and *Washington Post* are slimmer now, making competition even more fierce.

Local newspapers are sometimes open to travel pitches from freelancers and are worth a shot. If successful, you'll build up your portfolio and hopefully land more paying gigs and free trips in the future.

ONLINE PUBLICATIONS

Thankfully, the Internet has opened lots of opportunities for travel writers. Some travel websites and travel blogs pay for articles. Others accept guest blogs for free, which may be a good option when you're starting out and need writing credits.

If you've discovered a travel website or blog you admire, contact the editor, and offer to write content on a subject that features your special expertise.

COPYWRITING

As mentioned in the previous chapter, you can write articles, travel brochures, emails, press releases, and advertisements for businesses involved in the travel industry. Clients may include hotels, inns, vacation rentals, bed & breakfasts, restaurants, cruise lines, and travel agencies.

If you have marketing experience, this may be a good option. Often, these jobs are more profitable than other types of travel writing. You can search on job boards or approach clients directly.

SELF-PUBLISH OR START A BLOG

You can always self-publish your travel memoir or start your own travel blog. Who knows what might happen? Some writers who began this way went on to get book deals or published in a glossy magazine. Others have received offers of free travel and meals for recommendations on their blogs.

Even if none of that happens, you'll probably reach some appreciative readers who enjoy reading your book or stumble across your blog.

As a bonus, all your beautiful memories will be documented for your enjoyment later.

PART VII: PEN POETRY

CHAPTER 28:

WHY BECOME A POET?

Perhaps you don't want to commit to the discipline of writing a book, the challenge of monetizing a blog, or the deadlines of becoming a freelance writer. Your goal is not to earn money. You simply want to pursue your passion for writing in your spare time or whenever the muse hits.

Absolutely nothing wrong with that. In fact, be forewarned. If you try to make a living by writing, it can suck some of that joy right out of you. I truly believe that getting published or earning money is less important than the joy of writing.

The following few sections are for those who wish to write simply as a creative outlet. We'll start with a section on poetry.

WRITE FOR PURE PLEASURE

Making a living writing poetry is next to impossible. That's why I wouldn't recommend it if your goal is to earn an income. However, if you love the beauty of words and want to write for pleasure, poetry is a great option. Writing poems allows you to explore life through eloquent language, share your unique perspective, and release your deepest feelings.

If you're retired, you now have the time to experiment with this absorbing genre.

CHAPTER 29:
GETTING STARTED

Do you want to dive in and just start writing? Go ahead. You certainly have that option. Contrary to popular belief, poetry doesn't have to be about complicated formulas, rhyming schemes, or counting each syllable.

If you want to write freely without any rules or limitations, simply express your thoughts, feelings, and ideas. If desired, you can add some style and rhythm for bonus points.

On the other hand, perhaps you'd like to learn more about this art form. You have several choices.

LEARN ABOUT POETRY

Are you curious about writing poetry but don't know where to begin? You have lots of options when it comes to learning more:

- Consider a college course or an online class to learn about rhyming and meter (the number of syllables and a pattern of emphasis on those syllables).
- Read books, articles, and blogs on the subject.
- Of course, reading poems – both classic and modern-day – is not only enjoyable but will also help you learn about this genre and improve your writing skills. Analyze poems and dig for deeper meaning. Take note of the

subject, how the poems sound read aloud, and the strong feelings that are evoked.

- Many bookstores and coffeehouses have poetry readings, and these can be both fun and educational for aspiring poets. By listening to the rhythms of good poetry, you'll discover the beauty of this art form.
- If available, consider joining a poetry writing group where poets read each other's work, provide feedback, and recite poems aloud. Try to find a group that experiments with different types of poetry, discusses the art form, shares poetry exercises, brainstorms while jotting down ideas, and learns from the work of peers.

FIND INSPIRATION

What should you write about?

Think about what you want your poem to accomplish. Is it your goal to explore a personal experience, describe the beauty of nature, express your intimate feelings, or simply play with language?

Once you have an objective, grab a piece of paper, and write down all your ideas. Explore your memories, use your imagination, or express your deepest emotions. Nothing is off-limits.

Need a few ideas? You can write about:

- a regret
- a place that gives you peace
- your deepest fear
- a time when you had to say goodbye to a loved one
- a period of pure joy
- an object in nature considered ugly that you see as beautiful
- your spirituality
- gratitude
- something painfully out of reach

Subjects are limitless. If you need more inspiration, writing prompts for poetry abound on the Internet.

JUST WRITE

When you begin your poem, avoid getting stuck attempting to create the perfect first line. This is a mistake that some beginning poets make that causes them to give up right away. Keep writing and come back to edit that first line later.

As you write, be specific, open, and brave. Use all your senses. Create vivid imagery.

When you have a rough draft, have fun experimenting. Play with rhyme and meter. Organize your poem in different ways. Try shorter and longer lines. Add similes and metaphors.

Feel free to use tools that you find useful, including a thesaurus and a rhyming dictionary.

CHAPTER 30: DIFFERENT TYPES OF POETRY

Do you want to experiment with different kinds of poems? The following are some various forms of poetry you may want to try.

ALPHABET AND ACROSTIC POEMS

Alphabet poems, sometimes called ABC poems, are based on a section of the alphabet – or all 26 letters if you feel ambitious.

For example:

I LOVE YOU BECAUSE YOU...
Accept me as I am
Believe in me
Care for me unselfishly
Deepen my emotions
Enchant me

An acrostic poem is slightly different, with the first letter of each line spelling out a word or message. You may use the name of a loved one, a theme like "friend" or "grandmother" or "hope," or a message like "Happy Anniversary."

For example, if you want to use the word "hope," you might write:

Hold on to your vision.
Open your heart to possibilities.
Pave the way to success.
Earnestly make dreams come true.

BALLADS

Ballads are poems that tell a story, describe an event, or share a heartfelt experience. These poems are often about love, but you can create your ballad from any event that touched or deeply affected you.

Ballads frequently have a plot, characters, and a story arc, much like a short story, but with more elaborate and elegant language.

You can choose your own rhyme scheme, but these poems typically use a four-line stanza with lines two and four rhyming.

For classic examples, read ballads by John Keats, Edgar Allan Poe, Oscar Wilde, and William Butler Yeats.

FREE VERSE POEMS

Perhaps the most popular type of poetry, these poems don't follow any rules of rhyme, pattern, or meter.

Nonetheless, this type of poem should have some lyrical flow and rhythm. Consider using poetic devices like metaphors and similes.

HAIKU POEMS

This ancient form of Japanese poetry is the opposite of free verse in the sense that there are strict rules.

The haiku is a three-line poem that has five syllables in line one, seven syllables in line two, and five syllables in line three. The lines do not rhyme. For example:

A CALM LIFE
Peace like a river
Tranquility in my soul
Quiet contentment

These poems usually focus on the exquisiteness of nature and simple moments in life.

LIMERICKS

A limerick poem is a five-line fun or humorous poem with a set number of syllables and a rhyme scheme.

There are seven to 10 syllables in lines one, two, and five. These three lines rhyme and have the same rhythm. In lines three and four, there are five to seven syllables that have the same rhythm and rhyme.

This may sound complicated, but these poems can be fun. Here's one I wrote about my boyfriend and future husband:

There once was a guy named Scott
Who thought he was really hot.
His hair was so curly,
The image of Shirley,
But despite this, I like him a lot.

NARRATIVE POEMS

Narrative poems tell the story of an event in stanzas instead of paragraphs.

Like a ballad, novel, or short story, these poems usually include characters, settings, and a plot. A narrator relates the story using poetic techniques such as rhyme and meter, and often includes action and dialogue.

Examples of narrative poems are Edgar Allan Poe's famous *The Raven* and *Beowulf* by an unknown author.

CHAPTER 31: SHARE YOUR TALENT WITH OTHERS

You may want to write poems simply for your own enjoyment. If so, great! You do have a few options, however, if you want to share your poetry.

CREATE GREETING CARDS

Poems make wonderful and cherished gifts. You can write a poem and frame it for a special person.

Or create a homemade greeting card. A card with a special and unique poem you wrote will mean so much more than one you buy at a store. Do you have talent as an artist, photographer, or illustrator? Use your abilities on the cover of your card.

If desired, you could sell your homemade greeting cards on sites like Etsy or your own website if you have one.

SUBMIT YOUR POEMS FOR PUBLICATION

Print and online magazines accept poetry. For a list check out Writers.com or ReedsyBlog.

Remember that while some publishers compensate poets, many do not offer payment.

SELF-PUBLISH A POETRY BOOK

You can always self-publish a collection of your poetry. If you do so, you'll likely find others who will connect and relate to your words.

USE YOUR POEMS IN A NOVEL

If you're writing a novel, perhaps one of your characters enjoys writing poetry, and you can include a few in your book.

PART VIII: START A JOURNAL

CHAPTER 32:

BENEFITS OF JOURNALING

Today, you have social media and blogging as a way to express yourself. So, why use an old-fashioned journal?

For one thing, a journal is private, unlike the Internet. If you use a public platform as a journal, you'll lose the freedom to express your feelings without worrying about what others think. As a result, you'll probably start self-editing. This can interfere with the free flow of your creative thoughts.

Nonetheless, this is a personal choice. You may prefer an audience. Even so, consider keeping a separate private journal where you can express your most intimate thoughts without explanation, justification, or fear of judgment.

Aside from privacy issues, there are other reasons to journal. Consider some ways journaling can be life-changing.

GREATER SELF-AWARENESS

By journaling every day, you make a statement that you matter. That's a powerful thought. In addition, by regularly recording your thoughts and feelings, you learn about yourself and gain insight into your behaviors.

You get to know who and what makes you happy and what situations and people to avoid.

Taking note of patterns in your life can help you avoid repeating mistakes, which leads to personal growth.

HANG ON TO MEMORIES

Keeping a journal helps you capture details and remember important people, events, thoughts, and feelings.

If you don't put these precious memories into writing, they may fade or be lost altogether.

In addition, when you're having a bad day, you can pick up your journal and remember better times, improving your mood with happy and positive thoughts.

REDUCE STRESS

Write when you feel wretched. Write when you're on the top of the world. Let it all out. Writing helps process your feelings. Trust me, it's a wonderful outlet!

Journaling is downright therapeutic. Studies have shown that it can help you heal, reduce stress, and find inner peace.

By expressing sadness, fear, pain, jealousy, or anger, you release the intensity of those negative feelings. Journaling gives you a safe space to reflect on your emotions and what you can learn from it.

OUTLINE GOALS

Journals are a great place to identify, define, and outline your plans, ideas, goals, and dreams.

Once you know more about what you want out of life, it will be easier to find ways to reach your goals. What's most important to you and needs to take priority? What needs to change today for you to achieve your dream life?

Once you identify paths to success, you can create a realistic schedule. Not only will you be more motivated to accomplish your dreams, but detailing your goals in writing is a form of accountability.

When you achieve those dreams, it's so much fun to read about it later. I wrote in my diary 30 years ago: "I registered for a writing class. It's exciting. I might not get anything published, but at least I'm taking a step in the right direction of fulfilling a dream." How fun it is to look back and realize that three decades later, I'm living that dream!

Portions of my diaries were even used in my first young adult novel, *Just Call Me Goody-Two-Shoes*. Who knows what can happen? So, start documenting your life story and see where it takes you.

INCREASE SELF-CONFIDENCE

When you record significant life lessons, you gain a deeper understanding, insight, and hopefully, some wisdom to help you with future problems.

As a bonus, when a seemingly impossible situation arises, you'll be reminded that you have resolved and overcome previous dilemmas in the past and can do so again.

PROBLEM-SOLVE

Journaling can be used for problem-solving and resolving disagreements.

That is if you don't simply make your journal a place to rant and rave, blame others, wallow in self-pity, and justify yourself.

If you can avoid these tendencies, writing can clarify issues and help you understand another person's perspective.

IMPROVE WRITING SKILLS

If you dream of becoming a writer, keeping a journal can help you learn to write regularly and improve your skills. One entry may inspire a blog, poem, or even a novel.

CHAPTER 33: HOW TO JOURNAL

Those are some great reasons to journal, you may be thinking. But keeping a journal sounds like a chore or too big of a commitment.

It doesn't have to be.

MAKE IT FUN

Remember, there are no rules when it comes to journaling.

I don't believe in pledging to write in your journal every single day. That can rob you of the joy of writing and defeats the whole purpose. Diaries should be an escape from stress, not a dreaded homework assignment.

So, journal whenever you want. Relax and unwind. Write whatever comes to mind. Gush, vent, plan, remember, joke, or lament.

Forget about spelling and grammar. Resist editing yourself or worrying about whether your writing sounds eloquent. You don't need to create a literary masterpiece. Unless you're famous, no one is going to publish your journal.

Be creative. Don't limit yourself to a "dear diary" format. Draw pictures, include photos, or paste things in your journal. Experiment and make a mess. Start pages with a question, quote, or half-remembered dream. Maybe you'll include lyrics, poems, or book excerpts.

Again, there are no rules. If you discover you aren't enjoying yourself, you can always stop.

PICK THE PERFECT SPOT AND TIME

Be sure to seek a quiet, tranquil space to journal. Writing should be a time of reflection and peace.

That could mean lounging in bed with an inspiring playlist, sitting by a roaring fire with a mug of tea, finding a sunny place on your patio, or writing under your favorite tree.

It's also important to write when you feel the most creative. Maybe you'll write in the morning when your mind is fresh. Or you may prefer to write before you go to sleep to unload your mind. Whatever works best for you.

Avoid setting time limits. Write for a minute or spend an hour delving into your deepest thoughts and feelings. Whatever you feel like in the moment.

CHOOSE A SUITABLE METHOD

Pen and paper or a computer? That depends on your preference. Since everyone is different, explore different options to find the right choice for you.

To me, nothing beats putting pen to paper. I enjoy the luxurious feeling of sitting in a comfy chair with a cup of coffee to quietly reflect on my thoughts and write them down. Not to mention, a paper journal never needs electricity and can be personalized with drawings, tickets, and other mementos.

If this is your preferred method, tons of beautiful journals are available. Although a fancy or soft leather cover isn't necessary, you may feel that an attractive journal is part of the sensory experience and helps motivate you to write. Some journals include inspirational quotes and writing prompts to help get you started.

There are a few downsides, however, to recording your thoughts on paper. You won't have any backups if your journal is lost or destroyed. And privacy can be an issue. As a teen, I kept changing the hiding places of my diaries, but friends and family still found and read them.

Even with these risks, I'm still a pen-and-paper girl.

You may feel differently, however. Maybe security and privacy issues are a deal breaker. You may have bad handwriting that would make reading your journals later difficult. Admittedly, typing is faster and easier than writing by hand.

In that case, a computer may better suit your needs. You can use any word processing software. For privacy, take precautions. Password protect a computer-based journal or use an encrypted text file in Dropbox.

There are also tons of journal and diary apps you can use both online and offline, either from a web browser or on a mobile device. Many journal apps offer security and privacy features.

Recording your thoughts on a voice memo or using the note-taking app of your phone, if preferred, still counts as journaling.

CHAPTER 34:

EXPLORE DIFFERENT TYPES OF JOURNALS

When people think of journals, they often imagine writing about daily life. Usually, these kinds of journals record important events and experiences, express thoughts and feelings, list goals, or take note of life lessons.

However, a standard journal isn't your only choice. Many different types of journals are available. Here are some options you may want to consider.

GRATITUDE JOURNAL

What better way to bring positivity to your life than listing reasons you're thankful for and documenting happy moments?

When you're going through a difficult period, these journals can help you pause and think of life's simple pleasures. Yes, we all have them! Think of the moment you open your drapes and sunlight streams into your home. Or the aroma of coffee in the morning, the brisk air on your skin when you walk outside, the bright spring flowers exploding in your yard, the birds singing joyfully, or a kind word from a stranger.

As a bonus, if you're feeling depressed in the future, you'll have reminders of things you appreciate about life.

IDEA JOURNAL

If you're an aspiring writer, you can fill your journal with inspirational ideas for writing projects.

Jot down plots, characters, settings, or snippets of dialogue for your next novel. Or pen the beginnings of a poem, future blog topics, memories to include in your memoir, or ideas for articles.

Just think, when writer's block raises its ugly head, you'll have many ideas at your fingertips.

If you enjoy using writing prompts – which you can easily find on the Internet – an idea journal can help you keep track of them.

TRAVEL JOURNAL

These journals are a great place to make plans for a trip.

Once you've arrived, you can document your adventures, road trips, countries you visit, and delightful discoveries you made along the way.

These journals may even lead to a travel blog or travel memoir.

SCRAPBOOK JOURNAL

Are you crafty? Use pictures, magazine clippings, sketches, calligraphy, fabrics, photographs, mementos, and other materials to create a visual journal or type of vision board.

Of course, you can include a few words or short entries, but this style of journaling is focused more on indulging your artsy side.

For instance, you may have attended a great concert. Create a collage of photos, add your ticket and program, then write a short entry about your experience.

BUCKET LIST JOURNAL

These journals can help you break out of a rut, live consciously, dream big, unleash your imagination, and make your dreams a reality.

List places you want to travel and paste maps to inspire you. Take note of things you want to experience, like swimming with dolphins or riding a hot air balloon.

Write down fears you want to overcome, things you want to learn or achieve, or books you want to read.

Then, take note of the steps you need to take to achieve your dreams.

TOPIC JOURNAL

Create your own type of journal and give it a specific title. Here are just a few ideas:

- A "Dream Journal" can record your dreams, note themes and patterns, and provide insight into your thoughts and concerns.
- A journal titled "Moments that Changed My Life Forever" may help you write a memoir later.
- An "Inspirational Journal" can record inspirational quotes, spiritual lessons, quotes from books, or personal experiences that motivate you.
- A "Nature Journal" might include nature poems, a record of what you grow in your garden, or wildlife you observe, complete with sketches.
- A journal titled "Funny Things My Grandchildren Said" can bring back wonderful memories and make you laugh later.

PART IX: BECOME A PLAYWRIGHT

CHAPTER 35: CONSIDER YOUR OPTIONS

Just like making a living as a poet, earning money as a playwright isn't easy.

But even if your play doesn't end up on Broadway or on the screen, there are other possibilities.

Here are just a few:

TRY AMATEUR PRODUCTIONS

You may experience the thrill of seeing your work produced in community theaters, schools, or other amateur productions.

PRODUCE A FILM

Short films and full-length films from emerging playwrights are shown at festivals and online sites that host them. Or consider self-producing and distributing your film through the Internet.

ENTERTAIN GRANDCHILDREN

If you enjoy writing for children, try penning a fun play for your grandkids to perform. Bonus points if they help you write it!

HAVE YOUR OWN DINNER THEATER

Write a play, round up some friends to play the parts, and gather a small audience for some homestyle dinner theater.

VIDEOTAPE A PLAY AS A GIFT FOR LOVED ONES

When I was in my 20s, I wrote a humorous play for my parent's anniversary featuring aliens who thought their marriage and our family was hilarious.

I had fun writing and performing the short play with my siblings and some friends. We taped it on video and still laugh. My parents loved it!

CHAPTER 36:

GETTING STARTED

As with all aspects of writing, take the time to learn about the basics of writing a play.

LEARN THE DIFFERENCES BETWEEN A NOVEL AND A PLAY

Writing a novel and a play are similar. Both types of writing involve developing characters, settings, and a plot. However, there are a few differences:

- Novels rely heavily on revealing a character's inner thoughts while script writing depends more on dialogue. Unlike a novel, you don't have the luxury of sharing a character's thoughts and memories or filling in background information.
- A novel may have dozens of characters and settings. Plays usually simplify these aspects since too many scene changes, characters, and costumes makes the play more expensive and difficult to produce.
- The format for a traditional play is different than a novel, especially if you plan to submit your play to producers. A script includes actions of the characters and dialogue as well as describing the setting of the stage which can include backdrops, lighting, and props.

EDUCATE YOURSELF

Playwriting is distinct from other forms of writing, so if you're serious, take classes and read books, articles, and blogs about this genre. Attend workshops, conferences, and seminars both to learn about plays and to network. Read and watch as many plays as possible. Take note of the playwright's techniques and dialogue.

To become more aware of the practical aspects of producing a play, volunteer at a local theater. Watch how things work backstage. Make contacts with people who can give you feedback on your play and perhaps eventually help you get a play produced. Even if you plan to write plays purely for fun, watching plays and volunteering at a local theater can be enjoyable and rewarding.

If writing movie or TV screenplays is your dream, thoroughly research how to write and pitch a screenplay to producers.

JOIN A WRITERS' GROUP

A group of your peers who have different talents and are still learning can help you find inspiration. Writers' groups often share knowledge and provide support.

Look for groups that offer everyone the opportunity to have their work read and critiqued.

Some groups produce a play or film a story together, do table reads that include aspiring actors, or meet in local theaters followed by a lively discussion afterward.

CHAPTER 37: WRITE A TRADITIONAL PLAY

After you've learned about writing plays, you can begin writing. Where to start? Here are a few tips.

CREATE AN OUTLINE

Before writing an entire play from scratch, it helps to have a general idea of the type of play you want to write. Consider the following:

- Will your play be tragic, romantic, comedic, or mysterious?
- Who is your main character and who are your secondary characters? How do they relate to each other? What are their fears, dreams, and motivations? What kind of conflict will they face?
- Where does your story take place? During what time period?
- What's your basic plot? How will you create suspense and add unexpected twists?
- How does your play end?
- How many acts are in your play? For your first play, you may consider writing only one act with no intermissions to keep things simpler.

Once some of these decisions are made, create a general outline of your play. Briefly outline your scenes under each act using your synopsis. Note when characters are introduced. Add more details as you go along.

USE ELEMENTS OF NOVEL WRITING

You may want to review Chapter 7 on novel writing and apply some of the same techniques. That chapter describes how to choose a theme, create believable and interesting characters, craft a compelling plot, write gripping dialogue, establish a setting, and create suspense and conflict.

Just like a novel, you'll want an exciting beginning to hook your audience. Make sure the situation is explosive and dramatic, tensions are high, and tempers are short.

A play needs to command attention, so keep your story moving at a fast pace.

ADD STAGE DIRECTIONS

Within the script, note what each character is doing. Make it clear so actors understand your vision and what they need to do.

Keep in mind that a play must be told through actions that an audience can see from a distance. Body language is important since you can't zoom in on a face to see a character's reaction like in a movie.

The exception to this rule is if you're writing a screenplay for a movie or TV (see the next chapter for more information) or if you're simply videotaping a play for fun. In that case, a camera can easily zoom in to capture facial expressions.

Use brackets to set your stage directions apart from the spoken dialogue. Include:

- physical actions [Rachel paces nervously], [Robert violently punches the wall]
- emotional states [joyfully] [determined] [enthusiastically]
- conversations cues [hesitates a moment] [long, awkward silence]

Also include technical directions that may include set scenes, costume changes, props, and lighting.

EDIT YOUR PLAY

As with all forms of writing, edit and revise, paying attention to pacing, character development, and overall coherence.

Share your play with trusted friends, writing groups, or mentors. Constructive feedback can provide valuable insights and help you refine your work.

Consider performing a read-through of your play, either by yourself or better yet, with a group of friends. This can help you identify awkward dialogue, pacing issues, and areas that may need improvement.

FORMAT YOUR PLAY

Once you're satisfied with your play, make sure it adheres to the standard playwriting format. This includes proper formatting of dialogue, stage directions, and other elements. The general structure of a play is as follows:

- Title Page: Unless otherwise specified, keep it simple. Type the title of your play, the number of acts, your name, and contact information.
- Cast Page: List your character's names followed by a few tags that give the audience and director a basic idea of what the character is like. Example: (character's name): (gender), (age), (job) and characteristics such as "loner," "no-nonsense type," "short-tempered," etc.
- Scene Headings: Begin with Act (Number), Scene (Number). If you're writing a short play that only has one act, then simply include the scene number.
- Settings: Underneath the heading, you'll want to briefly describe your setting. Think about where and when the scene takes place. Is the character standing in a room overlooking a tranquil park or inside a classroom with rowdy students? Is it late afternoon, midnight, or daybreak?
- Action: Start a new line and describe the character's action. If characters are meeting for the first time, perhaps they enter from opposite ends of the stage. Maybe a teacher is writing on a chalkboard with the sound of students in the background. Be specific and detailed.
- Dialogue: Indicate which character is speaking by putting their name in all caps. Start a new line and begin the dialogue.
- End the Scene: Make a new line and describe how your character exits – if they exit. You can note "lights go down" to signify to the production team

that the scene has ended, and they can start preparing for the following one.

SUBMIT YOUR PLAY

Submitting plays is similar to submitting queries to agents (see Chapter 10). You'll need to draft a query letter to send to theaters, production companies, agents, and managers with open submission policies.

Keep the letter brief, and introduce yourself and your play in a concise but compelling way. Include a bio, noting any prior industry experience or a placement in any reputable contests. Do not attach your script; if the producer or rep is interested, they'll request to see more.

If submitting your play to a theater, keep in mind every theater is different. Follow submission guidelines. You may need to fill out an online submission form on a theater's website and upload your documents directly to their site.

CHAPTER 38:

WRITE A SCREENPLAY

Writing a screenplay involves a specific format and structure tailored for the visual medium of film. Industry-standard software like Final Draft or Celtx can assist you in formatting your script correctly.

In general, remember that a screenplay is organized into scenes. Every scene starts with a heading, sometimes referred to as a slug line. Scenes are simply a present-tense description of what the audience sees.

Here's an example of an action line from the movie L.A. Confidential:

Reporters scribble as the Chief speaks. Uniforms everywhere along with Exley and Loew. Bus sits in the back.

GETTING STARTED

When you're ready, you'll want to take the following steps:

- Develop a compelling concept or idea for your screenplay. This could be a unique story, an interesting character, or a thought-provoking theme.

- Outline the major plot points and structure of your screenplay. Consider the three-act structure commonly used in screenwriting: setup, confrontation, and resolution.
- Create well-defined and relatable characters. Consider their backgrounds, motivations, and arcs. Characters are crucial in engaging the audience.
- Draft a treatment, a summary of your screenplay. This will help you flesh out the story before diving into the script itself.
- Begin writing your screenplay using the established format. The first line of your script should be as good as the first line of any blockbuster. Make it count. Focus on visual storytelling and concise, engaging dialogue. Aim for an average of one page per minute of screen time.
- Introduce your characters with clarity, including their names and basic descriptions.
- Keep the audience engaged by introducing conflicts and obstacles that the characters must overcome. This creates tension and drives the plot forward.
- Use the classic "show, don't tell" rule. Use visual elements to convey information whenever possible. Remember, film is a visual medium, and showing actions can be more powerful than telling. Note: If you're writing a screenplay, skip detailed camera directions which can target you as an amateur.
- After completing your first draft, take the time to revise and polish your screenplay. Share your screenplay with others, such as writing groups, peers, or mentors. Constructive feedback can help you identify blind spots and areas for improvement.
- Ensure that your screenplay follows industry-standard formatting guidelines. This includes the correct placement of scene headings, action lines, dialogue, and transitions.
- Include a professional-looking title page with the title of your screenplay, your name, and contact information.
- Consider registering your screenplay with a copyright office or a screenwriters' guild for protection.
- If you're interested in getting your screenplay produced, research submission opportunities, or consider networking with industry professionals. You can also explore opportunities like film festivals and screenplay competitions.

Remember that writing a screenplay is a skill that develops with practice, so keep honing your craft and learning from your experiences.

BEWARE OF SCAMS

A word of caution if you plan to enter competitions for playwrights. Due diligence is needed since screenwriting competitions are usually expensive. Some competitions are legitimate and others are simply a way to make money for those who run them.

Ask yourself: Do winners really get the opportunity the promotors are promising? Is it a well-known, long-established competition? If not, don't waste your retirement money.

Remember, there are sincere people in Hollywood and on Broadway who may try to help you. However, there are also those in the entertainment industry who are unscrupulous and will happily take your money and offer nothing in return. Other wannabes who claim to be producers may make promises they can't fulfill.

CONCLUSION: TIME TO GET STARTED!

The Next Chapter: Writing in Retirement was written out of a sincere desire to help retirees who have always had the desire to write.

Whether you're ready to pursue your cherished dreams or simply looking for a creative and fulfilling hobby, this comprehensive book was meant to help you explore all your options and begin your writing journey. I've held nothing back and shared all my "secrets," often learned the hard way from decades of writing professionally.

You now have the tools to start down the exciting path of becoming a writer. It's time to quit reading and start writing! If you take anything away from this book, I hope it helps you discover the pure joy of writing.

If you enjoyed the book and found it beneficial, honest reviews are much appreciated! I'd love to hear your opinion and, as discussed earlier in the book, reviews strongly influence a book's success.

I hope this book inspires and motivates you to move forward. Please share any success stories with me so I can celebrate with you.

You can connect with me on my author website, blog, and social media sites:

Website: https://juliegorges.com/
Blog: https://babyboomerbliss.net/
Facebook: https://juliegorges.com/
Twitter: https://twitter.com/JulieGorges

I wish you much success in all your endeavors!

ABOUT THE CONTRIBUTORS

A big thanks to the retired writers who shared their stories and viewpoints, added valuable advice and insight, and provided inspiration:

Sandra Bennett, an international award-winning children's author, is a former primary school teacher and mother of three boys. She writes children's stories to engage and delight readers 3-12 years old and is an Australia Reads Ambassador. To learn more about Sandra visit https://sandrabennettauthor.com/.

Catherine Michaels, an award-winning author known for her feel-good stories and happy endings, transitioned to being a full-time Indie author in 2013 after leaving the 9-5 office grind. Writing as Cat Michaels, she has authored five children's books before turning to contemporary adult fiction. Look for her upcoming release, *Sand, Sea, and Second Chances*, a small-town, sweet romance coming in summer 2024. For more information about Catherine and to download your free copy of her short read, *The Wishing Stones*, a friends-to-lovers coastal romance, visit https://www.catmichaelswriter.com/.

Rosie Russell studied early childhood education and taught students in elementary and middle school for 15 years in the Midwest. In retirement, she began writing and illustrating children's books. A prolific writer, she has published 15 children's books. To learn more about Rosie, visit https://www.https://booksbyrose.com.

Barry Silverstein is a professional freelance writer and non-fiction book author with a background in brand marketing. After running his own direct marketing agency for 20 years, he began writing in retirement. He is also an active blogger at https://www.happilyrewired.com/. To learn more about Barry, visit https://www.barrysilverstein.com/.

RESOURCES

This book was meant to get you started on becoming a writer in retirement. I urge you to continue the learning process.

Many outstanding books, magazines, and websites are available to delve more deeply into the craft of writing and publishing. The following are some you may want to check out:

Books on Writing and Publishing:

- *How to Market a Book* by Joanna Penn: Drawing on her own experiences as a successful author and entrepreneur, Joanna Penn provides practical advice, actionable tips, and a step-by-step approach to book marketing.
- *On Writing: A Memoir of the Craft* by Stephen King: This book is part memoir and part writing guide. Stephen King shares his experiences and insights into the writing process, offering practical advice for aspiring writers.
- *ProBlogger: Secrets for Blogging Your Way to a Six-Figure Income* by Darren Rowse and Chris Garrett: This book provides practical advice on creating and monetizing a successful blog. It covers various aspects of blogging, from content creation to building an audience and generating income.
- *The Complete Guide to Self-Publishing* by Marilyn Ross & Sue Collier: A comprehensive and widely respected resource for authors looking to navigate the world of self-publishing
- *The Education of a Wandering Man* by Louis L'Amour: A delightful autobiographical work as L'Amour reflects on his life as a writer, experiences, and the various lessons he learned during his extensive travels and diverse pursuits.
- *The Elements of Style* by William Strunk Jr. and E.B. White: A classic guide to English writing style, this book is concise and packed with valuable tips on grammar, composition, and style.

- *The Writer's Compass* by Nancy Ellen Dodd: A comprehensive guide designed to help writers navigate the various stages of the writing process and develop their craft.
- *Writer's Market* published by Writer's Digest: This annually updated reference book is a go-to tool for writers seeking publication, representation, or freelance opportunities.
- *Writing the Memoir* by Judith Barrington: A guide offering writers the tools and inspiration needed to craft their personal stories with authenticity and literary merit.

Magazines for Writers:

- *Writer's Digest Magazine:* Offers tips, advice, and resources for writers.
- *Poets & Writers Magazine:* Focuses on creative writing, literary news, and publishing.
- *Publishers Weekly:* Provides news and reviews on the publishing industry.

Blogs and Websites on Writing:

- Writer's Digest: Offers writing tips, publishing advice, and information on the writing industry.
- The Creative Penn: Focuses on writing, self-publishing, and marketing for authors.
- Poets & Writers: Provides resources for creative writers, including a database of writing contests and literary magazines.
- Publishers Weekly: Targeted at publishers, librarians, booksellers, and literary agents.

Self-Publishing Resources:

- Alliance of Independent Authors: Provides guidance and support for self-published authors.
- Self-Publishing School: Offers courses and resources for authors interested in self-publishing.

GLOSSARY

Acrostic poems. A form of poetry in which the first letter, syllable, or word of each line or stanza spells out a word, message, or the alphabet.

Advance. A sum of money a publisher pays an author before the publication of a book.

Affiliate. A popular method for monetizing blogs by earning commissions using an affiliate link to promote a product or service from a retailer or advertiser.

Aggregator. A service or platform that aggregates and distributes digital books to various retailers and libraries.

AI. Refers to artificial intelligence, tools that can help writers brainstorm ideas, correct spelling, and grammar, develop story ideas, and much more. Some software will write entire passages or even books and must be used cautiously.

Alphabet poems. A type of poem in which each line or stanza begins with the successive letters of the alphabet.

Amazon ads. The advertising services provided by Amazon that allows authors and publishers to promote their books and reach a wider audience on the Amazon platform.

Anecdote. A short, interesting, and often humorous story or account of a real incident or person. Anecdotes provide insight into a particular event, experience, or character and often make a topic more engaging, relatable, or memorable.

Antagonist. A character, group of characters, force, or element in a story that opposes or conflicts with the main character.

ARC. Refers to advance reader copies, also known as galleys, sent to reviewers, booksellers, book bloggers, and influential individuals for testimonials.

Attribution. The act of giving credit or identifying the source of information, ideas, quotations, or data that is included in a piece of text.

Author bio. A brief written account of a writer's life, accomplishments, and relevant background information.

Author's platform. The author's overall visibility, influence, and presence in the literary and publishing world, both online and offline. May include an author's website, blog, email lists, professional associations, social media followers, public speaking engagements and events.

Backlinks. Hyperlinks on one website that direct users to another website. These links are crucial for search engine optimization (SEO) and play a significant role in determining a website's authority and ranking on search engine results pages.

Back story. Refers to the narrative history or background information about the characters, events, or world presented in a story.

Ballads. A form of narrative poetry or song that typically tells a story in a concise and rhythmic manner. Ballads have been a popular literary and musical form for centuries, with roots in various cultural traditions.

Barcode. Refers to the Bookland EAN scanning symbol that goes on the back of a book cover.

Beta readers. An individual who reads an early draft of a manuscript or written work before it is officially published and provides feedback to the author.

Blog. Short for "weblog," a blog is an online platform or website that presents regularly updated content in a chronological format. Blogs can cover a wide range of topics, including personal experiences, opinions, news, tutorials, reviews, and more.

Blog directories. Platforms or websites that organize and list blogs based on different criteria, making it easier for users to discover and navigate through a variety of blogs. Bloggers submit their blogs to these directories to increase visibility and attract a broader audience.

Blurb. A book endorsement or phrase promoting the book and its author.

Book bloggers. Individuals who share their thoughts, reviews, and recommendations about books on a blog or other online platforms.

Book promotional service. A professional service or platform that authors and publishers use to promote and market their books. These services are designed to increase the visibility of a book, attract potential readers, and drive sales.

Book proposal. A document that authors use to pitch their book idea to literary agents or publishers to secure a publishing deal.

Book trade publications. Periodicals that cater specifically to the publishing industry, often providing reviews and previews of upcoming books.

Books in Print. A comprehensive bibliographic database or catalog that provides information about books currently available for purchase or distribution.

Bowker. A prominent provider of bibliographic information and services to publishers, libraries, and the book trade. One of its key roles is the assignment and distribution of International Standard Book Numbers (ISBNs) in the United States.

Byline. Name of the author appearing with a published piece.

Character arc. The transformation or development of a character over the course of a story.

Character chart. A tool used by writers to organize and track details about the characters in their stories. The reference document helps writers maintain consistency in characterization and keep track of important information about each character.

Characterization. The process by which an author develops and portrays the personalities of the characters in a literary work.

Cliché. Overused expressions or ideas that have lost their originality and impact.

Climax. The pivotal point in the narrative where the tension and conflict reach their highest point. Typically, the main character faces a critical decision or undergoes a significant transformation.

Clips. Samples, usually from newspapers and print and online magazines, of a writer's published works.

Competitive book analysis. An evaluation, also known as comparative book analysis, by publishers, authors, or literary agents comparing books that are similar or competing in the same genre or market.

Conflict. The central struggle or problem that drives the plot of a story.

Copyediting. Editing a manuscript or article for grammar, punctuation, clarity, and accuracy.

Copyright. A means to protect an author's work.

Cover letter. A brief letter sent to an agent or editor with a manuscript.

Cross-promotion. The practice of promoting or publicizing one piece of written content in combination with another, with the goal of mutually benefiting both writers.

Description. The use of language to vividly portray the physical appearance of settings, characters, objects, and scenes.

Dialogue. The written conversation between characters, often used to reveal personality, advance the plot, or convey information.

Dialogue tags. Also known as attribution or speaker tags, dialog tags are words or phrases used to indicate which character is speaking in a written conversation or dialogue.

Distributor. A company or entity that acts as an intermediary between authors, publishers, and retailers, facilitating the marketing, sales, and distribution of books to bookstores, libraries, and other retail outlets.

Domain name. A web address that is used to identify and locate specific resources on the Internet.

Draft. A version of a manuscript or document before it is finalized.

eBook. Short for electronic book or digital version of a book.

Email list. A collection of email addresses gathered and maintained for the purpose of sending messages, updates, newsletters, or promotional content.

Embellishments. In the case of novels, writers may embellish the narration by expanding on certain aspects of the story, such as character traits, settings, or events. In the context of nonfiction and memoirs, embellishment refers to the inappropriate act of adding inaccurate, exaggerated, or fictional details to events, facts, or personal experiences to make the story more engaging, dramatic, or entertaining.

Endorsements. Statements of support, praise, or recommendations provided by individuals, often well-known or respected figures, expressing their positive opinions about the book. These endorsements are typically featured on the book's cover, back cover, or in promotional materials to lend credibility and influence potential readers.

Essays. A literary form that presents an argument, viewpoint, or perspective on a particular topic.

Exclusive rights. The rights granted by an author to a publisher, granting exclusive control over certain uses and distributions of the work typically in exchange for royalties or other compensation.

Expanded distribution. An Amazon service that makes a book available in bookstores, libraries, academic institutions, and other online platforms and retailers, allowing readers to purchase it from various sources outside of Amazon. By opting in, authors give Amazon exclusive rights.

External links. Refers to hyperlinks that lead to web pages outside the domain or website hosting the blog. These links connect the blog content to additional information, resources, or references on other websites.

Facebook advertising. A form of online advertising that authors and publishers often use to promote their books, blogs, services, or content on the Facebook platform.

Fact-check. The process of verifying the accuracy and truthfulness of statements, claims, or information presented in various forms of media.

Fair Use. Allows the use of copyrighted material under certain circumstances without obtaining permission from or paying royalties to the copyright owner.

Family history. Documenting and recounting the stories, experiences, and genealogical information related to one's family.

Fiction. Literary works created from the imagination rather than being based on real events or facts.

First person. The central character tells the story, using the pronoun "I." Everything a reader sees, hears, and experiences in the story comes through the main character.

Free association. A creative technique where the writer allows thoughts to flow freely without consciously controlling or censoring them. This method often involves jotting down whatever comes to mind, without worrying about coherence, grammar, or logical structure.

Free hosted sites. Blogging platforms that offer users the ability to create and publish blogs without the need to pay for hosting services or the technical complexities associated with self-hosted websites.
Freelance writer. A self-employed individual who writes content on a contractual basis for various clients, publications, or businesses.
Freelance writing sites. Online platforms that connect freelance writers with clients or employers looking for writing services.
Free verse. A form of poetry that does not adhere to a specific rhyme scheme, meter, or structured form.
Foreign rights. Refers to the rights held by a publisher or author to publish and distribute a book in languages and territories outside the book's original market or language.
Formatting. The process of arranging and structuring a book's content to meet the visual and technical requirements for publication.
Front matter. The pages that precede the main content or body of the book, providing information and details about the book and its publication.
Generalist. The practice of writing on a broad range of topics or subjects without specializing in a specific niche or industry.
Genre. A category or type of literature, such as fiction, nonfiction, mystery, or fantasy.
Ghostwriter. A writer who writes an article or book based on another person's ideas or knowledge, sometimes without receiving any credit.
Haiku. A traditional form of Japanese poetry, consisting of three lines with a specific syllable pattern.
Home Page. The main page of a website where readers first land when they visit a site.
HTML. Stands for HyperText Markup Language and refers to the coding language used to create documents for use on the Internet.
Hook. The opening line or lines of a story designed to grab the reader's attention.
Hybrid Publisher. A type of publishing model that claims to combine elements of both traditional publishing and self-publishing, but requires authors to contribute financially - often an exorbitant amount - to the publication process.
Hyperlinks. Links on a website that, when clicked, redirect the user to another location within the same website or to a different site.
Imagery. The use of vivid and descriptive language that appeals to the senses, creating a mental image or sensory experience for the reader.
Indie. Indie writers and publishers are independent entities, not affiliated with major publishing houses or corporate entities. They have full creative control over their works, from writing and editing to cover design and marketing.

IngramSpark. A publishing platform and service provided by Ingram Content Group, a major player in the global book distribution industry. IngramSpark is designed to assist independent authors and publishers in creating, publishing, and distributing print and e-book editions of their works. It offers a range of services, including printing, distribution, and access to various retail channels.

Internal links. Hyperlinks that connect one page or post on a website to another page or post within the same website.

ISBN. An ISBN, or International Standard Book Number, is a unique identifier assigned to a book, ensuring accurate identification in the publishing and bookselling industries.

Journal. A diary or record in which individuals document their thoughts, feelings, goals, experiences, and reflections.

KDP. Stands for Kindle Direct Publishing, which is a self-publishing platform provided by Amazon.

KDP Select. A program offered by Amazon that offers benefits to authors and publishers that make their eBooks exclusive to the Kindle platform for a minimum of 90 days.

Keywords. Specific words or phrases that people type into search engines to find relevant information online. Keywords play a crucial role in helping to drive traffic to a site.

Kindle Countdown Deals. A promotional tool offered by Amazon for authors and publishers who have enrolled in the Kindle Direct Publishing (KDP) Select program to help boost sales, increase visibility, and attract new readers. The Kindle Countdown Deals feature allows them to offer their eBooks at a discounted price for a limited time, creating a sense of urgency and encouraging readers to take advantage of the limited-time offer.

Kindle Unlimited (KU). A subscription service offered by Amazon that allows users to access a vast library of eBooks, audiobooks, and magazines for a monthly subscription fee. Authors can leverage Kindle Unlimited (KU) as a strategic marketing tool to increase visibility, reach a broader audience, and boost book sales. This program requires exclusivity, meaning the eBook cannot be available on other digital platforms during the enrollment period.

Launch party. An event organized to celebrate and promote the release of a newly published book.

Library of Congress Control Number (LCCN). A unique identification number assigned to books in the Library of Congress. It is used for cataloging and organizing the vast collection of books and materials.

Limericks. Limericks follow a specific rhyme scheme, with the first, second, and fifth lines rhyming with each other, and the third and fourth lines rhyming with each other. They often explore absurd or humorous scenarios and are a popular form of comic poetry.

Links. Refers to hyperlinks, which are clickable elements that connect one part of the blog (or webpage) to another, either within the same blog or to external sources on the Internet.

Literary device. Techniques used by writers to create specific effects in their writing, such as symbolism, metaphor, and foreshadowing.

LMP. Stands for *Literary Market Place*, an important publishing reference work.

Mainstream novel. A type of fiction that is intended for a broad and general audience.

Manuscript. A document that serves as the original copy of a writer's work before publication.

Marketing plan. A systematic approach to promote and sell a book effectively.

Marketing strategies. A combination of promotional activities designed to increase awareness, generate interest, and ultimately drive sales.

Media interviews. Interviews on television, radio, podcasts, or online platforms that can contribute to promoting a book.

Memoir. Unlike an autobiography, which is a comprehensive account of a person's entire life, a memoir typically concentrates on significant moments and events tied to a central theme.

Minor characters. Supporting roles in a novel that may not be as central to the plot as the main characters, but still contribute significantly to the overall narrative.

Monetize. The process of implementing specific strategies to generate income from blogs, books, and other forms of writing.

Motivation. The driving force or reasons behind a character's actions, decisions, and behaviors.

Multiple viewpoints. Also referred to as a "multiple perspective" or "multi-narrative" structure, this viewpoint presents the story from the perspectives of multiple characters.

Narrative. In a novel, a narrative refers to the overarching story or account of events presented by the author. It encompasses how the plot unfolds, characters evolve, and themes are explored throughout the book.

Narrative arc. The structure that shapes the progression of a story from its beginning to its conclusion. The narrative arc typically follows a specific sequence of events, building tension and engagement before reaching a resolution.

Narrative poems. A form of poetry that tells a story using verse. These poems unfold a series of events, often involving characters and a plot, and may include elements such as dialogue, description, and a clear structure like storytelling.

Newsletter. A communication tool that enables a writer to regularly engage with their audience, typically offering readers insights into the writer's world, including updates on their work, writing process, upcoming projects, and more.
Niche. A niche focuses on a specific topic, genre, or audience, rather than creating content that is broad and general.
Objectivity. The quality of being unbiased, impartial, and neutral in presenting information.
Online book retailers. E-commerce platforms or websites that specialize in the sale of books.
Online forums. These platforms, also known as discussion forums or message boards, provide a space for individuals to post messages, share information, ask questions, and engage in conversations on various topics.
Online magazines. Publications that are available on the Internet rather than in traditional print format.
Online marketing. The use of digital channels and strategies to promote and sell books in the online space.
Online retailers. E-commerce platforms or websites that specialize in selling books over the Internet.
Outbound Links. Hyperlinks that point to external websites or web pages outside the domain of the blog itself.
Outlines. A roadmap guiding writers in the development and organization of their works.
Overview. A concise summary that provides a book's key elements, including its main subject, themes, characters, and overall narrative.
Past tense. A grammatical tense used to indicate actions and events that have already occurred in the past.
Personality trait. A consistent and enduring quality or characteristic that defines and shapes a fictional character's behavior, thoughts, and actions.
Personal growth. The ongoing process of self-improvement, self-discovery, and development that individuals undergo throughout their lives.
Pitch. A concise and compelling description of a book's core elements, designed to capture the interest of literary agents, publishers, or readers.
Platform. The author's overall visibility, influence, and reach, both online and offline, especially in relation to their target audience.
Playwright. An individual who writes plays intended for performance on a stage by actors.
Plot. The sequence of events in a story.
Plug-ins. A piece of software added to a blog, designed to enhance, or add specific features, making it more versatile and customizable.

Point of View (POV). The perspective from which a story is told, such as first person or third person.

POD. Stands for print-on-demand, a publishing and book distribution method that only prints books after an order is placed.

Present tense. A grammatical tense used to describe actions, events, or situations that are currently happening or exist at present.

Press release. An official statement, also known as a news release, issued to members of the media (journalists, reporters, editors) to announce news and events.

PR firm. A professional organization that specializes in providing strategic public relations services tailored to the needs of authors, writers, and literary professionals.

Promotional services. A range of activities and strategies designed to increase the visibility and sales of books, and enhance the public image and recognition of authors.

Protagonist. The main character or the central figure in the story.

Public domain. Refers to creative works or intellectual property that is not under copyright protection or whose copyright has expired, allowing the public to use, share, and reproduce the works without obtaining permission or paying licensing fees.

Publishing house. A company or organization, often simply referred to as a publisher, that specializes in the production, distribution, and promotion of printed or digital materials, such as books, and other literary works.

Query letter. A letter that writers send to literary agents or publishers to pitch their work.

Release date. The specific date on which a book is officially made available to the public.

Resolution. The point in the narrative where the primary conflicts or issues faced by the characters are resolved or concluded.

Returns. A common bookstore practice to return unsold copies of books to the publisher or distributor for a refund.

Review. A critical evaluation of a book citing strengths and weaknesses.

Rough draft. An initial version of a written document, typically a piece of creative writing or manuscript.

Royalties. A percentage of the book's sales revenue serves as a form of compensation for the author's creative efforts.

Sales copy. Promotional and persuasive content to encourage readers to purchase a book.

Sample chapters. Instead of sending the entire manuscript, authors typically send sample chapters that represent a portion of the book. This allows agents to review a manageable amount of content during the initial evaluation.

Screenwriting. The process of writing a script for a film or television production.

Scrivener. A popular software application designed for writers, particularly those working on novels, screenplays, nonfiction books and other complex writing projects.

Self-hosted site. The website owner selects a web hosting provider, obtains a domain name, and sets up the website on their chosen hosting server.

Self-publishing. This term refers to authors who publish their own books without help from an established publishing house.

Sensory details. Specific elements in writing that engage the readers' senses, allowing them to vividly experience and imagine scenes, characters, or situations.

SEO (Search Engine Optimization). The practice of optimizing online content to improve its visibility and ranking on search engine results pages.

Setting. The time and place in which a story takes place.

Slush pile. Refers to a large collection of unsolicited manuscripts or submissions that a literary agent, publisher, or editor receives from writers who are seeking representation or publication.

Small press. A publishing house that operates on a relatively modest scale, often independent, that typically focuses on niche markets or specific genres.

Social media marketing. The use of social networks, online communities, blogs, or other Internet forms of media for marketing purposes.

Specialty books. These books are designed to meet the needs and preferences of a targeted readership with unique interests, expertise, or requirements.

Sponsored blogs. Blog posts or content created by bloggers that are paid for or supported by a third party, typically a brand, company, or advertiser.

Submission. The act of sending or presenting written work, such as articles, manuscripts, proposals, or queries, to publishers, literary agents, magazines, journals, or other entities for consideration or publication.

Subplots. Secondary storylines that run parallel to the main plot of a novel, film, play, or other forms of narrative.

Subsidy publisher. A publisher that charges writers to publish their work – usually at a high price while retaining ownership of the books. Sometimes referred to as a vanity publisher.

Synopsis. A summary of a book.

Tags. Distinctive features or qualities that help define and distinguish a character in the reader's mind.

Target audience. The specific group of readers that a writer aims to reach, connect with, and engage through their written work.

Traditional publishing. Refers to the old-fashioned process of getting a book deal with a commercial publishing company.

Theme. The central idea or message of a literary work.

Third person. A point of view where the narrator is not a character within the story but an external entity observing and narrating the events. This perspective uses pronouns such as "he," "she," "it," or "they" to refer to the characters, and provides a more objective view of the story.

Title generators. Online tools designed to assist authors, bloggers, and content creators in generating creative and compelling titles for their written works.

Twitter pitches. Concise and compelling book pitches or summaries that authors use to attract the attention of literary agents and editors at "Twitter pitch events."

Unsolicited manuscript. Refers to a written work that has been submitted to a literary agent, publisher, or editor without prior invitation or request.

URL. The web address that you type into a web browser to visit a specific webpage.

Vanity publisher. Sometimes referred to as a vanity press or subsidy publisher, a publishing company that requires authors to pay – usually an exorbitant amount - for the production and distribution of their books.

Viewpoint. The perspective from which a story is told, such as first person, third person, or multiple viewpoints.

Virtual launch party. An online event held to celebrate and promote the release of a new book.

Widget. A small, customizable module or component that can be added to a blog's sidebar, footer, or other designated areas to enhance its functionality or appearance.

INDEX

Made in the USA
Las Vegas, NV
20 October 2024

96665354R00164